# HOW TO BE YOUR OWN
# FINANCIAL PLANNER

# HOW TO BE YOUR OWN
# FINANCIAL PLANNER

Elliot Raphaelson
Debra Raphaelson West

SCOTT, FORESMAN AND COMPANY
Glenview, Illinois          London

Page 45; from pamphlet "A Word to Seniors About Securities
Fraud," Illinois Secretary of State Securities Department.
Reprinted by permission.


**Library of Congress Cataloging-in-Publication Data**

Raphaelson, Elliot.
    How to be your own financial planner / Elliot Raphaelson, Debra
Raphaelson West.
        p.   cm.
    Includes index.
    ISBN 0-673-24926-3
    1. Finance, Personal—United States.   I. West, Debra Raphaelson.
II. Title.
HG179.R3238    1990
332.024—dc20                                                89-10058
                                                                CIP


1    2    3    4    5    6    MUR    94    93    92    91    90    89


ISBN 0-673-24926-3

Copyright © 1990 Scott, Foresman and Company.
All Rights Reserved.
Printed in the United States of America.

Scott, Foresman professional books are available for bulk sales at quantity
discounts. For information, please contact Marketing Manager, Professional
Books Group, Scott, Foresman and Company, 1900 East Lake Avenue,
Glenview, IL  60025.

# Dedication

This book is dedicated to Senator Bill Bradley of New Jersey, whose efforts in tax reform have made this book necessary.

# Acknowledgments

We would like to thank Arline Raphaelson for waking up at all hours of the night to realign the printer and for mediating when necessary (and it was usually necessary). Also, appreciation goes to Stephen West for his trip to summer school, leaving us some peace and quiet.

Thanks to Robert Szpak and Terri Hudson for their assistance and encouragement.

Scudder, Stevens, and Clark generously provided us with valuable information on a variety of retirement issues. The No-Load Mutual Fund Association provided us with a glossary of mutual-fund terminology, of which we used, with adaptations, the most relevant portions, with their kind permission.

Thanks also to technical reviewers George E. Arocha, CFP, Director of the Institute for Financial Services Training at Roosevelt University, Chicago; Janet L. Gardner, Technical Analyst for Qualified Retirement Plan; and Gregg Wiemer, Director of Compensation and Benefits at Scott, Foresman and Company. We greatly appreciate their comments; the final responsibility for the writing, however, is our own.

# Contents

# Preface

It has never been easy to set up a financial plan for retirement. Unfortunately, it is now becoming more complicated. The new tax laws have not simplified the planning process at all. Moreover, it is very likely that more tax changes are in store for us that will make planning even *more* difficult because of the added uncertainty.

In the past few years, we have witnessed tremendous instability in the securities markets, for both bonds and common stocks, which also makes it very difficult to develop an investment plan that will assure us of a comfortable retirement.

The United States' huge budget deficit has forced Congress to look for new ways to tax its citizens. Unfortunately, some of the new methods have proven to be a burden on individuals and families planning for financial security in retirement. For example, Social Security income is no longer tax-free. Up to 50 percent of Social Security income, depending on income level, is now subject to tax, even though Social-Security taxes are not tax-deductible.

The maximum tax rate has been cut from 50 percent to 33 percent. However, this rate reduction is not as favorable as it may seem, because many previously acceptable deductions have been reduced—and others have been disallowed entirely. Furthermore, it is likely that there will be a steady increase in tax rates as time goes on. As Congress is pressured more and more to reduce the federal deficit, taxpayers will have a heavier obligation.

Another significant factor is that the percentage of retired individuals will increase in proportion to the percentage of working individuals. This may influence legislators to cut down on retirement benefits in order to reduce the tax burden on those who are working.

What is the impact of these factors on the financial planning process? If you are planning for financial security in retirement now, you need some flexibility. You should accept the fact that income tax rates are likely to increase. More of your Social Security income may be subject to income tax; Social Security income may not remain fully indexed to inflation. Inflation may not remain at the moderate 4- to 6-percent rate we have been enjoying lately.

Unfortunately, it is very difficult for retired persons to increase their sources of income. It becomes critical to preserve assets, obtain a reasonable rate of return, and develop a flexible plan for added protection during this era of great uncertainty.

There are many individuals and organizations eager to offer financial services. But you are your own most loyal ally. You can be your own financial planner, because you know best what your own needs are. There is no question that you may require and could certainly benefit from the expertise of lawyers, brokers, accountants, and other specialists. But you are the best architect of your own financial structure. The more you learn about tax laws, estate planning, Social Security, and market conditions, the easier it will be for you to develop and implement the most appropriate plan.

Our objective in this book is simple: We want to make you as knowledgeable as possible. We want you to be comfortable with the idea of becoming the foremost financial planner for the most important client in the world—you.

# Where You Are Now

**B**efore you can do any short- or long-term financial planning, you need to understand where you are now, and you should also identify future events that will have an impact on your financial situation.

To see where you are now, list all your financial assets and all your liabilities in two categories: short-term and long-term. Short-term assets can easily be converted to cash in one year or less. Examples of short-term assets are money-market accounts and money-market funds. A short-term liability is one whose payments are due within the next year. For example, if you have a 2-year car loan outstanding, the amount that you will pay off in 1 year is a short-term liability. (See Table 1-1.)

## Short-Term Assets

The following are assets that you could include in your list of short-term assets:

- Money-market accounts
- Money-market funds
- Savings accounts
- NOW accounts
- Checking accounts
- Certificates of deposit that mature within the year
- Common stocks
- Bonds
- Mutual funds

1

Table 1-1   SAMPLE PERSONAL BALANCE SHEET

| | |
|---|---:|
| Assets | |
| Short term | |
| Checking account | $      500 |
| Money-market accounts | 10,000 |
| Certificates of deposit | 25,000 |
| Mutual funds | 10,000 |
| Common stock | 15,000 |
| Bonds | 20,000 |
| Total short-term assets | 80,500 |
| Long term | |
| Cash value of life insurance | 5,000 |
| Real estate | 150,000 |
| Profit-sharing proceeds | 200,000 |
| IRAs | 20,000 |
| Total long-term assets | 375,000 |
| Total assets | $455,500 |
| | |
| Liabilities | |
| Short term | |
| Personal loans | $ 10,000 |
| Revolving credit | 3,000 |
| Margin account | 5,000 |
| Total short-term liabilities | 18,000 |
| Long term | |
| Personal loans | 10,000 |
| Mortgages | 15,000 |
| Life insurance loans | 5,000 |
| Total long-term liabilities | 30,000 |
| Total liabilities | 48,000 |
| Net worth (assets minus liabilities) | 407,500 |
| Total liabilities and net worth | $455,500 |

You should not include stocks, bonds, or any other securities you hold in retirement accounts such as IRAs or Keoghs, because you cannot withdraw from these accounts without incurring a penalty. These assets will be included in your list of long-term assets. If you have reached age 59½, you can include these assets as short-term ones because you can withdraw them without penalty.

## Long-Term Assets

This list should include all assets that cannot easily be converted into cash within a year. You should also include those assets that you could not convert to cash within a year without incurring a penalty. The following could be included in your list of long-term assets:

- Real estate
- Certificates of deposit that mature after a year
- Cash-value life insurance
- Securities held in pension and profit-sharing accounts that you cannot cash in within the year
- Automobiles
- Personal property

## Value of Assets

For each of the items included in your list you should indicate the current market value. For some assets, such as real estate, the value you supply will generally be a best-guess estimate.

## Short-Term Liabilities

All liabilities that you expect to pay in one year or less should be included in your list of short-term liabilities. Your list could include the following items:

- Installment debt
- Revolving credit
- Car payments due within the year
- Income tax liability
- Outstanding household bills

## Long-Term Liabilities

Any liabilities that cannot be categorized as short-term liabilities should be listed as long-term liabilities. This list could include the following debts that you do not intend to repay in the next year.

- Mortgage debt
- Home equity loans

- Installment loans
- Revolving credit
- Life insurance loans
- Family debt
- Car payments not due within the year

## Evaluation of Your Net Worth

The size of your net worth is an important factor in helping to evaluate your financial health. However, it is only one factor. In the next chapter we will be considering other factors, such as current income, expected income from pension and profit-sharing plans, and Social Security.

Your overall economic well-being can be ascertained by computing the combined income you can generate from all of your sources. Then you will be able to evaluate whether your net worth is adequate to provide a comfortable retirement for you.

## Your Assets as a Source of Income

Once you have developed your personal balance sheet, you will be able to approximate the amount of income that you can derive from your assets now and in the future. Select those items on your balance sheet from which you can derive income.

You will find that some of your assets, such as cars, furniture, and jewelry, will not provide income for you. For this exercise exclude these items.

For each asset that produces income, make a realistic estimate, using an annual percentage, of the income you can expect from that asset if you can keep the asset in that form.

For example: If your money-market account is returning 6 percent, use that percentage. If you keep some money in a demand account (from which you can make withdrawals at any time) bearing 5 percent interest, use that percentage, and so on. For the time being don't make any decisions regarding movement of assets.

You should develop a list of your income-producing assets, the current rate of return on these assets, and the yearly income you can expect from them. Use the format indicated in Table 1-2. Note that the categories of assets listed in Table 1-2 correspond to the categories of assets listed in Table 1-1. If you don't accurately construct your balance sheet, you will not be able to estimate and evaluate your income accurately.

Table 1-2  RETURN ON ASSETS

| Asset | Amount | Percentage | Yearly Income |
|---|---|---|---|
| **Short term** | | | |
| Checking account | $   500 | 5 | $   25 |
| Money market | 10,000 | 6 | 600 |
| CDs | 25,000 | 7 | 1,750 |
| Mutual funds | 10,000 | 7 | 700 |
| Bonds | 20,000 | 9 | 1,800 |
| Subtotal | | | 4,875 |
| **Long term** | | | |
| Profit sharing | 200,000 | 9 | 18,000 |
| IRAs | 20,000 | 9 | 1,800 |
| Subtotal | | | 19,800 |
| Total | | | $24,675 |

## Interest You Must Pay

In the same way you prepared a list of your income based on your assets, you should also prepare a list of your interest expenses based on your liabilities. (See Table 1-3.)

Table 1-3  INTEREST EXPENSE

| | Liability Amount | Percentage | Yearly Income |
|---|---|---|---|
| **Short term** | | | |
| Personal loans | $10,000 | 12 | $1,200 |
| Revolving credit | 3,000 | 15 | 450 |
| Margin account | 5,000 | 11 | 550 |
| Subtotal | | | 2,200 |
| **Long term** | | | |
| Personal loans | 10,000 | 12 | 1,200 |
| Mortgages | 15,000 | 8 | 1,200 |
| Life insurance | 5,000 | 6 | 300 |
| Subtotal | | | 2,700 |
| Total | | | $4,900 |

Now that you have listed all your assets and liabilities and the associated earnings and payments, you should review whether you want to reduce or eliminate some of your liabilities—specifically those for which you pay more than you are earning.

For example, if you are paying 15 percent or more for revolving credit, you should consider paying some or all of that liability from a money-market account that is earning approximately 6 percent. You do not, however, want to get into a position in which you have no short-term assets for emergencies. To the extent that you have sufficient short-term assets for contingencies, you should consider paying off or reducing liabilities that carry high interest rates.

To give yourself more flexibility regarding possible emergencies, you should establish lines of credit that you can use when necessary but that have no fees or charges until you use them. A line of credit is an agreement by a financial institution to guarantee a specified credit limit for a customer, subject to the customer's retention of a good credit rating. Most financial institutions offer such lines.

# Identifying Your Sources of Income and Establishing Financial Objectives

**B**efore you can establish long-term plans and objectives, you must be able to identify all your sources of income during retirement. Constructing a personal balance sheet is a necessary first step.

## Sources of Income

You should prepare a list of all the income you expect to receive during retirement. (See Table 2-1.) These sources may include Social Security, pension plans, and annuities as well as employment income if you plan to work part time during your retirement.

You should be able to estimate your earnings from Social Security. This topic is discussed in Chapter 11. Every 3 years you should request a statement of earnings from Social Security to ensure that your records are being maintained properly. Prior to your retirement you can ask the Social Security Administration to estimate your future earnings based on your earnings history. You can also estimate your Social Security earnings in advance of retirement yourself. The Social Security Administration provides free publications that indicate how you can compute your Social Security earnings and the expected earnings of your spouse.

Before your retirement, you should be able to estimate your pension income, if applicable, from your employer. All employers offering qualified pension plans must provide you with the essential information you can use to estimate your retirement income.

You should learn precisely how your pension benefit is computed. For example, if your employer sponsors a defined-benefit plan, you should examine the specific formula that is used. Your benefit will probably be

Table 2-1   SOURCES OF INCOME

| Source | Monthly Income |
| --- | --- |
| Social Security | $ 800 |
| Spouse's Social Security | 400 |
| Company pension plan | 1,000 |
| Income from other assets* | 400 |
| Part-time work | 500 |
| Total | $3,100 |

*The approximate yearly short-term income (see Table 1-2) of $4,800, divided by 12.

based on the total number of years you worked and some average of the last 3 or 5 years of your base salary.

Every plan is different, and you should know precisely how to estimate your benefits. Many companies offset part of your benefits based on the company's contribution to Social Security on your behalf. If that is the case, make sure you understand the computation.

If you are not sure exactly how your pension benefit is computed, meet with the plan representative well before you retire. It is critical that you understand every component of your retirement income well in advance of retirement.

You and your spouse will have to make a very important decision: whether to elect a lifetime pension benefit for yourself and your spouse or just for yourself. The level of income can vary significantly based on your ages. This topic is explored in detail in Chapter 12. Make sure you understand your options. Do not hesitate to discuss this with the plan representative well before you actually retire. This is a critical decision, and you should give it considerable thought. Unless your spouse has a high income and assets on his or her own, a joint option ordinarily makes more sense.

## Tax Considerations

You should calculate your income on an after-tax basis. The tax status of each major income source is discussed in various chapters of this book.

For example, Social Security income is tax free only for single taxpayers whose adjusted gross is less than $25,000. If you are single and earn more than $25,000, then up to 50 percent of your Social Security income is taxable at ordinary income tax rates. If you are married and file a joint return, up to 50 percent of your Social Security income is taxable if your joint income exceeds $32,000.

Before you prepare a budget, know what your after-tax income is.

## Establishing a Budget

Once you know what your after-tax income is, you can develop a family budget. On average, most family expenses during retirement are 70 percent to 75 percent of preretirement levels. Averages are meaningless on an individual family basis, however. You should develop a preliminary budget to get a feel for the standard of living you can afford during retirement. Develop a list of budget items that includes both the necessities and the luxuries you would like during retirement, such as travel, gifts, and entertainment.

If the total amount of your projected expenses is very close to your projected income, review alternate approaches on the income side as well as on the expense side. These options will be explored more fully in the next chapter.

A potentially significant problem during retirement is inflation. The preretirement budget that you develop will have to be modified throughout your retirement based on changes in the inflation rate. Obviously your budgeted expenses should change. In addition, however, your budgeted income should change also, because of inflation and inflation expectations. Accordingly, the budgeting process, because of inflation and other factors, should be an ongoing one for you.

## Establishing Financial Objectives

In order to develop a long-term financial plan, you should establish specific long-term financial objectives. Obviously, you should be realistic in establishing your objectives based on your expected income from sources such as Social Security, employer-sponsored retirement plans, IRAs, Keoghs, other pension and profit-sharing plans, and other assets.

The first step is to list your assets and liabilities and to examine and estimate the income you can expect from various sources. After you have gone through that exercise, you can evaluate whether you can meet your initial retirement objectives or whether you should look at other options. It would be ideal if you could retire early, for example, and still meet all your retirement objectives. What is most likely, however, is that you will go through many scenarios, with many options, before finally selecting a set of objectives that is realistic and consistent with your desired lifestyle in retirement. Some of the options and trade-offs you may want to consider are early retirement, part-time work during retirement, and electing that Social Security payments begin before age 65.

## Starting Point

A reasonable place to start is with some traditional assumptions, for example:

- Work until your pension begins
- Initiate Social Security payments at age 65
- Postpone receiving any income from personal and employer-sponsored retirement until age 65
- Make an assumption regarding your required income after retirement, for example, 75 percent of current after-tax income, adjusted for inflation
- Assume an annual inflation rate of 6 percent
- Assume 8 percent average rate of return (before taxes) on investable assets between now and age 65

### SCENARIO

Harry Smith is 60 now and anticipates that he will continue to work until age 65. Mary, his wife, is 58 and expects to retire at age 63 so they can retire together. Both are covered by guaranteed employer-sponsored pension plans and have worked in the Social Security system long enough so that they both have more than 40 quarters of coverage; hence they are entitled to Social Security income at retirement. They both have individual retirement accounts, which are currently worth $30,000 combined. They also have $50,000 in certificates of deposit and $50,000 in common stocks.

The Smiths earn $70,000 after taxes and believe that in retirement they could live comfortably on $35,000 after taxes in today's dollars.

Table 2-2 illustrates the Smiths' estimated income in retirement. The computations in this table are based on the assumption that Mr. and Mrs. Smith will continue working for 5 years and retire in 1994. The income

Table 2-2  THE SMITHS' ESTIMATED DISPOSABLE INCOME AFTER RETIREMENT

|  | Per month | Per year |
|---|---|---|
| Social Security—Mr. Smith | $1,000 | |
| Social Security—Mrs. Smith | 750 | |
| Employer retirement plan—Mr. Smith | 1,200 | |
| Employer retirement plan—Mrs. Smith | 800 | |
| Income on assets of $100,000 @ 8% | 665 | |
| Income on IRA assets of $35,000 @ 8% | 235 | |
| Subtotal | 4,650 | $55,800 |
| Nontaxable Social Security income | (875) | (10,500) |
| Gross taxable income before deductions | $3,775 | 45,300 |
| Deductions | | |
| Two exemptions @ $2,000 | | 4,000 |
| Standard deduction | | 5,200 |
| Total deduction | | 9,200 |
| Net taxable income | | 36,100 |
| Total federal taxes | | (6,085) |
| Net income after taxes (including Social Security income) | | $30,015 |

shown is based on the formulas used by the Smiths' employers and the latest Social Security information available as well as on the Smiths' work history and estimated contributions for the next 5 years.

The Smiths estimate that at retirement age they will have $100,000 in investable assets. Assuming a before-tax average rate of return of 8 percent, these assets will provide income of $2,335 per month.

Including Social Security income, employer retirement plan income, income on personal assets, and income on IRA assets, the total estimated income the Smiths can expect in 1994 is $4,650 per month. Unfortunately, most of that income will be taxable. Based on existing tax law, 50 percent of their Social Security income will not be taxable. Therefore, $875 per month was subtracted from the $4,650, resulting in $3,775 per month of taxable income.

Net taxable income was then computed by subtracting allowable deductions ($4,000) and the standard deduction ($5,200) based on current tax law, which allows that these deductions will be adjusted for inflation. However, to allow for the possible if not likely increase in taxes, these deductions have not been adjusted for inflation.

## Estimating Gap

The Smiths would like their 1994 income after taxes to be equivalent to $35,000 in 1989 constant dollars. Assuming an inflation rate of 4 percent, $35,000 of income in 1989 is equivalent to $42,580 of income in 1994. Thus, as indicated in Table 2-2, there is a gap of $12,565 per year.

## Alternatives

You have several alternatives if you are facing a gap similar to that of the Smiths:

- Accept the fact that you will not be able to generate $43,000 in after-tax income and revise your expected standard of living to reflect a lower expected income, that is, $30,015 per year (Table 2-2).
- Work a few years longer, accumulate more assets, and earn more retirement benefits in order to increase your standard of living.
- Consider an annuity for your personal savings. This could provide a higher retirement income. However, it would reduce the size of the estate you can leave your beneficiaries.
- Save more now so that you will have a larger asset base when you retire.
- Invest more aggressively now so that you may have a larger asset base when you retire, recognizing the risk that you may suffer capital losses.
- Move to less expensive housing at retirement, creating additional investable assets. This alternative is likely to reduce your recurring operating and maintenance costs too.
- Supplement your income during retirement by working part time.

## Reviewing Alternatives

Obviously, each individual will have different reactions to these alternatives. It would be pleasant if there were no gap to face, if there were no unattractive alternatives. However, it is important to face any possible gap as early as possible. This will give you much more flexibility.

For example, if saving money in advance for a more comfortable retirement is one option that appeals to you, you are better off starting early. The sooner you modify your savings program, the less radical the increase in savings will have to be. The importance of starting such an investment program early is demonstrated by Table 2-3, which indicates the value of investing a fixed monthly sum for different time periods at a constant rate of return.

<hr>

Table 2-3   FUTURE VALUE OF INVESTMENT PLAN

Assumptions
$100 per month invested
9 percent earned on investment compounded monthly

Value of investment at end of

| | |
|---|---|
| Year 1 | $ 1,250 |
| Year 3 | 4,115 |
| Year 5 | 7,540 |
| Year 10 | 19,350 |
| Year 20 | 66,790 |

## Developing Alternative Approaches

It is unlikely that the first plan you develop will be your final one. It is not important that your first plan be your final one. What is important, however, is that you develop an initial plan, make some realistic assumptions, and revise your plan — and your assumptions — until you are comfortable with the result.

## Revising the Plan

The plan you develop will certainly change over time. At least once a year you should review your situation, compute your assets, look at the assumptions you made, and reevaluate your plan. This should be an ongoing process. Although it may seem burdensome now, you will have comfort in knowing that you will have a financially sound retirement, partially because of your initial planning and your subsequent review process.

The fact that we live with a dynamic market with constant fluctuation in inflation rates, interest rates, and stock and bond prices should not deter you from planning. In fact, it is these changing conditions that require you to establish an initial preretirement financial plan and to modify it on a regular basis.

# Impact of Inflation

The rate of inflation in effect after you retire will undoubtedly have an impact on your lifestyle. Obviously, you would like the rate of inflation to be very low in your retirement years. Although you have no control over the inflation rate, in some ways you will be partially protected from inflation. In other ways you will not have sufficient protection, however. In this chapter we will be examining various aspects of retirement from a viewpoint of inflation.

## Inflation Level

We are fortunate that the level of inflation has dropped from the double digits of 1981 to the relatively stable levels of 4 percent to 6 percent. There is no guarantee, however, that the inflation rate will remain at its current level.

There are indications that the inflation rate may increase again. The vast budget deficit and the growing trade deficit are both inflationary. The Reagan administration helped put a lid on inflation by taking a tough stand to control the labor costs of both the military and civil service workers. A different administration might not control costs as well, which would be inflationary.

Moreover, there is much industry pressure to restrict imports from Japan and other countries that have favorable trade balances with us. To the extent that these pressures influence Congress to limit imports, this will cause additional inflation, because United States businesses will be able to raise their prices more easily.

If the rate of inflation increases, it will be more difficult for you to maintain your standard of living during retirement. The more you know about the effects of inflation, the easier it will be for you to plan, to develop strategies for coping, and to inform your congressional representatives as to your concerns.

## Social Security

Social Security income is now partially indexed to the consumer price index (CPI). When the CPI exceeds a specified level, Social Security income is automatically increased to reflect the higher cost of living. It is possible that Congress will do one of three things that would reduce your Social Security retirement income:

1. Delay the adjustment for inflation, resulting in a longer wait for the extra money.
2. Reduce the indexed increase. For example, Congress could mandate that if the CPI increased by 4 percent, Social Security income would be increased by 2 percent.
3. Stop Social Security income indexing completely.

There is no way to know with certainty whether Congress will exercise any of these options. History tells us, however, that Congress has been willing to delay and reduce the indexing of Social Security income. Accordingly, you should not assume that this type of change cannot happen again. You should not depend on the assumption that the existing indexing policy will remain. If you object to a change, communicate with your representatives in Congress. Let them know that you do not want indexing changes that are unfavorable to you. Your representatives should protect you, but sometimes they need reminders.

## Military and Civil Service Retirement Plans

The pensions of military and civil service retirees are indexed somewhat to changes in the CPI, but generally not completely indexed. The trend recently has been for reductions in pension adjustments based on inflation. For example, all civil service workers hired after 1984 are covered by the Federal Employee Retirement System (FERS), which does not provide as much protection against inflation as the old retirement system. The old system, the Civil Service Retirement System (CSRS), covers civil service workers hired before 1984 who did not transfer to FERS.

## Future Adjustments

There is no guarantee that these pension adjustments will continue in their current form. For your own protection you should understand how these adjustments work. You should also keep abreast of any proposed changes that can affect you and let your Congressional representatives know your position.

## Corporate Pension Plans

Most corporate pension plans are not indexed to inflation. Some, because of union contracts, are indexed, but this type of corporate pension plan is not common. Some corporations do voluntarily adjust pension benefits periodically based on inflation rates. This type of adjustment is becoming infrequent, however. Most corporations are concerned more with their overall profitability than they are about increasing pension benefits. Accordingly, you should not expect any adjustment to your corporate pension plan due to inflation.

If there are periods of high inflation, you should not expect your former employer to supplement your retirement income. You have to anticipate that there will be some periods of high inflation. Your overall preretirement plan should take into consideration the fact that some or most of your retirement income will not be fully—or even partially—indexed to inflation.

## Inflation and Your Investments

High rates of inflation can play havoc with some of your investments. In subsequent sections of this book, there are detailed analyses of various forms of investment. In this section the discussion will be limited to an overview of the impact that high levels of inflation would have on your investments.

Certain forms of investment generally do well during periods of high inflation or anticipated high inflation. These include real estate and precious metals such as gold. You should seriously consider maintaining some of your assets in real estate, for example in the form of condominium ownership. Your maintenance responsibility would be at a minimum, and you would have some protection against inflation.

During periods of high inflation, interest rates rise. Bond prices have an inverse relationship with interest rates. When interest rates increase, the value of bonds falls. The bonds with the longest time to maturity fall in value by the highest percentage. It is not unusual for bonds with 30-year maturities to fall more than 10 percent in market value when interest rates increase.

This does not mean you should not invest in long-term bonds. It does mean, however, that you have to pay close attention to the structure of your investment portfolio during periods of high inflation. Investors in long-term bonds who sold them in 1980 or 1981 suffered very substantial losses. As an investor, you should understand all the investment risks, and the inflation risk in particular.

During periods of high inflation, you should be a little more conservative with your portfolio mix by investing in shorter-term instruments. This will minimize your investment risk. Many times as an investor you have to make a trade-off between rate of return and capital risk. To earn more interest, you have to be willing to take higher risks. If you do not wish to expose your capital to high risks, you have to be willing to invest your money in shorter-term instruments. These issues will be explained in more depth in Chapters 5 and 6.

## Impact of Inflation—Various Scenarios

It is important that you understand the potential impact of inflation during retirement, since you will find that you may not be able to increase your income very much but that your expenses will increase.

There is a fairly simple technique for you to estimate the effect of inflation on your cost of living. The *rule of 72* lets you compute the effect of inflation within various scenarios.

Divide 72 by the expected rate of inflation; the resultant number indicates how long it will take for prices to double. For example, if the rate of inflation is 6 percent, then prices will double overall in about 12 years (72 ÷ 6). If the rate of inflation is 8 percent, then prices will double in 9 years (72 ÷ 8). You can use the same formula to compute how long it will take for your investments to double in value.

Not every item in your budget will increase in cost at the same rate. However, changes in the consumer price index should give you a pretty good idea as to the direction of prices.

Even though you cannot control changes in the cost of the items you need, you can protect yourself from the ravages of inflation.

## How to Protect Yourself

Some things you can do will help during inflationary periods. This is true of both investments and expenses.

From an investment viewpoint, some assets have done well during inflationary periods. Investment in real estate has generally been advantageous during high levels of inflation.

During retirement you probably do not want to maintain a large residence, but you may want to consider purchasing a condominium in an area where you like the living conditions and where property values have been increasing. Purchasing rather than renting will give you protection from sharp increases in housing costs.

If you do purchase a new residence during retirement, you should use a conventional mortgage. You want to eliminate as much uncertainty as possible. A fixed-rate mortgage assures you that your mortgage payments for principal and interest are fixed regardless of what happens to inflation and interest rates.

You may want to consider other forms of investment that have traditionally been hedges against inflation. Gold has historically been an effective inflation hedge because it increases in value during inflationary periods. However, dramatic price changes make this investment form dangerous for investors with limited capital. If you have a $100,000 investment portfolio, you may want to keep 5 percent of your investments in gold as an inflation hedge.

An investment program during retirement can also be an effective inflation hedge. Rather than invading your capital in the early years of retirement, you should consider investing part of your retirement income. If you are able to increase your capital base during the first few years of retirement, it will be much easier for you to survive inflation in subsequent years.

## Potential Problems

There are some pitfalls that can make retirement difficult for you because of inflation. You should be able to avoid these problems.

You should avoid any long-term debt with a variable interest rate. Most variable debt is tied to very volatile interest rates. For example, a variable mortgage or other form of debt can be tied to the Treasury-bill index. If this index goes up 3 or 4 percentage points, which is quite possible, so does the interest rate you have to pay. You are much better off paying a percentage point or so higher to ensure that the rate will not increase.

If interest rates in general fall dramatically, you can always take out a new loan at a lower rate and retire your old debt.

Another pitfall is the fixed-rate annuity. For individuals who have many other assets and are not concerned about inflation, fixed-rate annuities may be appropriate. For retirees whose income level is very close to their expense level at retirement, fixed-rate annuities can be a problem. Once you accept a specific income from a fixed-rate annuity, you will be unable to increase your income from that source. This can be a problem during periods of high inflation if your income is close to your expenses at the beginning of retirement. If that is the case, you should consider other investment alternatives that will give you more flexibility. Annuities are discussed in depth in Chapter 17.

# Establishing Investment
# Objectives

**R**egardless of where you are in your career, it is critical to establish the investment objectives that are most important to you. The most important investment objectives are

- Safety of capital
- Liquidity
- Income
- Growth potential
- Tax considerations

We will analyze each of these objectives from both a general perspective and a preretirement financial planning perspective.

## Safety of Capital

An investment that provides safety is simply one that preserves your capital. Many investments fit this criterion. If you invest $1,000 safely, you will always receive at least your original $1,000 when you liquidate your investment. In the next chapter, we will discuss money-market accounts, money-market funds, short-term certificates of deposit, and Treasury bills. All of these investments are safe, primarily because they are short-term investments. Investments whose maturities exceed one year are not quite as safe as these short-term investments.

The reality of investing is that you must sacrifice certain investment attributes if you want safety. The investment that will provide you with a high rate of return, guaranteed for 30 years, and refund your full principal whenever you want it is still in the fantasy stage of development. In other words, you must decide which investment objectives are most important for you and then select the available investments that best meet your objectives.

Obviously, during retirement, preservation of capital is important because it is not easily replaced. Nevertheless, other investment characteristics are also important.

Safety of capital is a relative term. You must consider inflation. For example: Assume you invest $10,000 for 5 years, receive a rate of return of 5 percent, and get your $10,000 investment back at the end of 5 years. If the inflation rate for the 5 years averaged 8 percent, did you truly protect your capital with this investment? You did not, because at the end of 5 years, the purchasing power of your investment had eroded, and the level of income that you received rose more slowly than the inflation rate.

Although you do not want to take unnecessary risks during retirement, you should not be too conservative if the end result is a loss in purchasing power and a drop in your standard of living.

## Liquidity

Liquidity simply refers to the ease of converting an asset to cash. If you can sell an asset quickly, for example within a week, and receive cash without incurring penalties, then the asset is liquid. Bonds, stocks, most mutual funds, money-market funds, money-market accounts, and NOW accounts are all examples of liquid assets.

Assets such as real estate, limited partnerships, IRAs, and retirement plan accounts owned by people under 59½ are examples of nonliquid assets. They can be liquidated, but they may take longer to sell at fair market value, or there may be penalties associated with the liquidation.

Some insurance products, such as single-payment annuities, are not liquid in the first few years after you purchase them because of surrender charges. (*Surrender charge* is insurance company jargon for early-withdrawal penalty.)

Some mutual funds, specifically in-house funds sold by large brokerage firms, are not very liquid because the selling broker cannot transfer funds without charging costly exit fees. Ask your broker if there are any such restrictions before you purchase any fund.

Some investments, such as real estate, have many attractive attributes despite their nonliquidity. When you develop your investment portfolio, you want to use a balanced approach to achieve a good rate of return, preserve your capital, and maintain liquidity.

## Income

An effective way to evaluate an investment with respect to income is in comparison with inflation. For example, for long-term bond investments a good rule of thumb is that the rate of return should generally be 3 percentage points higher than the rate of inflation. A rate of return that is lower than the inflation rate is simply not adequate, since the owner of the asset is losing ground to inflation. In the long term, an investor who continually invests in assets earning 5 percent when the inflation rate is 9 percent is going to face financial difficulty.

It is difficult if not impossible to predict future rates of inflation and resultant changes in interest rates. An effective strategy is to spread your investments over different time periods in order to provide higher income as well as some flexibility as interest rates change. This is discussed in more detail in Chapter 6.

In order to be a successful investor, you must monitor the direction of inflation and interest rates. If one of your primary objectives is a high income, then you should make sure that the rate of return you are earning in the aggregate is keeping pace with inflation.

For most individuals planning for retirement, and for those already retired, high income is an important investment objective. Investments that generally provide high rates of return are Treasury notes, Treasury bonds, federal agency bonds, corporate bonds, mutual funds that specialize in income securities, and specific categories of common stocks such as utilities. These investment vehicles generally pay higher rates than date-of-deposit-to-date-of-withdrawal savings accounts, NOW accounts, money-market accounts, and money-market mutual funds. These types of investments will be discussed in detail in Chapter 6.

## Growth

Growth investments are those that increase in value faster than other forms of investment. Such investments do not necessarily pay high incomes or dividends, however. One example is the common stock of a rapidly growing company—especially one that invests most of its earnings in the company rather than paying it to common-stock shareholders in the form of dividends. Growth investments are most important when an individual is trying to make capital grow faster than average.

For persons close to or in retirement, growth in capital is generally not as important as other objectives. Investments that are growth-oriented generally fluctuate more in value than other investments. Thus, they are generally not a significant part of an investment portfolio for an investor with retirement close at hand. Growth investments are discussed in depth in chapter 7.

## Tax Factors

Tax considerations should never be primary in an individual's investment strategy. However, it is imprudent to pay more taxes than necessary.

As a result of the Tax Reform Act of 1986, tax rates were cut substantially and capital gains taxes have been eliminated. In addition, the tax advantages of limited partnerships have been severely restricted. Accordingly, many of the old tax reduction strategies have been either severely curtailed or eliminated.

There still remain, however, several alternatives, such as IRA rollovers, employer-sponsored retirement plans, Keogh plans, municipal bonds, and Treasury securities, that still provide some tax advantages. The advantages and disadvantages of all of these investments will be explained in later chapters.

Because of tax reform it is safe to say that you should look at any investment first and foremost because of its investment value. Tax considerations should be a truly secondary factor. This has always been true, but it can now be stated with even more assurance.

## Matching Investments to Your Objectives

Various forms of investments and investment strategies will be explained in the next few chapters. The major advantages and disadvantages of each of these investments will be identified.

You will get the most value from the next few chapters if you have already established your long-term objectives and identified the objectives that are most important to you now. Your primary objectives may change as events occur in your life and as general financial conditions change. Thus, you should be open to change both in your objectives and in your portfolio mix. But at any point in time, you should know what your primary investment objectives are so that you can review each available investment form intelligently, determining which ones are appropriate for you.

# CHAPTER 5

# Low-Risk Investments

**S**everal low-risk investment options will be reviewed in this chapter. Opting for such investments means that you incur practically no capital risk other than the risk of inflation. Regardless of the size of your investment, you will obtain a nominal rate of return, and when you sell the investment, or when it matures, you will receive your principal essentially unchanged in value.

It is likely that during retirement you will invest a portion of your investments in this category. However, if you were to place most or all of your investments with such low risks, you would be sacrificing some income that you could receive by investing your money on a longer-term basis. Investments with longer maturities are discussed in subsequent chapters.

## Money-Market Accounts

Money-market accounts provide you with safety of principal and immediate liquidity. They are offered by banks and other financial institutions and are generally insured up to specified limits. In financial institutions insured by the FDIC (Federal Deposit Insurance Corporation) and FSLIC (Federal Savings and Loan Insurance Corporation), for example, your accounts are insured for up to $100,000. You should limit the total of all accounts in that bank to the amount of the insurance coverage.

The rate of return that financial institutions offer on money-market accounts will vary based on prevailing interest rates and competitive conditions. Returns will vary among financial institutions, although not generally by very much. Banks generally establish these rates based on their cost of funds and local competitive conditions. Unless you are investing several thousand dollars, it usually will not be worthwhile to switch from one financial institution to another as rates change among them. A difference of half a percent on $1,000 results in a difference of approximately 50 cents a month.

You may find, however, that certain financial institutions consistently pay higher rates than their competitors. If this is the case, then you certainly should maintain your balances with the bank that does pay consistently higher rates. Banks generally review and change their rates weekly. Local newspapers generally publish these rates regularly, and you should periodically review them.

You should not maintain large sums of money in money-market accounts or money-market funds on a long-term basis. You will be able to obtain higher rates of return by extending your maturity to 6 months, a year, or longer. Your investment in money-market funds should be restricted to savings that you want ready access to. For assets that you know you will be investing for longer than 6 months, you generally can obtain a higher rate of return.

Some financial institutions charge service fees if your balance falls below specified levels, even if only for an hour. If you cannot maintain the specified minimum balance, invest your funds elsewhere. Many financial institutions have no such restraints.

Financial institutions can establish their own minimum investment requirements. Although some institutions have no minimum requirements, many require a $1,000 initial investment.

## Money-Market Funds

A money-market fund is a specific type of mutual fund that pools your money with that of other investors and invests the proceeds in highly liquid, high-quality, short-term investments. Fund investments include Treasury bills, certificates of deposit, and bankers' acceptances. A *banker's acceptance* is a time draft issued by a bank. On the face of the draft the word *accepted* is written along with the date and place payable. An authorized banker signs the instrument. A *draft* is an instrument similar to a check that may be payable at a future date and need not be payable at a bank. The rate of return you receive is based on the fund's return from these investments.

From an investor's viewpoint, money-market funds are equivalent to money-market accounts with respect to risk and rate of return. Although money-market funds are not insured, they are safe investments because of the conservative nature of the fund investments. You can provide more protection for yourself by investing only in well-established funds that have been in business for many years. In some locations you will find that money-market funds offer a slightly higher rate of return on the average than money-market accounts. Local newspapers generally publish weekly the latest average yields for money-market funds for the last 7 days and the last 30 days. Most funds also have a recording on a toll-free number you can call to obtain the latest rate information.

Most funds provide you with check-writing options with specified minimums such as $250 or $500. There is generally no sales commission or fee associated with redemption. Accordingly, these funds are quite liquid. If you write a check on a money-market fund, you receive interest until the check clears.

Each fund establishes its minimum initial and subsequent investment. These minimums vary, although many funds require an initial $1,000 minimum investment, allowing smaller minimums for subsequent investments. Some funds have no minimum investment requirement.

The Association of No Load Funds publishes a directory of no-load funds that are members. The directory contains basic information about the funds, including minimum purchase requirements. A *no-load mutual fund* is one that does not charge a sales commission when mutual fund shares are purchased. Other information includes purchase and selling options, retirement plan options, and fund objectives. The directory covers other types of no-load mutual funds in addition to money-market funds. You can obtain this directory by sending $5 to

> The Association of No Load Funds
> Suite 1632
> 520 N. Michigan Ave.
> Chicago, IL 60611

## Tax-Free Money-Market Funds

Tax-free money-market funds were started to provide tax-free income to individuals in high tax brackets who wanted to invest in short-term municipal bonds. These funds generally offer a lower pretax rate of return than regular money-market funds, but for individuals in a higher tax bracket they can provide a better after-tax return. For most taxpayers these funds do not provide a high enough rate of return. Income is tax-free at the federal level but can be taxable at the state level depending on where the bondholder lives, where the issuer of the municipal bond is located, and the laws of the particular state.

## Treasury Bills

Treasury bills, Treasury notes, and Treasury bonds are debt obligations of the United States Treasury. Treasury bills have the shortest maturities and accordingly are the safest. Treasury notes and bonds are discussed in depth in Chapter 6. Treasury bills are obligations of the United States Treasury that are issued in maturities of 3 months, 6 months, and 1 year. The 3- and 6-month bills are auctioned weekly, and 12-month bills are auctioned monthly. The yield you receive is based on market conditions at the time the bills are sold. Because the bills are backed by the United States government and the term of the maturity is short, they are one of the safest forms of investment.

Treasury bills are sold on "discount," which means that you receive your interest in advance and the face value of the security at maturity. The minimum investment in Treasury bills is $10,000, with additional purchases in $5,000 increments.

You can purchase bills directly from a Federal Reserve bank without paying a sales commission. You can also purchase bills from a financial institution or broker, paying a sales commission such as $50 for a $10,000 investment.

If you decide not to hold your bill until maturity, you can sell it in the open market through a financial institution or broker, in which case you will incur a sales commission. The price of Treasury bills changes daily based on market conditions. If you sell bills before maturity after holding them for a short time, you could lose some money if interest rates have gone up since you purchased the bill. The best strategy is to hold the bills to maturity to ensure a gain in value and to avoid sales commissions.

If you purchased a 1-year $10,000 bill yielding 10 percent, you would receive your interest, approximately $1,000, in advance. If you hold the bill until maturity, you will receive the $10,000 face value. At your option you could roll over your investment at maturity, purchasing a new Treasury bill at prevailing rates. If you roll over your investment directly with the Federal Reserve, you do not pay any sales commission.

Investments in Treasury bills, as well as other Treasury-issued securities, have a tax advantage that many other investments do not have. No interest is taxable at the state and local level. This can be an important factor if you live in a state with high state and local income tax rates. Income from Treasury bills is taxable on your federal return, however.

The rates of return on Treasury bills, especially after taxes, are generally higher than on money-market accounts or funds if you hold the bills until maturity. You do, however, have to commit at least $10,000, and bills are not quite so liquid as money-market accounts or money-market funds.

If you do not plan to hold the Treasury bill until maturity, you may be better off investing in a money-market fund or account. With either of these, you will always obtain a positive return, and you do not pay a sales commission. If you do not hold the Treasury bill to maturity, its value can fall to less than what you paid for it, and you will have to pay a sales commission.

The Federal Reserve banks issue free circulars indicating how you can purchase Treasury securities. You can call your local Federal Reserve bank or write to

The Federal Reserve Bank of Richmond
Public Services Department
Box 27622
Richmond, VA 23261

Ask for the booklet called *Basic Information on Treasury Securities.*

## United States Savings Bonds

United States Series EE savings bonds are another vehicle for conservative investors. These bonds are issued in denominations of $50 to $10,000. The bonds are sold at a 50 percent discount from their face value, and they mature in 10 years. The difference between the discounted purchase price and the face value is considered to be interest. If you redeem the bond prior to maturity, you will not receive the full face value of the bond. The Treasury maintains a schedule that specifies the redemption value of each bond denomination based on the length of time the bond is held. The longer the bond is held, the more it increases in value.

At a minimum you will receive your initial capital back. If you hold the bonds for a minimum of 5 years, you will receive a rate of return of either 85 percent of the average yield for 5-year Treasury notes, or 5.5 percent, whichever is higher. This means, in effect, that the bonds offer a minimum or floor rate of 5.5 percent, and if interest rates increase, you will earn a higher rate of return based on the return on Treasury notes.

If you do not keep the bonds for at least 5 years, however, you will receive a lower rate of return than 5.5 percent. Within that period the specific rate will be based on a sliding scale—the longer you hold the bond, the higher the rate of return. Once you purchase a bond, you must wait a minimum of 6 months before you can redeem it.

A logical question is: "Hmmm. If I only receive 85 percent of the rate for 5-year Treasury notes, why don't I buy Treasury notes instead?" Good question. In order to purchase 5-year Treasury notes, you have to invest a minimum of $1,000. If you are investing at least $1,000 and you expect to hold the note until maturity, the note will generally be a higher-paying investment. In periods of low interest rates, the 5.5 percent return for savings bonds may be higher than even 100 percent of the Treasury note rate. This would be highly unusual, however.

Over a shorter time savings bonds have some advantages over Treasury notes. If interest rates rise, Treasury notes will fall in value. Accordingly, you could have a capital loss if you sell notes before maturity. If you bought savings bonds, however, you would always receive at least the amount of your investment after the minimum 6-month holding period.

There are also tax advantages associated with savings bonds. Interest on the bonds is not taxable at the state or local level but is taxable at the federal level. You can elect one of two options regarding federal taxes. You can pay tax annually on interest earned, or you can report your income when you cash the bonds. The option you select should be determined by your personal situation. However, in most situations postponing the tax liability is the best tax strategy.

At maturity EE savings bonds with a redemption value of at least $500 can be exchanged for HH bonds. If you exchange EE bonds for HH bonds, you defer the accumulated interest you earned. HH bonds currently pay 6 percent interest on a semiannual basis for 10 years. If you buy HH bonds, you have to pay taxes on the interest from them, but you may still defer payments on interest from your EE bonds until you sell the HH bonds. HH bonds can only be purchased on an exchange basis.

Investments in savings bonds are appropriate only if you intend to invest for at least 5 years. For time frames shorter than that, other investments such as money-market accounts and money-market funds or certificates of deposit are more appropriate.

As a result of the Tax Reform Act of 1986 there is in certain circumstances an additional tax advantage in purchasing savings bonds for children. The Tax Reform Act of 1986 specifies that when children under the age of 14 earn more than $1,000 in interest, the interest is taxed at the parents' rate, not the child's. Gifts of securities to grandchildren are also taxed at the parents' rate. For traditional investments interest is taxed as earned and would be taxable at rates as high as 28 percent or 33 percent once the child's earnings exceeded $1,000. If savings bonds are purchased for the child, however, and the bonds are held until the child reaches the age of 14 or older, then the interest is taxable at the child's tax rate, not the parents'. Since the child is usually in a lower tax bracket than the parents, there is a family tax savings. If you elect to defer the payment of taxes on savings bond interest, you will be able to save taxes in this situation.

## Certificates of Deposit

Certificates of deposit (CDs) are another example of a conservative investment. You invest your funds in a financial institution for a specific period in order to obtain a specified rate of interest. If you invest your money until maturity, you will receive your principal as well as interest.

You should purchase CDs only from financial institutions that are insured by a federal or governmental agency. You should not deposit more than the maximum amount guaranteed by the agency.

As a general rule, the longer you are willing to invest your funds with a financial institution, the higher your rate of return will be. Thus, if you are willing to invest your money for 7 years, you will generally receive a higher rate of return than if you were willing to tie up your funds for only 6 months. The exact differential between rates will change as expectations regarding the inflation rate change. If high rates of inflation are expected, you will generally find a larger differential between short-term rates and long-term rates.

Banks and other financial institutions generally offer a variety of investment options with different interest rates based on different time frames. Most financial institutions offer many options for CDs. Terms often range from 6 months to 5 years, but they can be higher or lower depending on the institution.

If you knew whether interest rates were going up or down, then you would know whether to invest your money in short-term or long-term investments. But you never know, and neither does anyone else. Accordingly, you should consider investing in instruments of various maturities so that regardless of whether interest rates go up or down, you have retained some flexibility. If interest rates go up when your short-term investments mature, you can invest the proceeds in higher-yielding CDs. If interest rates go down, you still receive higher yields on CDs with longer maturities.

There are no tax advantages in investing in certificates of deposit.

## Tax Factors

There are no tax advantages when you invest in money-market funds, regular money-market accounts, or certificates of deposit. Interest income from Treasury bills and United States savings bonds is tax-free on the state and local level but is taxable at the federal level. Interest income from tax-free money-market funds is tax-free at the federal level but may be taxable at state and local levels, depending on applicable law.

## Summary

You may find that the conservative investments discussed in this chapter can satisfy your objectives and that you do not need any investments that carry more risk. On the other hand, you may require a higher income, and you may wish to place some of your assets in investments that will provide some growth potential for you and protect you from inflation. In the next few chapters we will discuss other forms of investment, some of which could provide you with more income and better growth potential. Keep in mind, however, that when you select an investment that does provide more income or better growth potential, it is quite likely that there will be more capital risk associated with it.

# High-Income Investments

**I**n this chapter we will review investment options that can provide a higher rate of return than the conservative investments discussed in Chapter 5.

It is important for you to understand that you cannot obtain higher income without some potential disadvantages. In the case of high-income investments, that price is the risk of loss of capital. If interest rates increase, the value of your investments will decrease in value in direct proportion to the increase in interest rates. If you are forced to sell this type of investment while interest rates are rising, you can lose some of your initial investment.

High inflation creates high interest rates. Thus, when inflation is at high levels, you must be especially concerned about the risks inherent in long-term debt instruments. A continuation of higher inflation will result in higher interest rates and further decrease the value of your investment in long-term debt instruments.

Even if high income is your primary investment objective, you should consider a wide range of maturities, including some shorter-term conservative investments, so that if interest rates do increase, you will be able to invest the proceeds of your shorter-term maturities in other investments at higher interest rates.

Maturity refers to the length of time you have to hold a security before the lender repays you the principal amount of the debt. A 25-year Treasury bond is so called because it matures in 25 years. The maturity date is the specific date you will be repaid. You receive no interest on your principal after the maturity date.

## Debt Instruments

A debt instrument, or "debt," is a promissory instrument; debts are issued by the United States Treasury, governmental agencies, and corporations. From an investor viewpoint there are three types of risk associated with any debt instruments: issuer risk, interest rate risk, and call risk. Before reviewing any specific investment, the three types of risk will be discussed. You should not purchase any debt security unless you understand the associated risks.

### Issuer Risk

The first risk is the possibility that the issuer will default, or postpone payment of interest or principal. When you buy a bond or equivalent debt instrument, you are lending money to an issuer for a specific interest rate for a given length of time. As long as the issuer is financially able to pay you the required interest on time and is able to pay your principal back at maturity, you will have survived this risk. You should not make any loan to any party without understanding the nature of this risk.

The United States Treasury is the issuer with the best credit, since it has the backing of the United States government. Therefore, you do not have to be concerned with issuer risk when you lend to the United States Treasury. Similarly, if you lend money to a federal government agency, you do not incur very much issuer risk. On the other hand, if you lend funds to a corporation that is in poor financial condition and faces bankruptcy, you incur a great deal of risk.

Rating services such as Standard & Poor's and Moody's continually rate corporations' and municipalities' financial condition. You should not lend money to any entity if you cannot obtain up-to-date information regarding its financial condition.

Even if an issuer has an acceptable rating at the time you lend it money, this does not mean that its financial situation will not deteriorate. For example, Moody's can give its best rating, Aaa, to a corporation today, based on the current financial condition of the corporation. This does not guarantee that the company's financial situation will not become worse in a few years—in which case the company's rating would be downgraded.

When a company's credit rating is downgraded, the bonds it has issued drop in price. This is why it is very important for you to be careful about whom you lend money to. If a corporation has to pay 3 percent or 4 percent higher on a debt instrument than does the United States Treasury for a security of the same maturity, then you should consider that a danger signal. The higher the differential between the rate on a United States Treasury security and that of another issuer, the higher the risk for you.

If it is important for you to obtain a higher rate of return than that which is available from Treasury securities, consider purchasing a diversified portfolio. A portfolio is the holdings of securities by an individual or institution. If you have insufficient assets to build an independent portfolio, you can purchase shares in a mutual fund that specializes in debt instruments.

Through diversification you can minimize your overall risk because you spread your risk over many securities. If out of a hundred in a portfolio, one or two securities decrease in value because of financial difficulties, the value of your total holdings will be only minimally affected.

## Interest Rate Risk

Regardless of the financial strength of an issuer, you are subject to possible decreases in the value of your instrument because of interest rate fluctuations. Even if you purchase Treasury instruments, the value of your holdings will fall if interest rates increase overall. The market value will fall not because anyone believes that the government will default on its obligations but because no logical person will be willing to purchase your instrument at the same price for which they could purchase a new instrument that is paying a higher interest rate.

For example, assume you purchased a Treasury bond that matures in 25 years. A bond is a debt instrument whose term is generally 10 to 25 years and that is issued by a governmental agency or corporation. The issuer normally pays interest at a specified rate semiannually to the purchaser of the bond. At maturity the issuer repays the investor's initial investment — the face amount of the bond.

---

### SCENARIO

You paid $1,000 for a bond with a 10 percent interest rate. Interest rates for new $1,000 bonds went from 10 percent to 11 percent. Would anyone be willing to pay $1,000 for your bond if he or she could purchase a new bond that pays 11 percent per year ($110)? Remember, your bond pays only 10 percent per year ($100). The answer is *of course not.* You could sell your bond only if its price fell far enough to compensate for the lower interest rate.

An investor may be willing to pay $950 for your bond, even with the lower interest, because he knows the Treasury will redeem the bond at maturity for $1,000.

---

The longer the interval before maturity, the more significant the changes in interest rate and accordingly, the associated risks. A bond that will mature in a year or less will not fluctuate very much because of changes in interest rates. A bond that does not mature for 25 years, however, will be very sensitive to changes in rates.

No one can predict with certainty how and when interest rates will change. By staggering your maturities, as discussed in the previous chapter, you should be able to obtain a reasonably high rate of return and have some flexibility. You want to avoid being in too extreme a position. If you have all your funds in short-term securities, for example, your income will be lower than it could be. If you have all of your money in long-term bonds, you run the risk of having to sell securities at a loss if interest rates increase.

You can develop a mixed-maturity portfolio either on your own, through your broker, or through mutual funds. You can't eliminate interest rate risks completely, but you can invest in ways that will minimize the effects on you.

### Call Risk

Many corporate bonds have what are known as callable provisions. If a bond you purchase is callable, you may have to sell your bond back to the corporation before it matures. When a bond is issued with callable provisions, it means that the issuing corporation has the right to retire—that is, repurchase from you—the bond before the maturity date. Corporations exercise this option when it is in their best interest to do so, specifically when interest rates have fallen.

For example, assume a corporation issues 30-year bonds for $1,000 each at 10 percent interest. Assume also that the provisions allow the corporation to retire the bonds after 10 years at $1,050. If interest rates fall after 10 years to 8 percent, the corporation will certainly retire the bonds. If the corporation still needs funds, it can issue new bonds at 8 percent, thereby saving considerable interest expense.

From an investor's viewpoint, when you purchase a callable bond, the risk is that you may not receive interest at the specified rate for the complete interval up to maturity. If you purchase a 30-year bond that is called after 10 years, you will have to reinvest the proceeds and receive a lower rate of return. In that case the only way to obtain a higher rate of return is to incur more risk by investing in a lower-quality bond.

When a bond is issued, all callable provisions have to be identified and documented. Accordingly, you should ask your broker, before you purchase a bond, whether there are any callable provisions and if so, what they are. If the callable provisions will deny you a guaranteed interest rate for a guaranteed length of time consistent with your investment objectives, you should ask your broker to find another investment that does meet your objectives.

Callable provisions protect corporations, not you. If interest rates increase, corporations will not exercise the callable option, and you will have the choice of keeping a bond paying a low interest rate or selling the bond and suffering a capital loss.

## Treasury Notes and Bonds

Treasury notes are United States Treasury debt obligations that are issued in maturities from 2 years to 10 years. For 2-year and 3-year notes the minimum purchase price is $5,000; above $5,000 they are sold in $1,000 increments. For longer maturities the minimum purchase price is $1,000. Treasury bonds are issued in maturities between 10 years and 30 years. The minimum purchase is $1,000. Interest rates are fixed when the debt instruments are issued.

For both notes and bonds, interest is paid semiannually. Interest paid will be based on existing economic conditions and expected inflation rates. The rates of return on notes and bonds will generally be greater than the rates on Treasury bills.

You can purchase notes and bonds directly from the Federal Reserve without paying a sales commission. You can also purchase them from brokers or banks and pay sales commissions such as $25 or $50 per note or bond. If you hold the notes and bonds until maturity, you will receive the face value. You can sell these securities at any time, but if you sell before maturity, the price you will receive will be based on prevailing interest rates at the time you sell. If interest rates have gone up since your initial purchase, the price of your securities will undoubtedly be lower than what you paid for them. The further the securities are from maturity, the more volatile the price movements will be. Not only debt instruments issued by the Treasury but also all other debt instruments will fluctuate in value based on changes in interest rates and the length of the interval before maturity.

If you sell Treasury securities before maturity, you will have to sell them through your broker or banker, and you will have to pay a sales commission. The Federal Reserve redeems notes and bonds only at maturity.

Securities issued by the Treasury are the safest debt instrument you can buy because they are backed by the United States government. If you hold these securities until maturity, you can rest assured that you will be paid the face value of the security. The rate of return you obtain from Treasury notes and bonds will not be as high as those you can get from securities issued by other governmental agencies and corporations for the same maturity. The reason is that Treasury instruments are the safest. You may be able to get a higher rate of return on a security from some other issuer, but the instrument will not be as safe.

At times the rate of return on Treasury bills (See Chapter 7) is close to the rate of return available from Treasury notes and/or Treasury bonds.

Interest on all Treasury instruments, including notes and bonds, is taxable at the federal level. They are tax-exempt, however, at the state and local level.

## Government Agency Bonds

Many federal agencies also issue debt securities with varying maturities. You can generally obtain a slightly higher rate of return, perhaps half a percentage point more, from a government agency bond. These bonds are almost as safe as Treasury instruments. There has never been any situation in which a federal agency has defaulted on its bonds. You can purchase such bonds from a broker or banker.

Agencies that issue debt securities include the Farm Credit Association (FCA), Federal Home Loan Banks (FHLB), Federal National Mortgage Association (FNMA), Federal Home Loan Mortgage Corporation, and the Student Loan Marketing Association (SLMA). Many agency securities have tax advantages. For example, securities issued by the FHLB and SLMA are exempt from state and local taxes.

One disadvantage of agency bonds is that they do not have as wide a market as Treasury securities. Accordingly, if you sold these bonds before maturity, you might not obtain a fair price because of the lack of market. If you think you will not hold the bonds until maturity, you are probably better off with Treasury securities with the same maturity.

## Mortgage-Backed Securities

Some federal agencies also issue mortgage-backed pass-through securities. These securities are bonds that have collateral in the form of pools of mortgages. Financial institutions package these pools of mortgages, which are guaranteed by the federal government. These packages are generally sold in units of $25,000, although you can purchase them from mutual funds with smaller investments.

The Government National Mortgage Association (GNMA), a governmental agency, underwrites some of these securities, which are known as Ginnie Maes. The Federal National Mortgage Association (FNMA) also underwrites such securities, known as Fannie Maes. Both Ginnie Mae and Fannie Mae securities, known as pass-through certificates, are very safe because they are insured by the federal government. If you invest in these securities, you will receive interest and principal each month until the certificates are paid off. They normally pay a slightly higher return than Treasury securities of the same maturity.

The average life of these securities is approximately 12 years. The length is uncertain because it is determined by individual homeowners, who decide whether to pay off their mortgages and when. You do not deal with the individual homeowner, however. You receive your payment directly from the brokerage firm or financial institution that markets the security.

Many mutual funds now offer funds that specialize in pass-through certificates. If you purchased a fund, your minimum investment would generally be much smaller than $25,000—normally $1,000, sometimes less. Moreover, you can have your interest and return of capital automatically reinvested in the fund. If you purchase the units outside a fund, you will have to reinvest the income and capital you receive independently.

One of the advantages of the pass-through certificates is that you receive interest and part of your capital back each month. That works to your advantage when interest rates are rising because you can reinvest the proceeds in investments that produce higher returns. The fact that you get part of your capital back each month provides more protection for you because you receive your investment regularly over time, and your capital is not as exposed to increases in interest rates.

You can sell your investment in these securities in the open market whenever you wish. As is true for all debt instruments, however, the price will fluctuate, and if you sell when interest rates have gone up, you may lose some of your initial capital investment.

Overall, pass-through certificates offer many attractive features such as high income, an active secondary market, and a relatively short maturity. If you purchase shares in a mutual fund specializing in these securities, you will also have flexibility regarding reinvestment of interest and capital as well as lower minimum investment requirements.

## Corporate Bonds

Corporate bonds are generally issued in units of $1,000 with maturities of 10 to 30 years and usually pay interest semiannually. The highest-quality long-term corporate bond will generally provide approximately 1 percent more than a Treasury bond with the same maturity date. Corporate bonds provide higher rates of return than Treasury securities because they are not as safe. Even the strongest corporation does not have the financial strength of the United States government.

Corporations that do not have the strongest financial ratings have to offer much higher returns than Treasury bonds in order to encourage investors to purchase them. Higher rates will undoubtedly appeal to you, but you have to consider the risks of investing in securities that are rated poorly because of the financial condition of the issuing corporation.

If you are willing to accept the risk of purchasing bonds from a financially troubled company in order to obtain a higher return, you should consider investing in mutual funds that specialize in corporate bonds. The risk of investing in low-quality bonds is too high for most individual investors. If you invest in a mutual fund, you are spreading your risks across many bonds, perhaps more than a hundred.

Even if you are purchasing high-quality bonds, you may want to consider mutual funds rather than individual bonds. Many brokerage firms consider any purchase of individual bonds to be small, and this may be reflected in their sales commission structure. Find out how your brokerage firm computes its commission on bond purchases. If your purchase is considered an odd lot, then you may want to reconsider whether you want to buy individual bonds. An odd-lot purchase is an order for less than the normal units of trading—fewer than 100 shares of stock or fewer than 5 bonds. The odd lot differential is the price differential that is often charged when an odd lot order is executed on an exchange. If you purchase an odd lot, the spread between the purchase price and the sale price is wider than otherwise. In short, you pay more if you are buying or receive less if you are selling.

## Municipal Bonds

If you are in a high tax bracket, municipal bonds may provide you with a higher after-tax return than corporate bonds that have the same maturity and risk. Municipal bonds are issued by a municipal government. Interest on municipal bonds is tax-free at the federal level. Many municipal bonds are also exempt from state and local taxes in the state where they are issued.

Municipal bonds can be general obligation bonds, which means that the municipality can use general tax revenues to pay interest and principal. Revenue bonds are municipal bonds that derive their revenue from a specific project such as a toll road or a toll bridge. A municipality can offer more than one bond issue, each of which is rated individually by the same rating services that rate corporate bonds. Municipalities provide lower yields than taxable securities of the same maturity and risk rating. You should compare the rate of return on a municipal bond only with the after-tax return of an equivalently rated taxable security.

For example, assume you can purchase a 30-year bond yielding 10 percent with the excellent rating of AAA. If you are in the 28 percent tax bracket, a yield of 7.2 percent on a municipal bond of the same rating and maturity will offer you the same after-tax yield. For every $100 interest that you earn, you have to pay the IRS $28 in federal taxes. If the yield on a municipal bond is more than 7.2 percent, the after-tax yield on the municipal bond will be higher than the yield on the corporate bond. If the yield on a municipal bond is less than 7.2 percent, you will obtain a higher after-tax yield by purchasing the corporate bond.

Municipal bonds fluctuate in value based on changes in interest rates in the same way that other bonds do. Thus, you should not purchase long-term municipal bonds, which have a greater fluctuation in prices than short-term bonds, if you cannot afford any loss in your capital base and you do not expect to hold the bond until maturity.

Municipal bonds in general have historically been safe investments from the viewpoint of on-time interest payments and repayment of principal at maturity. There have been exceptions, however. You should not jeopardize your retirement capital by investing too much of your assets in one bond, even if it does have an excellent rating. Ratings can fall, and when they do, your bonds fall in value also, placing your interest payments and principal in jeopardy.

One way to protect your capital is through the purchase of a diversified portfolio. If you do not have sufficient assets to build a diversified individual portfolio, or you prefer not to, you can purchase shares in a municipal bond fund or units of a unit investment trust. These investments are discussed in this chapter.

## Insurance for Your Portfolio

One way to cover the risk of a specific bond is to purchase insurance. Some large insurance companies provide insurance for specific bonds. The insurance company does not offer you any protection against any fall in the price of your bond resulting from general increases in interest rates or any other market factors. What the insurance company does do, however, is pay you the face value of the bond if the issuer cannot continue to pay interest and repay your principal. If your bond decreases in value before the issuer defaults, you will be protected in the sense that you will be paid the face value of the bond. The insurance company does not guarantee you that you will receive all interest payments. It guarantees principal only.

The cost to you for insurance is approximately half a percent. Normally, when a specific issue, or group of bonds, is protected by insurance, the rating of the bonds is Standard & Poor's AAA or Moody's Aaa, the highest possible ratings. Insurance is generally more useful if you have a small portfolio. If you purchase shares of a municipal bond mutual fund, however, your fund will not have insurance, and you will not need it because the size of the portfolio makes insurance unnecessary.

## Income-Producing Mutual Funds

If you are investing less than $100,000, it will be difficult for you to develop an individualized diversified portfolio in order to minimize your risks. A diversified portfolio will allow you to minimize all three of the risks discussed earlier in the chapter—issuer risk, interest rate risk, and call risk. Moreover, if you are making small individual purchases, you will likely be paying higher sales commissions and higher prices than if you were to use the same dollars to purchase shares of a large mutual fund.

There are many mutual funds for you to choose from that specialize in income and bonds. Some of these funds are very conservative, and some are aggressive. For example, there are funds that invest only in shorter-term government securities and others that invest only in high-risk bonds known as junk bonds. The investment objectives of most funds lie between these two extremes. Be assured, you will be able to select a fund that meets your investment objectives.

In Chapter 8 mutual funds are covered in depth, providing you with sources of information, guidelines for selecting a fund, and ways to monitor fund performance.

## Unit Trusts

A unit trust is a professionally selected fixed portfolio of securities designed to meet specific investment objectives. The portfolio is kept in trust for all the individual investors by a trustee. A trustee has the responsibility to manage the portfolio on behalf of the individual investors. The trust is sold in specific units with a minimum investment, which varies based on the specific trust.

Unit trusts that are designed to meet retirement objectives could include investments in municipal bonds, corporate bonds, government securities, GNMAs, FNMAs, utility stocks, and zero-coupon bonds. A zero-coupon bond is a fixed-income security issued at a discount. It does not pay interest but is redeemable at face value upon maturity. For example, if you purchased a 30-year zero-coupon bond paying 10 percent with a face value of $1,000 at maturity, you could purchase the bond at a cost of approximately $54. (A detailed discussion of zero-coupon bonds is contained in Chapter 10.)

Unit trusts can provide the advantages of professional selection, diversification, high yields, a fixed rate of return, monthly income, a secondary market for resale, and a specific end date when the capital is returned to the purchaser.

The unit trust differs from the mutual fund in that the trust has a specific point when the trust will be terminated. Income from the trust and returns of capital are distributed to you. They cannot be reinvested in the trust. If you invest in a mutual fund, you can reinvest returns of capital and interest.

Unit trusts and mutual funds have some similarities and a significant difference. They are similar in that both offer diversified portfolios and professional management. The significant difference relates to the portfolio. With the trust the portfolio is fixed, and no new securities are added. The trust has a specific end point when the capital is returned.

The mutual fund has no end date. The management of the fund continuously buys and sells securities based on the flow of money into the fund. Although you can sell your fund shares at any time, there is no guarantee that you will get your initial investment back because the value of the shares will change continuously based on changes in the value of the securities in the fund, which in turn fluctuate because of changes in interest rates.

Before you invest in a unit trust or mutual fund, it is important that you understand the differences between the two. Which is best for you depends on your primary objectives. It is possible, however, that both vehicles can be useful to you simultaneously.

## High-Income Common Stocks

Another type of security that can provide you with high income is common stock. You have to be selective when it comes to common stocks. Consider only those corporations that have a history of paying a significant portion of their earnings to their stockholders in the form of dividends. Corporations in certain industries such as utilities, financial services, and auto manufacturing have consistently paid high dividends.

There is a significant difference between bonds and common stocks regarding the obligation of the corporation. When a corporation issues bonds, it has a legal obligation to pay interest on the debt and to retire the debt at maturity. Regarding common stocks, corporate management has no obligation to pay dividends. Once a corporation has a reputation as a company that pays high dividends, management generally tries hard to continue to pay dividends at established levels and to increase dividends wherever possible. Corporate management is under no legal obligation, however, to pay dividends. Therefore, if a corporation undergoes financial difficulties, management may decide to reduce or eliminate its dividend.

If you are considering purchasing the common shares of an individual company for income purposes, look carefully at its recent performance and associated industry prospects. Make sure that recent earnings comfortably exceed the size of the latest dividend.

There are many reliable sources of information that can help you review the financial condition of a corporation. Moody's, Standard & Poor's, and Value Line all analyze corporate performance and prospects on both an individual basis and an industry basis. Your broker should be able to provide this type of information to you. If you invest with a full-service brokerage firm, the research department should be able to make individual recommendations to you.

There are a few advantages that common stock investments provide for you that bonds would not. Over time, if a corporation performs well and increases its earnings, corporate management can elect to increase its dividend for its common stockholders. Bondholders will never obtain a higher interest rate on a bond than is specified in the initial agreement.

A second advantage is that the price of the common stock can increase because of economic conditions and because of the performance of the individual corporation. When you purchase a bond and hold it to maturity, you will receive the face value of the bond regardless of how well the issuing corporation may have performed.

## Preferred Stock

A preferred stock, despite its name, is more like a bond than it is like a common stock. When you purchase either common or preferred stock, you have an ownership share in the corporation. Preferred shareholders receive fixed dividends at a specified rate. Preferred stockholders generally do not have voting rights (as common stockholders do).

Both types of shareholders are owners of the company. In both cases dividends are declared at the option of the Board of Directors. However, preferred shareholders have priority over common shareholders for dividends. Common shareholders receive a dividend that varies depending on the performance of the company.

For an investor interested in income, preferred stock has some advantages over common stock in that the company is required to pay preferred stockholders for as long as it is financially able to do so. Most preferred stock is cumulative, which means that dividends accumulate if for any reason they have not been paid out. They must be paid before common stock dividends are paid.

If preferred stock is noncumulative, dividends passed — that is, not paid in a specific year — are not paid at all. Dividends are passed when earnings are poor and there are insufficient liquid assets to pay dividends. Avoid purchasing noncumulative preferred stock.

Preferred stock is different from bonds in that there is no maturity date for preferred stock. You can sell preferred stock on the open market through your broker. The price of preferred stock will fluctuate in the market in the same way that bonds do.

There is one category of preferred stock that gives you some protection against increases in interest rates — adjustable-rate preferred stock. The rate of return on adjustable-rate preferred stock can vary based on changes in a preestablished index such as Treasury bills. From an investor standpoint, this gives you flexibility and capital protection. As interest rates increase, you automatically receive a higher interest rate on a schedule, for example, quarterly. Moreover, the adjustable feature will provide price stability.

Historically, preferred stock has not been a particularly attractive vehicle for retirees. The adjustable-rate feature, however, makes it much more attractive than it used to be. Thus far, however, such stocks have not been issued by very many corporations, and they generally have been sold to institutions.

Before you consider the purchase of any preferred stock, make sure you understand the rights of the issuing corporation regarding retiring the stock.

## Securities Fraud

Although the majority of securities salespeople and the firms they work for are ethical, there will always be sales representatives who are unethical. Accordingly, in order for you to avoid being a party to a fraudulent transaction, it is necessary for you to take certain precautions before you enter into any securities transaction.

Before you complete any securities transaction, take into account the following considerations:

- Ask your sales representative about his or her qualifications and how long he or she has been employed in the securities field.
- Know the history of the firm the sales representative works for and which state and national organizations the firm is registered with. Call your local Better Business Bureau for a reliability report on the company.
- Obtain and review a written proposal or prospectus on the venture and the company, including financial statements if available.
- Consult an accountant, attorney, or other knowledgeable person whom you trust if you have questions or do not understand the deal.
- For tax shelter deals, ask the promoter for a written legal opinion as to the tax consequences of the venture.
- Contact your state securities department to determine whether the selling organization has obtained all proper licenses or has a history of problems with authorities.
- Avoid promoters using random telephone calls, high-pressure tactics, or messenger services that pick up money from investors. Be wary of salespeople who urge "immediate action."
- Never mail payment by certified check, give credit card numbers over the phone, or send payment via a messenger service arranged by the promoter.
- Beware of pyramid schemes, in which recruitment of new members is more important than the product being distributed. Those in the scheme early may profit; those in late always lose.

## Sources of Information

Before you select a specific common stock, you should examine the fundamentals of the industry and any available specific information regarding the company. Financial services companies such as Value Line, Moody's, and Standard & Poor's offer services that can be very helpful to you. If their reviews show that earnings prospects are poor for a particular industry, you should be cautious regarding investing in stocks in that industry.

These services also look at earnings prospects for specific companies. Certainly, industry reviews and individual company reviews are not foolproof in terms of predicting future earnings, but they are basically reliable sources of information that you should take advantage of.

Be sure to select a brokerage firm with a good research department. It should be able to provide you with industry analyses as well as individual evaluations.

All major corporations prepare annual reports that contain useful financial information. These reports are available directly from the corporation at no cost to you. You can obtain full names and addresses from your broker or from a public library. The financial information contained in the annual report has been verified by an independent accounting firm. Accordingly, you can rely on its accuracy because of the independence of the accounting firm. The nonfinancial information in the annual report is prepared by the corporation, and therefore it will be presented in as favorable a light as possible. Nevertheless, this information should be valuable to you because it provides you with an insight as to how existing management looks at the corporation and how it views the future prospects and trends of the company.

## Summary

There are many options available to you if your primary objective is high income. These include debt instruments issued by the United States Treasury, other governmental agencies, and corporations. You can also consider common stocks, which have a long history of paying out high levels of dividends.

An important factor for you to remember is that whenever an investment seems to be providing an extremely high interest rate, you can be certain that there is some type of risk, either issuer risk or interest rate risk. You should consider these risk factors before you purchase a security.

You should also take tax considerations into account and compute your expected return on an after-tax basis. Treasury securities and some federal agency securities provide tax advantages at the state and local level. Municipal bonds provide tax-free income at the federal level, and they sometimes have state and local tax advantages as well.

# CHAPTER 7

# Investments with Growth Potential

**I**n this chapter we will discuss investments that are likely to provide a high rate of growth for you. You might consider these types of investments if one of your investment objectives is capital growth. In this chapter we will discuss common stocks and mutual funds that specialize in growth. Real estate, gold, zero-coupon bonds, and other investments with growth potential will be covered in subsequent chapters.

There are a few reasons why growth investments may be important to you. One important reason is so that you can build up a significant capital base prior to retirement. A second important reason is to provide a hedge against inflation. Even during retirement it may be necessary for you to apportion some of your assets into growth-related instruments to ensure that your capital base will remain large enough throughout your retirement.

## Preretirement Investing

When more than 5 years away from retirement, most people find it reasonable to invest in growth common stocks and growth mutual funds. You are still building an asset base for retirement, and you are more interested in capital growth than you are in producing income.

As you approach and enter retirement, however, your situation changes. You should be more concerned about preservation of capital and producing income. Accordingly, the percentage of your total assets that you allocate primarily to growth-related investments should generally be reduced as you approach and enter retirement.

## Common Stocks

Historically, common stocks in United States equities have been an excellent investment. In the long run investment in common stocks, also known as equity investment, has been superior to investment in fixed-income securities. There have been many periods, however, some of which have lasted more than 5 years, in which investments in common stock have not been good, both in general and in comparison with other forms of investment.

In October 1987 many investors found out that stock prices could go down in value in much less time than it takes for them to increase in value. In only one day, October 19 to be exact, common stock prices fell an average of 23 percent. For corporations with a small number of common shares outstanding, stock prices fell even further on average. Even though prices recovered from these levels, many investors were unable or unwilling to wait, and they sold their stock at low levels, suffering major capital losses.

No one can guarantee that the value of common stocks will be any more stable in the future. When the stock market fell in October 1987, just about every common stock fell significantly in value. You were not protected if you invested in common stock mutual funds or if you invested only in the highest-quality stocks.

The volatility in the stock market is likely to remain for some time. Despite various studies and recommendations by different parties, the interests of powerful lobbies make it very difficult to make structural changes in the securities markets. The result is that volatility will remain, and investors who are concerned about preservation of their existing capital base—mainly persons already retired—should not be investing significant portions of their portfolios in growth-related common stocks.

### Basics of Investing in Common Stocks

When you purchase shares of common stock, you are purchasing a share of ownership in a specific corporation. Your share of ownership can be computed by dividing the number of shares you own by the total number of shares outstanding at a particular time.

Most investors buy common stock in units of 100 shares. The primary reason is that for most corporate issues fewer than 100 shares is considered an odd lot. If you purchase stocks in odd lots, you pay more per share than you would if you were to purchase shares in units of 100.

Most financial information is reported on a per-share basis, which makes it easier for you to keep track of your investment. For example, the price of common stock is listed in the financial pages of most daily newspapers on a per-share basis. If you purchased 100 shares of common stock, and the price is quoted at $50 per share, the value of your investment is 100 × $50, or $5,000.

You can benefit from purchasing common stock in two ways: through dividend payments and through increases in the value of common stock. The foundations of both dividends and common stock prices are current earnings and projected earnings of the corporation and in some cases the availability for sale of marketable assets owned by the corporation.

### Fundamental Analysis

Regardless of whether you are purchasing common stocks primarily for growth or for income, fundamental analysis is important. When you choose a common stock, it should be based on specific criteria concerning the earnings capability of the company, the price of the common stock, and the overall financial strength of the company. Some of these fundamental factors are industry prospects, earnings, the ratio of price to earnings, return on equity, and dividends. These fundamental factors will be discussed further.

To evaluate whether a company pays high dividends, examine the ratio of dividends to earnings over the last few years. A true growth company will have a ratio of less than 50 percent on a consistent basis for several years.

## Sources of Information

The fundamental data discussed in this chapter are available from a variety of sources. Historical information regarding earnings, dividends, and security prices is available at no cost to you in the form of annual and quarterly reports prepared by the company. You can obtain these reports by requesting them from the corporate communications or public relations department of the company you are interested in.

Fundamental data are also available from publications maintained and issued by Standard & Poor's, Moody's, and Value Line. This information is produced for individual companies and for specific industries. You can obtain this information from a full-service broker or through a major public library. You can subscribe individually, but you may find the cost to be prohibitively high if you are a relatively small investor.

The research departments of full-service brokerage firms regularly prepare reports of individual companies and specific industries. You can ask your broker to have these reports sent to you.

Following are addresses of companies you may wish to contact:

Standard & Poor's Corporation
25 Broadway
New York, NY 10004

Moody's Investors Service
99 Church Street
New York, NY 10007-2796

Forbes Inc.
60 Fifth Avenue
New York, NY 10011

Value Line Inc.
711 Third Avenue
New York, NY 10017

### Dividends

The dividend is the portion of earnings that is paid to common stockholders. Generally the dividend is declared quarterly.

It is important for you to understand that the management of a corporation is under no obligation to pay dividends. Dividends can be omitted, reduced, or increased. Management makes its recommendations regarding dividends based on the financial condition of the corporation at a point in time and based on expectations of future prospects.

If you are investing in a company primarily for growth purposes, you should be looking for companies that *do not* pay high dividends. If a corporation pays high dividends, those earnings cannot be reinvested in the company to foster growth. Companies that generally achieve the fastest growth are those that are investing the majority of their earnings in the company in a profitable manner.

### Earnings per Share

Earnings per share are the total earnings of the corporation divided by the number of shares outstanding. You should review the historical trend of earnings per share. A company that is growing and investing a good portion of its earnings in the company should be reporting growth in earnings per share. If you observe a drop in earnings per share in the last year or so, you should be wary of purchasing common stock unless you are convinced that there were special circumstances and that earnings will increase in the future.

### Price-Earnings Ratio

The best measure of the price of the stock is the price-earnings (P/E) ratio. Simply stated, the P/E ratio is the market price per share of the common stock divided by the annual earnings per share of the company.

For example, if the current price of a company's common stock is $30 and the earnings over the last year were $3 per share, the P/E ratio is 10 ($30 ÷ $3).

The P/E ratio is listed in most daily newspapers on the same line as the latest common stock prices in the financial section of the newspaper. Historical P/E ratios are generally included in company annual reports and in the other sources identified earlier in the chapter such as Standard & Poor's, Moody's, and Value Line.

The P/E ratio of a stock is generally a pretty good indication of how the financial community judges the future prospects in earnings of a company. If a company's P/E ratio is low in comparison with the industry's average P/E ratio, it is an indication that the financial community does not think highly of a specific company's prospects. On the other hand, a high P/E ratio is an indicator that a company's earning prospects are better than average. Generally, you will find that the major companies in a specific industry will have P/E ratios fairly close to one another. The leading or best-managed company in an industry will usually have the highest P/E ratio. You should be concerned that you do not purchase stocks whose P/E ratios are *too* high, however, because you may be paying too much. Before you purchase a stock that has a high P/E ratio, satisfy yourself that the company has above-average prospects for future earnings growth. Ask your broker to provide you with the latest available research reports for both the company and the industry.

Before you purchase a stock, you should examine the history of P/E ratios for that company. If the P/E ratio is at an all-time high or close to it, you should be wary of purchasing the stock unless there are new positive fundamental factors. For example, if a pharmaceutical company with a high P/E ratio has just found the cure for AIDS, then a high P/E ratio is justified. You should consider purchasing stocks in companies with high P/E ratios only when there are fundamental reasons to expect higher than average earnings in the future.

The P/E ratio of most common stock is between 10 and 20. P/E ratios above 20 generally indicate that earnings projections are favorable for the corresponding company. High P/E ratios generally last only as long as earnings for the company remain high. For that reason you have to be cautious about investing in companies whose P/E ratio is abnormally high, since a fall, or even a leveling off in earnings, usually leads to a sharp fall in the price of the common stock.

### Return on Equity

Return on equity is a very important measure of a company's profitability. This measure is an indication of the profitability of the company relative to total stockholder investment. Return on equity is computed by dividing net income by net worth. Net worth is the amount of common stock investment plus retained earnings from prior years. Net income is simply the income remaining after all expenses and taxes have been paid. Figures for return on equity are available from annual reports as well as from the various investment services.

Return on equity is most valuable if you are comparing stocks in the same industry. A company that consistently shows higher rates of return on equity than its competitors can safely be considered a well-managed company. On a long-term basis you will be a successful investor if you invest only in companies that consistently provide high returns on equity. For example, Philip Morris Companies, Inc. consistently has a high return on equity.

## Growth Mutual Funds

For most investors it is difficult to build and manage diversified common stock portfolios. If your common stock portfolio is less than $50,000, you should seriously consider using mutual funds rather than managing your own portfolio. In fact, many professionals suggest that even a $100,000 portfolio is not large enough to manage individually.

There are many well-run mutual funds that specialize in growth securities. These funds provide many advantages such as diversification, liquidity, professional management, and low fees. If you are dissatisfied with a specific fund's performance, you can switch funds or decide to manage your assets yourself whenever you wish. You can invest in as many funds as you want. Another advantage of using a fund manager is that your time and effort will be minimized. If you manage your own assets, you should regularly—if not daily, then certainly weekly—monitor the prices of the securities in your portfolio. The volatility of the markets today makes this necessary.

Except under extraordinary conditions, the value of your investments in a fund, because of its wider diversification, will not fluctuate as much as it would in a small individual portfolio.

Mutual fund investments will be explored in more detail in the next chapter.

## Summary

Investing in common stock equities can provide you with growth potential in addition to dividend income. When you invest in debt instruments, you are limited in two ways: your income level is fixed, and you will receive only the face value of your investment at maturity. When you invest in common stocks, whether individual ones or as part of a mutual fund, the amount of the dividend can be increased and the value of the common stock can increase in value.

On the other hand, dividends are not guaranteed at any level, and common stock prices go down as well as up. Moreover, there is *never* a point in time that corporations will redeem a common stock at a specified value.

In short, common stock investing has advantages as well as disadvantages. If it is important for you to have some capital appreciation in your assets, then you should consider common stock investments. If you do not expect to have a common stock portfolio greater than $100,000, consider well-managed mutual funds whose objectives are consistent with yours.

CHAPTER

## 8

# Mutual Funds

**A** mutual fund is an open-end investment company that pools the money of its shareholders to invest in a diversified portfolio of securities.

For example, Dreyfus Corporation is one of the nation's largest mutual fund management companies. The Dreyfus Corporation manages approximately 25 individual mutual funds. Each of these funds is an individual open-end investment company with unique investment objectives. If you look at the mutual fund listing in the financial section of a major newspaper, you will see all the mutual funds that are managed by the Dreyfus Corporation under the Dreyfus heading.

An open-end investment company is one that continually buys and sells ownership shares based on investors' demands. Accordingly, the number of shares outstanding in mutual funds varies daily. This open-endedness gives investors maximum liquidity because the fund is always willing to buy shares back from investors. The price that investors receive is based on the value of the securities held by the mutual fund. The securities in the mutual fund are selected according to the investment objectives of the fund. These securities include common stocks, corporate bonds, government bonds, municipal bonds, money-market instruments, and foreign securities.

## Advantages

There are many advantages for an investor in mutual funds. They include diversification, wide selection, professional management, flexibility, liquidity, low management and administrative costs, possible tax shelter, convenient

55

options for purchase and sale, and automatic reinvestment of interest and capital gains at your option.

In many types of investment small investors are not treated as well as large ones, sometimes paying higher sales commissions or paying higher prices for the same securities. Mutual funds, however, generally treat all investors in the same way. The individual who invests $1,000 is treated exactly the same as the individual investing $1,000,000. Mutual fund investing is an excellent way for small investors to build up an investment base without incurring large sales commissions or administrative costs.

Another significant advantage of investing in mutual funds is that there is a great deal of reliable historical information available. Accordingly, you can select a mutual fund based on unbiased historical performance data. Past performance is available for various periods of time from various sources.

Some sources of information are Wiesenberger's *Investment Companies, Money* magazine, and *Forbes. Forbes* publishes a special issue annually, generally the last week of September or the first week in October, that contains a detailed review of new developments in the mutual fund field and an in-depth review of the performance of individual funds.

Since past performance is one of the most important criteria for selecting a mutual fund, ready availability of historical data is an important advantage to you.

Another is the option to reinvest any interest, dividends, or capital gains to purchase additional shares. When you initially purchase shares in a fund, you will specify whether income or capital gains distributed by the fund are to be sent to you or reinvested in the fund. You can change this option whenever you wish. This option is significant because it gives you flexibility. Even if you choose to reinvest earnings in the fund, the earnings will be taxable unless you are investing in a tax-free fund.

Another important advantage is flexibility in switching from one type of fund to another. Most mutual funds offer investors more than one type of fund. At different times, based on market conditions and your personal objectives, you may want to move your money from one type of invest- ment to another. For example, you may have made a reasonable profit investing in a common stock mutual fund. If you wanted to lock in some of these profits, you could sell some of the shares you own and reinvest the proceeds in a safer money-market fund. With most funds you could do this as simply as calling the toll-free number of the fund and informing the representative of the dollar amount of the transaction and the names of the funds you are selling and purchasing. Your transaction will be exe- cuted at the closing prices in the market that day.

## SCENARIO

You own shares in two funds that are part of the Scudder Family of Funds. You have $10,000 invested in the Japan Fund, which invests exclusively in Japanese-managed companies. You also have $5,000 invested in the Scudder Cash Investment Trust, a money-market fund. You want to sell $5,000 worth of the Japan Fund and invest the proceeds in the Scudder Cash Investment Trust.

You can execute this transaction by calling a Scudder Fund representative on a toll-free number supplied by Scudder. You inform the representative as to the transaction you want to execute and the account numbers of the funds you are executing transactions for. These transactions will be executed at the closing prices of the funds on the day you call in your transactions. In a few business days you will receive a confirmation of your transaction, specifying the number of shares bought and sold, the price per share of the funds bought and sold, and the number of shares that you own in each of these funds after the transactions were executed.

You will find that buying and selling shares in your fund is very simple. You can execute your transactions by mail, dealing directly with the mutual fund representative without any contact with an intermediary such as a stockbroker.

If you want faster service, you can execute all your transactions by telephone, dealing directly with the fund. When you open your account, you select the purchase and the selling options you wish from the fund's available alternatives. You will find that most funds offer a wide selection of convenient options. For example, if you may need immediate availability of funds, you can request wire-transfer capability. This will give you the opportunity to sell shares and have the fund wire the money to your bank the next day. You will have access to those funds immediately thereafter.

Another advantage of investing in funds is the ability to invest specific dollar amounts rather than purchasing a specific number of shares. For many investors it is convenient to invest a specific dollar amount periodically. For example, you may wish to invest $100 per month, or $300 per quarter. With most investment vehicles, this type of transaction would be either prohibitively expensive or impossible. Mutual funds accept any amount as long as it meets the minimum investment requirement established by the fund. You will receive a regular statement from the mutual fund confirming either the purchase or sale of shares, records of transactions and present holdings in thousandths of a share, for example, 100.653 shares.

Moreover, there can be advantages to periodically investing a specific amount. This technique, known as dollar-cost averaging, is examined in detail below.

Perhaps the most significant advantage to mutual fund investors is diversification. A small or medium investor simply cannot afford to purchase a diversified portfolio independently. However, *even the smallest investor in a mutual fund obtains the same diversification as the largest investor.* Moreover, the smallest investor receives the same rate of return as the largest investor: If the fund increases in value 10 percent, the investor who owns one share receives the same 10 percent increase in value as the investor who owns a million shares. Obviously, the small investor has good reason to invest in mutual funds.

## Dollar-Cost Averaging

Dollar-cost averaging is a technique in which you periodically place a constant dollar amount in one specific investment. The period can vary according to the desires of the particular investor. The advantage of the technique is that it allows you to purchase more shares when prices are low and fewer shares when prices are high. Dollar-cost averaging is effective only when the securities you are purchasing have a long-term upward price trend. The technique is effective for small and large investors, particularly if there is a great deal of volatility in prices as with common stock and bond investments.

This technique works well with mutual funds because you can invest constant dollar amounts with funds very easily. The technique cannot be used very effectively with forms of investment in which you have to purchase a specific number of shares rather than a constant dollar amount.

If you have a large sum of money that you would like to invest in common stocks gradually, you can initially invest your resources in a money-market account or money-market fund. Then you can periodically invest whatever amount you wish—there are no limits at all.

The technique is a good one, but it requires discipline on your part. You must be able to invest a fixed amount when prices are falling. At times like these, many investors find it difficult to invest, but that is when you must invest in order to take advantage of dollar-cost averaging.

If you expect a lump-sum distribution—the distribution of an individual's benefit in one payment rather than in installments—you may want to consider using dollar-cost averaging. You may wish to invest a portion of your distribution in common stocks, for example, but are concerned about timing. You can place your distribution initially in conservative investments such as money-market funds or certificates of deposit. Then you can gradually invest a fixed dollar amount in one or more well-managed common-stock funds.

## No-Load and Load Funds

Some mutual funds are sold to you without a sales commission. These funds are called no-load funds. A true no-load fund has no back-end charges—known as redemption fees—or marketing fees associated with 12(b)1 funds. 12(b)1 refers to a portion of the IRS code that allows a mutual fund to charge advertising and promotion expenses to its shareholders. If a fund elects to do this, it must be disclosed in the prospectus. These fees will be discussed later in this chapter. These are sold either directly by the company managing the fund or through an authorized distributor. Funds for which you must pay a sales commission are called load funds. The sales commissions vary, but they generally fall between 3 percent and 8 percent of your investment. Most commissions are closer to 8 percent than 3 percent.

The only time you should purchase a load fund is when you believe that the performance of the adviser for the fund is superior to that of the managers of the available no-load funds.

When you invest $1,000 in a no-load fund, you have $1,000 working for you. If you invest $1,000 in a fund and pay an 8 percent sales commission, you have only $920 working for you. The investment adviser of the load fund must have a performance that is worth the extra $80 to you. If the no-load fund earned 8 percent, the value of your investment would be $1,166 at the end of 2 years. If the load fund increased in value by 12 percent each year, the value of your investment at the end of two years would be only $1,155.

Another problem associated with investing in load funds is buyer reluctance to sell. If you pay an 8 percent sales commission, you may hesitate to sell your shares, even if the fund is performing poorly, because you would lose the 8 percent sales commission. You could much more easily afford to sell a no-load fund.

If you review the past performance of mutual funds, you will find that many of the best performers have been no-load funds. Do not be misled by a salesman who tells you, "You get what you pay for," to justify paying a sales commission. Mutual-fund advisers are compensated by investment advisory fees. They do not receive sales commissions. Therefore, do not purchase a load mutual fund because you think you will get better treatment from investment advisers. As an investor, you are better off if 100 percent of your investment is working for you.

## Mutual Fund Listings

When you read the financial section of most newspapers, you can immediately determine whether a fund is load or no-load. You can tell that a fund has no associated commissions if the bid price and ask (buy) price are identical, or if the paper uses the initials NL, which stand for no-load. The bid price in many newspapers is listed as NAV, which means net asset value. If the bid and ask prices are different, then the fund is evidently a load fund. You can determine the sales commission by the spread between the bid price and the ask price.

Assume the bid price for a fund is $18.40 and the ask price is $20. This means that if you bought the fund, you would pay $20 per share and that if you sold the fund you would receive only $18.40. The difference is $1.60. If you divide $1.60 by $20, the result is 0.08, or 8 percent. Thus, if you purchased shares in this fund, you would be paying an 8 percent sales commission.

The listing in the newspaper will also indicate to you the net change in price from the previous day. For example, if the cost of a fund share went from $9.80 to $9.90, the 10-cent difference would be indicated in the right-hand column, next to the specific fund:

|          | NAV   | Buy   | Change |
|----------|-------|-------|--------|
| Fund ABC | 9.90  | NL    | +0.10  |
| Fund DEF | 18.40 | 20.00 | +0.20  |

Fund ABC is a no-load fund, as indicated by the initials NL. The purchase price and sale price are the same. Its net asset value (NAV) increased by 10 cents per share from its closing price the previous day. If you owned 100 shares, the value of your shares would increase by $10 (100 shares times 10 cents). Net asset value is the current market price of one share of the mutual fund. The net asset value is computed daily by taking the value of the fund's assets, subtracting any liabilities, and dividing the remainder by the number of shares outstanding.

It is evident that fund DEF is a load fund because of the difference between the NAV and the buy price listed in the paper. If you were to purchase fund DEF, you would pay $20 per share. If you sell shares in fund DEF, you receive $18.40. The difference between the purchase and sale price, $1.60, is the commission that goes to the selling organization.

## Open-End and Closed-End Investment Companies

Most investment companies are open-end ones. This means that the number of shares outstanding will change each business day. The management of open-end companies, that is, mutual funds, will issue new shares daily based on customer demand and will also redeem shares daily based on customer demand. The purchase price is the NAV for no-load funds and the NAV plus sales commission for load funds. The selling price is the NAV for all mutual funds, both no-load and load funds. Existing shareholders and new customers can complete these transactions by dealing directly with fund management.

A closed-end investment company is one with a fixed number of shares outstanding. The investment objectives of closed-end companies can be the same as those of open-end companies. Shares are sold on exchanges such as the New York Stock Exchange and the American Stock Exchange. The price of shares is based on supply and demand. Thus, the share price can be either higher or lower than the net asset value per share. You will find as wide a performance variance among closed-end funds as you would among open-end funds.

You will generally find that you have more flexibility with open-end funds, however, than with closed-end funds. If you invest in an open-end company, you can reinvest fund distributions—either interest or dividends—in the fund automatically. Most closed-end funds do not offer you that feature. Moreover, each time you purchase or sell shares in a closed-end investment company, you incur a sales commission.

## The Prospectus

Before you purchase a mutual fund, you must receive a prospectus from the selling organization. You can request a prospectus from the fund management directly or from a sales agent such as a stockbroker. The prospectus contains very useful information, which you should review prior to purchasing a fund. This information includes the investment objectives of the fund, sales commission if any, how investment advisory fees are computed, minimum purchase requirements, options for purchase and sales of the fund, and a description of the backgrounds of officers of the fund. If the fund has a sliding sales commission, that is, the sales commission is lower for larger investments, it will be specified in the prospectus.

One of the most important pieces of information in the prospectus is the investment objective of the fund. It is almost always on the first page of the prospectus. You should not purchase any fund whose investment objectives are not consistent with yours.

## Investment-Advisory Fees

Whether you purchase a load or no-load mutual fund, your fund will be managed by an investment adviser who charges an investment advisory fee. Usually, the fee is nominal and generally averages about half a percent of the fund's assets a year. The fee is automatically taken out of your fund balance, generally monthly. You are not billed for this fee separately.

The investment advisory fee is generally reasonable. Even if you had a large enough portfolio to hire your own investment adviser, you would generally pay a higher fee than the one charged by a mutual fund investment adviser. You would not necessarily get better investment advice, either.

## Other Fees

Some funds that seem to be no-load are not, because of specific unusual fees they charge. Some funds, although they do not charge an initial sales commission, do charge a fee when you sell your shares. These fees are known as back-end fees. Other funds charge marketing expenses to the shareholders. These expenses can be considerable over a long time. Known as 12(b)1 fees, they must be specified in the prospectus, as must all fees.

Unless you are convinced that the management of a fund is superior to the management of true no-load funds, do not purchase shares in any mutual fund that has sales commissions, back-end fees, or marketing fees. As indicated earlier in this chapter, many well-run funds have excellent performance histories and are truly no-load funds.

## Sources of Information

There are more than 2,000 funds available, so it will probably not be simple for you to select the fund or funds that meet your needs. Before you select a fund, you must establish your investment objectives carefully. For example, an objective of the Select fund, one of the funds in the Twentieth Century Fund Family, is to invest in securities that primarily provide growth potential. A secondary objective is income. All securities selected by the fund must have a record of paying cash dividends or interest.

You can review the best-performing funds in the categories of funds that meet your investment objectives. Fortunately, there are many reliable sources of information that you can select from:

1. Wiesenberger Services, Inc., 1 New York Plaza, New York, NY 10005. Wiesenberger publishes *Investment Companies.* This yearly contains in-depth information regarding every major mutual fund, including information on past performance, investment objectives, and sales commission. Wiesenberger also publishes a monthly report of which funds have the best performance over the last month or longer. This source is available at most major public libraries or through your brokerage firm.

2. *Money* magazine, Rockefeller Center, New York, NY 10020. Each month *Money* runs a summary of the leading mutual funds, frequently including detailed articles about mutual funds. This is available at newsstands.

3. *Forbes* magazine, 60 Fifth Avenue, New York, NY 10011. In September or October each year *Forbes* publishes a comprehensive summary of the performance of various mutual funds. Performance is measured on an annual basis as well as over longer periods. Funds that have shown above-average performance over long periods are identified in the *Forbes* honor roll. *Forbes* is available at newsstands.

4. Association of No Load Funds, 520 N. Michigan Avenue, Suite 1632, Chicago, IL 60611. This association publishes a directory which contains comprehensive data regarding no-load mutual funds. The directory includes detailed definitions and a listing of funds by category. It provides addresses, telephone numbers, investment objectives, asset size, purchase requirements, redemption procedures, and services provided by each fund that is a member of the association. The directory does not contain performance history. You can obtain this directory from the association for $5.

## Categories of Funds

There are several categories of funds. You should select a fund or funds whose investment objectives are consistent with yours. When you compare the performance of various funds, you should base your comparison on funds within the same category. In the following paragraphs the major categories of funds will be defined, and they will be matched to specific investment objectives you may have.

### Capital-Growth Funds

Capital-growth funds are funds whose primary objective is to invest in securities that are expected to increase in value. You would expect most of the investments to be in common stocks of companies that reinvest most of their earnings in the company. Therefore, you should expect very small dividends, if any. You can also expect a great deal of volatility in prices. Accordingly, if your primary investment objectives are preservation of capital and high income, you should avoid this category of fund.

It is not unusual for the best-managed capital-growth funds over ten years to increase the value of shareholder investments by 15 percent to 20 percent per year. However, in some years even the best-performing funds lose value.

### Growth-and-Income Funds

The growth-and-income funds take a middle-of-the-road approach. Fund managers select securities that will provide some income and also have some capital-growth potential. The portfolio could be a mixture of common stocks and bonds. The prospectus of the fund specifies the types of investments included in its portfolio. The price of this fund is generally less volatile than that of a capital-growth fund and it does not increase as much on a long-term basis.

### Income Funds

The primary objective of an income fund is to provide you with high current income. The portfolio of such a fund generally includes bonds and common stocks paying high dividends. Some funds use conservative-option techniques, which also provide higher income. (See Chapter 10.) If the portfolio consists of long-term bonds, an increase in interest rates could cause a significant drop in the value of the fund shares.

## Money-Market Funds

The objective of the money-market fund is to preserve capital while providing the investor with a moderate amount of income. All investments in this type of fund have short maturities. Typical examples of this type of investment are Treasury bills, bankers' acceptances, and certificates of deposit. Regardless of how long you invest in a money-market fund, you will not suffer a capital loss.

## Tax-Exempt Money-Market Funds

The objective of the tax-exempt money-market fund is to provide tax-free income while preserving capital. All investments are in short-term municipal securities. This form of investment is designed for individuals in high tax brackets who want tax-free income and preservation of capital. The rate of return is generally much lower than it is for money-market funds. Middle-income and low-income individuals can obtain higher rates of after-tax return with money-market funds.

## Municipal Bond Funds

The objective of municipal bond funds is to provide a high level of tax-free income. The portfolio of this type of fund usually contains a mix of municipal bonds of different maturities. Investors receive a higher rate of return from a municipal bond fund than from a tax-exempt money-market fund because of the bonds' longer maturities. However, there is more capital risk in bonds, since if interest rates increased, the value of the medium-term and long-term bonds in the portfolio would decrease in value.

## Socially Conscious Funds

Some mutual funds, in addition to selecting investments that meet traditional investment standards, also restrict their choice of investments to those that are consistent with specific "socially conscious" objectives. For example, The Pax World Fund, Inc. operates "to make a contribution to world peace through investment in companies producing life-supportive goods and services." The Dreyfus Third Century Fund, Inc. purchases stocks of companies that "show evidence in the conduct of their business, relative to other companies in the same industry or industries, of contributing to the enhancement of the quality of life in America...."

### Special-Purpose Funds

Many funds are organized to specialize in a particular segment of the market. Examples of these are energy stocks, international securities, and financial-services stocks. Some of these funds generally have more volatility than other categories of funds, since in general the stocks in the fund tend to move in tandem. If you understand a particular sector of the market especially well, these funds can be profitable for you. You should recognize, however, that there are additional capital risks when you invest in a narrow market sector.

## IRA and Keogh Investments

As a result of the Tax Reform Act of 1986, many employees are no longer eligible to make tax-deductible IRA contributions. However, IRA investments are still applicable to a sizable number of individuals:

1. Employees who no longer contribute to IRAs but established accounts when eligibility requirements were more lenient
2. Employees who are not participants in qualified pension or profit plans
3. Employees whose incomes are low enough to still make the tax-deductible contributions (single filers who earn less than $25,000; joint filers whose income is less than $40,000)
4. Individuals who will be receiving a lump-sum distribution from their employer (see Chapter 16)

The Tax Reform Act did not change the eligibility requirements for self-employed individuals. Thus, if you are self-employed, you can participate in a Keogh plan (see Chapter 14).

In this section we will be discussing mutual funds as IRA investments. These observations about IRAs also apply to Keoghs.

Mutual funds are an excellent vehicle for IRA investments. (See Chapter 13.) Most IRA investment forms do not provide as much flexibility as mutual funds provide. Specifically, mutual funds that manage several funds with different investment objectives, commonly called a mutual-fund family, are especially attractive as IRA investments because of their flexibility. Mutual-fund families allow you to transfer your investments from one fund to another as often as you wish by simply picking up the phone.

Most funds charge nominal annual fees to maintain individual retirement accounts. Although some funds do not charge a fee, the average fee is about $10 a year.

You will find a detailed examination of IRA and Keogh alternatives in Chapter 15.

## Disclosure Regulations

Until July 1988 investors in mutual funds may have been confused by advertisements and sales literature issued by funds. Previously there were no standards established to ensure consistency among advertisements. Effective July 1, 1988, however, under rules established by the Securities and Exchange Commission (SEC), all funds are required to use a standardized formula when computing yields.

Effective May 1, 1988, funds started to use a standardized formula, developed by the SEC, to disclose total return for 1-, 5-, and 10-year periods. The formula for total return is [capital gain] + [interest or dividends].

These standardized formulas benefit mutual fund investors who could otherwise be misled by selective or deceptive advertising and sales promotions.

## Disadvantages of Mutual Funds

There are a few disadvantages associated with mutual funds, and you should be aware of them. One disadvantage is a potential tax liability that you have no control over. When a mutual fund sells securities in its portfolio at a profit, it is creating a tax liability for you. Even if you elect to invest all fund distributions back in the fund, you will have a tax liability for that tax year.

At the end of each year you will receive a tax statement from the fund summarizing the earnings you received, itemized according to interest, dividends, and capital gains. You have to report this income on your tax return. Keep these statements as part of your permanent records to avoid double taxation when you ultimately sell your shares.

### SCENARIO

You invest $1,000 in fund A in 1989. You ask the fund to invest all distributions. In 1989 the fund distributes $200, which you reinvest. On your 1989 tax return you must report $200 in income even though you reinvested the $200 in the fund.

In 1990 you sell all of your shares for $1,100. On your 1990 tax return you should report a loss of $100. After you reported a $200 gain in 1989, your initial investment base changed from $1,000 to $1,200.

Because you have included this $200 as part of your base investment in 1990, you will not be taxed on it again.

---

Whenever you pay taxes on a distribution, your investment base changes to reflect the tax you have already paid. If you do not take into account the amount already paid in tax, you will pay more tax than you should.

So you can see that a disadvantage of mutual fund investing is that you have to pay tax earlier than you would like to. When you purchase securities independently of a mutual fund, you make the decisions about when to sell securities and create a tax liability. When you purchase shares in a fund, you relinquish those decisions to the management adviser of the fund.

A second disadvantage of mutual funds is that you may have a tax liability based on an increase in value of stocks in the portfolio that occurred *before you purchased it.* You are buying mutual fund shares at a certain price, but this price is based partly on stocks that have already increased in value. Your liability occurs when the mutual fund sells such stocks. The fact is that you originally paid more because these stocks had increased in value, and now you are being taxed because of that same increase.

## Summary

The advantages of investing in mutual funds far outweigh the disadvantages. There are many well-managed no-load funds that offer you a wide variety of alternatives, regardless of your tax bracket, your objectives, and the amount of money you have available to invest.

# Real Estate

**A**lthough the Tax Reform Act of 1986 eliminated many tax shelters, many tax advantages of investing in real estate were either left unchanged or were changed so slightly that investment in real estate still has many attractive features. This is true whether you are buying real estate as a residence or for income production.

## Your Residence

There are still many reasons why even during retirement you may want to consider remaining a property owner, especially with respect to your primary residence. Your residence will probably continue to be a good inflation hedge, and there are still many attractive tax advantages. Specifically, these tax advantages pertain to (1) interest; (2) postponing of tax payment on gains if you continue to own your own residence; and (3) a special one-time $125,000 exclusion from taxable profits on the sale of your residence(s) after you reach age 55.

### Interest

Although the deductibility of many forms of consumer interest was reduced or eliminated by the Tax Reform Act of 1986, the interest on residential mortgages is still fully tax-deductible. The specific benefit to you is based on the tax bracket you are in.

For example, if you are in the 28 percent tax bracket, then 28 percent of your interest payments are tax-deductible. For each $100 in interest you pay on your residential mortgage, you pay $72 in actual after-tax costs. The federal government subsidizes the other $28. If you live in a state that has a state income tax, you will probably have additional tax advantages.

## Real Estate Taxes

Tax reform did not have an impact on the deductibility of real estate taxes on your residence. All real estate taxes are still tax-deductible, even if you own two homes.

## Postponing Gains

If you continue to own your own residence without a gap of more than two years, you can postpone profits on the sales of your residences as long as you continue to purchase property at least as expensive as the property you sold.

### SCENARIO

You purchased a home for $100,000 and sold it 5 years later for $200,000. If you purchase another residence within 2 years for at least $200,000, whether it be a house, condominium, or cooperative, you have postponed the income tax liability on your gain, in this case $100,000. Under the current law you can indefinitely sell your residence at a profit and postpone your tax liability as long as you continue to purchase a new home at least as expensive. If you do not purchase a home within 2 years, your profits are then taxed.

If you purchase a new residence for less than the selling price of the old one, you have a tax liability. In the previous scenario, if you had purchased a home for $175,000 instead of $200,000, you would have an income-tax liability of $25,000, the difference between the selling price of your old home and the purchase price of your new one.

Note that you are postponing your tax liability when you purchase a home. You may decide at some point in your life that you no longer want to own a residence. At that point you will either have to pay the income tax due or elect the one-time $125,000 exclusion available when you have reached age 55.

## $125,000 Exclusion

When either you or your spouse becomes 55, you are eligible for a one-time $125,000 exclusion from any profits that you made on the sales of all properties that you have lived in. You may elect this exclusion whether you continue to own a residence or not.

### SCENARIO

You are in the 28 percent tax bracket. You purchased a home for $100,000, including improvements, sold it for $200,000, and then purchased a new residence for $200,000. Subsequently, you sold that property for $250,000, and you no longer wish to own a residence. The total profit on the sale of your two homes is $150,000, since you made a profit of $100,000 from the first house and $50,000 from the second. If you or your spouse is 55 or older, you can elect to take the $125,000 exclusion, and you have to pay taxes only on $25,000, the $150,000 total profit minus the $125,000 exclusion.

The specific tax you owe is based on your tax bracket in the tax year you sold the property and elected to take the exclusion. Since you are in the 28 percent tax bracket, you have a $7,000 tax liability.

## Retirement Strategies

As you approach retirement, you may want to consider moving to a smaller residence in order to provide more capital and also to reduce your maintenance responsibilities.

### SCENARIO

You live in a $275,000 home that you purchased for $150,000. You can purchase a $150,000 residence and claim the $125,000 exclusion. By so doing you create $125,000 in capital for your use without any tax liability.

One of the advantages of purchasing a smaller home is that you will be freeing up additional capital to invest. For example, if you sell a $250,000 home and move into a smaller one for $150,000, you have an additional $100,000 of capital to invest. If you earn 10 percent on the $100,000, you have an additional $10,000 a year of income.

If you do purchase a smaller home, your real estate taxes, insurance costs, heating, and general maintenance costs will probably also be reduced.

Obviously, this is a personal matter, but you may want to consider purchasing or renting a smaller home if your expected income in retirement is small in relation to your desired standard of living. Of course, your standard of living is partially based on the home you live in, so think carefully before making such a decision.

## Condominiums

You may want to consider living in a condominium during retirement. Under this form of ownership, you own and maintain your living area yourself, and you contribute monthly fees to maintain common property and grounds. Your maintenance fee covers items such as building exterior, landscaping, possibly a swimming pool, and other recreational areas.

The primary advantages of condominium ownership are inflation protection because property values are likely to rise, fixed costs if you obtain a conventional mortgage, low maintenance costs (which may rise with inflation), and a good social environment if you are careful about where you live.

The primary disadvantage is that you may not always agree with condominium rules, but you can counteract this disadvantage by becoming an active member — perhaps even an officer — in the condominium association.

## Your Tax Base

When you compute your profit on the sale of any home, be sure to include all improvements approved by the IRS when you establish the base price of your home. The following items are considered improvements to a home and should be added to the base price you paid for the home when you compute the profit you make when you sell your home:

- Adding a room or garage
- Finishing an attic or basement
- Adding a fence
- Replacing or making a major improvement to heating, air conditioning, or plumbing systems or a water heater
- Constructing a new roof
- Landscaping

- Resurfacing a driveway
- Installing a swimming pool

## Shopping for a Mortgage

When you purchase a new residence, you will have the option of applying for either a fixed-rate or adjustable-rate mortgage (ARM). A fixed-rate mortgage is one in which the interest rate and time frame are fixed. An adjustable-rate mortgage (ARM) is one in which the interest rate is variable based on the movement of a preestablished index. The time frame in some ARMs is adjustable also.

In retirement you are probably better off with a fixed-rate mortgage. An adjustable-rate mortgage may seem attractive initially because of a lower rate, but even if you have to pay 1 percent or so higher initially, a fixed-rate mortgage is better because you want to be able to control your own expenses. With an ARM the index, and accordingly the interest you pay, is not within your control.

If you are tempted to use an ARM, make sure you are not tempted by an artificially low rate that will increase dramatically later. With an ARM you want an index that is stable, not volatile. Ask the lender for a history of the index. The Treasury bill rate is a volatile index and should be avoided if possible. Federal Home Loan Bank Board's national average mortgage rate and Moody's Aa corporate-bond index are much less volatile than other indexes.

Another important variable is the limit an adjustment rate can increase to. Regulations require that limits for new ARMs be established, but they do not specify an upper limit. The ideal ARM for you is one that has a narrow limit. For example, if an ARM agreement specifies that your rate cannot go up by more than 4 percent, you know the maximum rate you would pay would be 14 percent if you obtained a mortgage at 10 percent.

Many ARMs have annual limits on rate increases as well as a limit for the complete time frame of the agreement. For example, an agreement may stipulate that rates cannot increase by more than 2 percent in any year and 4 percent for the total length of the mortgage. ARM agreements can be very complex, and the provisions can vary greatly among financial institutions. You should not enter into an ARM agreement unless you understand all of the provisions.

In general during retirement most individuals are better off with fixed-rate mortgages because they can control their costs better. As you approach retirement, it is a good idea to avoid all types of loans that are variable.

## Individual Reverse-Mortgage Account

Some families find that they are unable to afford the home they are living in upon retirement but would like to stay there. One option allows a family that owns the property outright to live in the same home and get some financial relief. This is an individual reverse mortgage account (IRMA). There are several disadvantages and pitfalls associated with IRMAs. Moreover, this type of account takes many different forms, and the agreement is generally a very complicated one. You definitely need an attorney's guidance if you are considering this type of account.

With one variation of an IRMA account the lender pays you a specific monthly sum for life. The amount of the monthly payment is based on the value of the home, the life expectancy of you and/or your spouse, and the expected appreciation of the property. Any appreciation on the value of your home goes to the lender.

If you live beyond your life expectancy, your estate must repay the lender the value of your home upon your death. If you die before your life expectancy, the bank is entitled to the amount of money you borrowed, plus interest, plus appreciation in the home from the time you signed the agreement.

In summary, the advantages for you are that you receive income for life and you can remain in your home. The disadvantages are that you are giving up the equity built up in your home and any subsequent appreciation value. If you do decide to move, you must pay the lender the amount of money you were paid, plus interest, plus appreciation. Thus, you may not have sufficient equity to move after you have accepted payments for a long time. Moreover, there is no financial advantage in making improvements, since the added appreciation goes to the lender, not to you.

Not all of these loans provide lifetime payments. You must be wary of a reverse mortgage that requires payment after a specified time. At that time you would have to repay the loan, which could mean having to sell the home under crisis conditions. Only under extraordinary circumstances should you consider this type of transaction.

## More Than One Residence

You may want to consider owning more than one residence. If you own a second residence, the mortgage interest and real estate taxes for both homes will be fully deductible. If you own more than two residences, you have to designate which two you would like to qualify for the exemption.

## Vacation Homes

Besides the obvious advantage of improving your lifestyle, there are tax advantages associated with owning a vacation home.

If your vacation home is used exclusively by you, then all interest expenses and real estate taxes are deductible. If you rent out your vacation home for part of the year, you have additional tax advantages. You may be able to declare a loss on your income-tax return based on a number of factors, which will be discussed in the next section.

## Renting Out Your Vacation Home

The tax rules that apply to vacation homes depend on how the home is used. The rules are precise. Therefore it is important for you to decide in advance which of three basic approaches you plan to use:

1. Renting for 14 days or less
2. Personal use of 10 percent or less
3. Personal use of more than 10 percent

### Renting for 14 Days or Less

If you rent your vacation home for 14 days or less, you do not have to declare any rental income. All of your mortgage interest and real estate taxes are deductible in full as long as you do not own more than two residences. However, you cannot deduct any maintenance expenses.

### SCENARIO

You rented your vacation home for 10 days for $4,000. Your interest expenses are $2,000 a year, and your real estate taxes are $2,400 a year. The cost of maintaining the property is $1,200 a year. The major tax considerations are as follows:

Rental income declared $       0
Interest expenses              2,000
Property taxes                 2,400

---

## Personal Use of 10 Percent or Less

If you rent your vacation home for more than 14 days, different tax rules apply. The proportion of the time that you use the property for personal use relative to the proportion that you rent the property becomes critical. If you use the property 10 percent or less of the total time the home is occupied either by you or your renter and less than 15 days during the year, then you can deduct some depreciation expenses and operating costs in addition to interest expenses and property taxes. Depreciation is the annual amount the IRS allows a property owner to deduct for income-producing property independent of whether the property increases or decreases in value.

All operation and depreciation expenses are prorated based on the proportion of the time the property was used for personal versus rental use.

The depreciation computation is based on when the property was purchased and placed in service. For example, if you start renting property in 1988 or later, you may depreciate the property over 27.5 years, as specified by the Tax Reform Act of 1986. This means that if you paid $275,000 for the property, you would be allowed to deduct $10,000 per year in depreciation cost. If the property was placed in service between 1981 and 1987, the property can be depreciated over 19 years.

You may also deduct operating expenses. These expenses include maintenance, utilities, property insurance, advertisements, and any other marketing expenses associated with property rental.

These expenses are prorated based on the proportion of rental to personal use. Based on the expense level and the rental income, you may have a profit or a loss on your rental property. You can declare a loss before you sell the property only under specific conditions. The maximum loss that can be written off in one year is $25,000. That loss can be taken only if your income is within specified limits.

If your adjusted gross income is greater than $150,000 a year, you do not qualify for any part of the $25,000 write-off. If your income is below $100,000 a year, you can write off your annual loss up to $25,000. If your income is between $100,000 and $150,000, you can prorate part of your loss. If the adjusted gross income is $120,000, you can write off 40 percent of your annual losses up to a $25,000 maximum loss per year.

---

### SCENARIO

| | | |
|---|---|---|
| Total rental days | 100 | |
| Personal use days | 10 | |
| Rental income | | $10,000 |

EXPENSES

| | | |
|---|---|---|
| Mortgage interest | $8,000 × (100 ÷ 365) = | 2,190 |
| Property taxes | 2,500 × (100 ÷ 365) = | 685 |
| Operating expenses | 2,000 × (100 ÷ 110) = | 1,820 |
| Depreciation | 8,000 × (100 ÷ 110) = | 7,280 |
| Total expenses | | 11,975 |
| Loss | | ($ 1,975) |

---

In this example the owner of a vacation home lost $1,975 based on IRS rules. If the owner's gross income was under $100,000, then the entire $1,975 could be deducted as a loss.

Note that mortgage interest and property taxes can be prorated over the complete year, and operating expenses and depreciation are allocated based on the ratio of rental days to the sum total of rental days and personal-use days. The proportion of property taxes and mortgage interest that is associated with personal use can be deducted separately on Schedule A on your itemized return.

Regardless of how high your income is, you are allowed to declare a loss on your rental property *after you sell it,* if in fact the investment was unprofitable. Thus, even if your income is greater than $150,000, you should keep proper records of all your operating expenses and depreciation expenses. After you sell your property, these expenses should be used to determine whether you made a gain or a loss on your rental property.

### Personal Use Greater than 10 Percent

If you use your property for more than the greater of 14 days or 10 percent of the time you rent the property, different rules apply. You may not claim an annual loss from the property. You can, however, carry any loss to succeeding years to offset rental income you receive on the property.

## SCENARIO

**1989**

| | | |
|---|---|---|
| Total rental days | 100 | |
| Personal use days | 20 | |
| Rental income | | $10,000 |

| EXPENSES | | |
|---|---|---|
| Mortgage interest | $8,000 × (100 ÷ 365) = | 2,190 |
| Property taxes | 2,500 × (100 ÷ 365) = | 685 |
| Operating expense | 2,000 × (100 ÷ 120) = | 1,665 |
| Depreciation | 8,000 × (100 ÷ 120) = | 6,660 |
| Total expenses | | 11,200 |
| Loss | | ($1,200) |

The total loss for 1989 was $1,200. Because the owner's personal use exceeded 14 days, the loss is not deductible. The loss can be carried forward, however, to successive years. The portion of mortgage interest and property taxes that were associated with personal use are deductible on Schedule A.

Suppose the owner sells the property in 1990 for a gross profit of $5,000. He or she can deduct the loss of $1,200 incurred in 1989. The net profit, which is reportable income on the 1990 tax return, is $3,800.

## Summary—Rental Property

There are still many advantages associated with investing in real estate, including personal enjoyment, protection from inflation, and tax incentives. As you can see, however, some of the alternatives, especially those associated with the rental of a vacation home, are complicated. The personal use of a vacation home for just one additional day can be remarkably significant. Accordingly, it is important that you keep meticulous records. Before you decide how to apportion rental versus personal use of a vacation home, it would be a good idea to consult a tax specialist.

The financial advantage of owning a nonrental home arises when the property value increases significantly. Taxes and interest are deductible. In general, however, the primary advantage is personal unless a family is spending a great deal on rentals for vacation.

# Miscellaneous Investments

**I**n this chapter we will discuss several forms of investment that do not fall into the standard investment categories covered in other parts of the book. *It is unlikely that you should invest a substantial portion of your available funds in these vehicles.* Based on your overall objectives and the other investments you select, however, some of these instruments could help you meet your goals.

## Zero-Coupon Bonds

A zero-coupon bond is a security that is sold at a significant discount of its face value. No interest payments are made. The amount of the discount determines the rate of return of the bond. At maturity the bondholder receives the face amount of the bond.

Corporations may issue zero-coupon bonds. Brokers create the majority of these bonds, many of which are backed by federal government issues, mortgages, or municipal bonds. The safest zero-coupon bonds are those backed by United States Treasury bonds.

A broker creates a zero-coupon bond backed by the Treasury by buying Treasury bonds and separating each bond into the components principal and interest. In reality each of these components is a separate zero-coupon bond, which is sold separately by the broker.

The primary advantage of the zero-coupon bond is that you obtain a guaranteed rate of return on your investment if you hold the bond to maturity.

For example, assume you purchase a regular 30-year $1,000 bond that has a 10 percent coupon rate. In 6 months you will receive an interest payment of $50. It is unlikely that you will be able to get such a high rate of return as 10 percent if you reinvest the $50. However, if you were to invest $1,000 in several discounted 30-year bonds, you would receive compounded interest on your investment when the bonds mature.

Purchasing $1,000 worth of zero-coupon bonds with a 10 percent rate of return is similar to buying a $1,000 regular bond with a coupon rate of 10 percent with the guarantee that you will be able to invest your interest payments at the same rate. There is one significant difference, however: You do not receive any annual interest payments with a zero-coupon bond. Your interest is the difference between what you paid for the bond and the face value you receive at maturity. Over time the value of the bond increases. At maturity the bond is redeemable at face value.

You have the option to sell the bond before maturity. If you sell the bond before maturity, however, you will not receive the face value of the bond. The value you receive will be based on prevailing interest rates and the time left to maturity.

There are two disadvantages associated with zero-coupon bonds.

One disadvantage is that interest is not paid. You receive income only if you sell your bond or hold it to maturity. Although you do not receive interest, the IRS claims that you do have an annual tax liability on the imputed interest. Imputed interest is the expected increase in the market value of a bond because the time to maturity is shorter.

A second disadvantage of zero-coupon bonds is that the market price will drop sharply in periods of rising interest rates. The prices of zero-coupon bonds are even more volatile than those of regular bonds, because all of what would be reinvestable interest is tied up for the entire term of the bond. If in general interest rates fall, the market price of an already-issued bond will increase sharply. Regardless of what happens during the interim, you will receive the face value of the bond if you hold it until maturity.

Zero-coupon bonds are excellent for tax-deferred investments such as IRAs and Keogh plans. They are ideal because of the tax-deferred nature of these plans; you would not be subject to an annual tax liability. Moreover, because you would normally invest in retirement plans on a long-term basis, short-term volatility would not be a significant disadvantage. When you purchase zero-coupon bonds for retirement plans, you can select the specific maturity to coincide with your expected withdrawal schedule. For example, if you plan to withdraw funds in 10 years, you can purchase 10-year zero-coupon bonds; the following year you can purchase 9-year zero-coupon bonds, and so on down the line. The major brokerage firms can generally offer you a wide range of maturities to meet your objectives.

Zero-coupon bonds are also excellent vehicles to fund college needs or any future need in which you can predict the expected cost with some degree of reliability.

For example, assume you wanted to have $40,000 in a lump sum in 16 years to help fund the college expenses for a family member. If you contact your broker, he can tell you, based on current available rates on zero-coupon bonds, how much money you would have to invest today to have $40,000 in 16 years. If bonds were available at 8 percent, you could invest approximately $10,000 today to receive $40,000 in 16 years. Your broker should be able to provide you with a table indicating the specific discount for different interest rates and time frames.

Tax-free zero-coupon bonds are also available. These bonds will pay lower interest rates, but they may be better for you if you do not want to incur a tax liability each year. Such tax-free bonds do not belong in a tax-deferred account such as an IRA, since the total amount of your withdrawal is taxable when you take it out regardless of how you invested your funds.

You could purchase zero-coupon bonds as a hedging technique.

For example, assume you have sizable investments in CDs that will mature in a few years. You are concerned that when they mature, you will not be able to reinvest the proceeds and obtain the same rate of return you are now getting. You can purchase long-term zero-coupon bonds as protection. If interest rates do fall in the next few years, the increase in the value of the zero-coupon bonds will make up for the lost interest. If you inform your broker as to the amount of funds that are maturing, he or she should be able to advise you as to the quantity of zero-coupon you will have to purchase to protect your position.

If interest rates increase, the value of your bonds will decrease, but you will be able to reinvest the proceeds of your maturing securities at higher interest rates to counteract the drop in value of the bonds.

## Gold

During periods of high inflation and uncertain international conditions, the price of gold generally increases, as do the prices of other precious metals such as silver and platinum. You can hedge your portfolio against the risk of inflation by investing a small percentage of your portfolio, such as 5 percent, in precious metals. To provide you with diversification, you can purchase shares in a no-load mutual fund that specializes in this field. Select a fund that has a good long-term performance. Some of the better-performing funds have low minimum investment requirements. This allows you to use dollar-cost averaging to build up a modest holding.

One of the hazards of investing in precious metals is the high volatility of prices, even in mutual funds. It is not unusual for funds to go up and down 100 percent or more in the course of one or two years. Because of this volatility, you should not invest a large percentage of your holdings in precious metals.

## Convertible Bonds and Preferred Stock

A convertible bond is a hybrid instrument. It has some features of a bond and some of a common stock. The instrument pays income at a specified rate of interest during a specified time frame just as ordinary bonds do. The difference is that the convertible bond can be exchanged for a predetermined number of shares of the common stock of the issuing corporation. Thus, if the common stock of the company substantially increased in value, the holder of the convertible bond would benefit. The price of the bond increases in value as the common stock increases in value. You do not have to convert your bond to shares of common stock to make a profit. You can simply sell your bonds whenever you wish at the existing market price.

If the common stock does not increase in value, then the value of the bond in the market will be based on the same criteria used to determine the price of other bonds, that is, the coupon—annual interest—rate of the bond, the financial strength of the issuing corporation, and the general level of interest rates.

The coupon rate on convertible bonds is somewhat lower than the coupon rate for regular bonds issued by corporations of equivalent financial strength. This is because the possibility that the bond will increase in value as a result of an increase in the value of the common stock makes the bond a more attractive security than an ordinary bond. Thus, when you purchase a convertible, you give up some income for the possibility of growth. You should purchase convertible bonds issued by corporations that have sufficient financial strength to support the payment of interest on the bond and repayment of principal. Convertible bonds are rated by the same rating services that rate traditional bonds and common stocks.

Another desirable attribute you should look for in the issuing company is high growth potential that will support an increase in value of the common stock.

Some corporations issue convertible preferred stocks. The fundamentals are identical to those of convertible bonds. A preferred stock is convertible into a fixed number of shares of common stock for a specific time frame.

Many mutual funds specialize in convertible issues; that is, they invest exclusively in convertible bonds and convertible preferred stock. Several sources identify this type of mutual fund. Among them are the Forbes annual mutual fund issue, generally published at the end of September or early October; the Association of No Load Fund Directory; and Wiesenberger's *Investment Companies*.

If convertible issues appeal to you, mutual funds are an attractive option. Investing in convertibles is complicated, and a well-run fund will give you both required expertise and diversification. There will be substantial variations in past performance among the funds, however. Accordingly, just as you should do before you purchase any fund, you should review its past performance.

## Foreign Securities

There are many periods during which the dollar is weak relative to other currencies, especially the Japanese yen and the German mark. During these times both bonds and common stocks of companies in foreign countries generally perform better than comparable United States securities. When the United States has large balance-of-trade deficits with certain countries, the currencies as well as the securities of major companies in those particular countries generally increase in value relative to the dollar and United States-based securities. In recent years the United States has had large trade deficits with many countries, especially Japan.

One way you can hedge your investment portfolio is by investing in foreign securities. The simplest and safest way to do this is to invest in a mutual fund, preferably a no-load fund, that has a diversified portfolio of international securities. You will find that many of the well-run mutual funds such as Scudder, T. Rowe Price, and Fidelity manage such diversified funds and have had excellent results.

When the common stocks of United States-based companies dropped in price dramatically in October 1987, the common stocks of most other countries fell also. However, in some countries stock prices fell less dramatically and recovered faster. Japanese common stocks are one example of this.

It is not unusual for both United States stocks and United States bonds in the aggregate to decrease in value on the same day that foreign securities increase in value. If you scan price movements on the mutual fund listings in the financial section of the newspaper, you will be able to observe such occurrences. In fact, it is not unusual for foreign-based securities to be the only ones to increase in value on a particular day.

You can minimize your overall portfolio risk by investing 5 percent or 10 percent of your holdings in international securities through mutual funds. Since foreign securities can be just as volatile as United States securities, you should not commit a large percentage of your investment portfolio. Purchase only mutual funds that have an excellent performance history. Use dollar-cost averaging to avoid making a large investment at the wrong time.

## Real Estate Investment Trusts

Real estate investment trusts (REITs) are similar to mutual funds. When you purchase shares in a REIT, you are essentially pooling your money with other investors either to finance or to purchase income-producing property. The shares are liquid, as they are sold on the major stock exchanges. The rental income from the property flows to the REIT. Expenses are paid, and the net income is sent to you in the form of dividends.

There are two basic types of REIT, equity and mortgage. Equity REITs own property such as shopping centers, apartment houses, and warehouses. In an equity REIT you may obtain income from two sources—renting and sale of the property. Some equity REITs reinvest their income in other properties, and others will send you the net income in the form of dividends. For new issues the investment objectives and type of property to be purchased by the REIT management will be explained in a prospectus. Participating brokers who are selling shares in new issues can provide you with a prospectus.

Mortgage REITs specialize in mortgage loans. Accordingly, the value of this type of REIT will vary based on movements in interest rates. As interest rates go up, share values go down, and vice versa. If your primary investment goal is high income, you can consider mortgage REITs, but you should recognize that the instrument has the same capital risks as long-term bonds.

## Real Estate Limited Partnerships and Syndications

A syndicator is an individual or group that organizes partnership ventures for investors. The syndicator is essentially a middleman between the investor and the developer. He or she is responsible for selecting property, arranging for its purchase, and working with the developer during the construction stage. The syndicator in some situations is also the developer.

Prior to the Tax Reform Act of 1986, and the Omnibus Budget Reconciliation Act of 1987, limited partnerships could provide significant tax advantages, even if the venture was not profitable in the first few years of a project. Under tax reform, however, losses associated with limited partnerships are not deductible unless they can be matched against income from the same partnerships in subsequent years.

An investment in a limited partnership is a passive activity. Passive activity is defined as any activity that involves the conduct of any trade or business in which the taxpayer does not materially participate. Interest and dividends, however, are not considered passive income. The intent of Congress was to make it difficult for investors to deduct losses from investments in limited partnerships and other passive investments.

You should consider an investment in a limited partnership only if you believe that the investment is sound. Tax advantages should not be a major consideration.

Congress has indicated through the Tax Reform Act of 1986 that it intends to cut back or eliminate various forms of tax-advantaged investments. Congress commonly eliminates tax advantages retroactively. Accordingly, it is important that your investments be economically sound and able to withstand any possible tax changes that Congress may introduce in the future.

If you seriously consider a limited partnership investment, you should use the services of an experienced tax accountant.

## Options

There are several different types of options that can be used by investors in the various securities markets. An option is the right to buy or sell specified securities for a specified time frame at a set price. The cost of options will vary based on these conditions and the expected volatility of the specified security. Many options are speculative and have no role for the conservative investor. However, some options are very conservative and can serve as an effective hedge for you.

There are two basic options: a call option, which allows you to purchase securities at a specific price for a specific time frame; and a put option, which allows you to sell securities at a specific price for a specific time frame.

There are times when the use of a put option is very conservative and can protect a gain in a stock you own.

### Purchasing Puts to Protect Profits

With many employer-sponsored investment plans, employees can make sale or purchase decisions only once in a quarter or even less frequently. In such an environment you may at times have a "paper profit" on stocks in your plan but have no flexibility to sell those shares until the end of the quarter or the end of the year. By that time your paper profit may not be there. Through the use of put options that you can purchase *outside the plan* you can protect your gain.

---

### SCENARIO

Your company allows you to purchase common stocks through a tax-deferred profit-sharing plan. You can make changes in your portfolio only at the end of June and December. At the beginning of 1987 you owned 1,000 shares of common stock valued at $100 per share. By September 1, 1987, the price of the common stock was $120 per share. You would have liked to sell your common stock at $120, but your plan does not give you the flexibility to sell until the end of the year.

You could purchase 10 put options of 100 shares each from your broker. This would give you the right to sell a total of 1,000 shares of common stock until December 31, 1987. By executing this transaction, you are effectively selling 1,000 shares of stock at the September 1 price of $120. If the value of the shares goes higher than $120, then the increase in the value of the stock you hold in the plan will counteract the loss you would have had on the options you purchased. On the other hand, if the value of the shares falls below $120, the increase in the value of the option will counteract the loss in value of your shares held in the plan.

In short, by purchasing the put options, you have locked in the $20 gain per share, or $20,000 profit.

---

In 1987 many investors lost a great deal of potential profits in pension plans and profit-sharing plans because they did not take advantage of options. The net cost to you of using this technique is the sales commissions to purchase and sell the option. These costs are nominal in comparison with their potential value in volatile markets.

## Selling Calls for Income

There is one other option technique that is also conservative: you can sell call options. When you sell a call option, you receive a specific amount for granting the buyer of the call option the right to purchase securities you own at a specific price for a specific time frame. Your broker will provide you with the proceeds from the sale of the option, minus his or her own commission.

One of two things can occur at the end of the option period. If the price of your stock increased to at least the price specified in the option agreement, your stock would be sold, and you would be given the proceeds of the sale, minus commissions. If the price of your stock did not increase to the price specified in the option, the option would expire and you would keep the stock. You could then, if you wish, sell another option for a subsequent period.

---

### SCENARIO

You own 100 shares of an automotive stock now selling for $90 a share. You sell a 180-day call option at $95 per share, receiving $300 from your broker, who has handled the transaction for you. At the end of 180 days, the price of your shares is $91 each. The option is not executed, you still have your shares, and you have an extra $300.

The disadvantage for you is that if the stock does rise above $95, your stock is already sold. When you sell a call option on stock you own, you limit your selling price and accordingly your potential for profit. In this scenario you limited your maximum selling price to $95.

---

The technique of selling call options can be useful to you if your primary objective is to obtain higher income. You should not use the technique if one of your primary investment objectives is to maximize capital growth.

Some mutual funds use options in a conservative manner. If the technique appeals to you but you would prefer to be passive, you can invest in funds specializing in this field.

If you decide to take advantage of these techniques, be sure to use a broker who has a great deal of expertise in options.

# Social Security and Supplemental Health Coverage

Social Security was initiated in Congress in 1935 to provide retirement benefits for wage earners. Since its initiation Social Security has been expanded to provide benefits for spouses and dependents, disability benefits, and medical benefits such as hospital coverage.

You should look at Social Security as a base to build on. Social Security benefits, although generous in many instances, seldom provide all of the benefits you require for retirement income, disability coverage, and health insurance. It is important that you understand your Social Security benefits so that you can establish other investment plans and insurance coverage to meet all of your investment objectives and insurance requirements.

## Social Security Credits

You earn Social Security credits by working in a job covered by Social Security. A Social Security credit is also called a quarter of coverage. You earn one credit if you have a certain amount of covered earnings. The amount of covered earnings needed for a credit automatically increases each year to keep up with increases in average salary levels.

You can earn up to four Social Security credits each year. No more than four credits can be counted for any year, regardless of your total earnings.

In 1989 you earn one credit for each $500 of your covered annual earnings, up to a maximum of four credits for the year. The required amount of covered earnings for the 5 prior years is

| | |
|------|--------|
| 1988 | $470 |
| 1987 | $460 |
| 1986 | $440 |
| 1985 | $410 |
| 1984 | $390 |

A maximum of four credits could be earned in each of those years. (Source: Social Security Administration.)

Almost all jobs in the United States are covered by Social Security, but special rules apply to some types of work.

## Domestic Employees

If you work as a domestic employee in a private household and one employer pays you $50 or more in a 3-month calendar quarter, your wages are covered by Social Security.

## Farm Employees

Suppose someone hires you to do farm work, including domestic work on a farm. Your wages are covered by Social Security if:

- You receive at least $150 from that employer during a year *or*
- You are employed for 20 or more days during a year

## Self-Employment

If you are self-employed, your self-employment income is covered by Social Security whenever you have a net profit of $400 or more in a year.

## Employees of Nonprofit Organizations

Most employees of nonprofit organizations are covered by Social Security if they are paid at least $100 a year. However, employees of certain churches and church-controlled organizations are treated as self-employed persons for Social Security purposes.

A church or qualified church-controlled organization can elect exemption from Social Security taxes if it is opposed to paying them for religious reasons. If you are an employee of a church or organization that chooses exemption, you are still covered by Social Security if you earn $100 or more in a year from the church or organization. However, you are considered self-employed, and your earnings are self-employment income even if they are less than $400.

### Federal Employees

Federal employees hired on or after January 1, 1984, are covered by Social Security.

### Family Members

Work done by a child under 21 for a parent, by a husband for his wife, or by a wife for her husband is not covered by Social Security. However, work done by a parent for a son or daughter in connection with the son's or daughter's business is covered.

### Military

Basic pay received while on active duty or training for active duty in the military service in 1957 or later is covered by Social Security. If you are in the military, you earn Social Security credits in the same way that civilian employees do.

Also, you may receive additional earnings credits for your military service if you or your family need them to qualify for benefits or if they would result in a higher benefit amount.

Table 11-1   CREDIT FOR FULL INSURANCE

| For workers reaching age 62 in | Years of credit needed |
|---|---|
| 1984 | 8 |
| 1985 | 8 |
| 1986 | 8¾ |
| 1987 | 9 |
| 1988 | 9 |
| 1989 | 9 |
| 1990 | 9¾ |
| 1991 or later | 10 |

Note: You are fully insured if you have one credit for each year after 1950 up to the year you reach 62, become disabled, or die. In counting the years after 1950, a person born in 1930 or later would omit years before age 22.
Source: Social Security Administration

Table 11-1 shows how much credit for work covered by Social Security you need to be fully insured. As you can see from this table, if you have already reached age 62, the years of credit you needed to be fully insured is less than that is required for workers who will subsequently be 62.

## Nonprofit Organizations

If you work for a nonprofit organization that was covered by Social Security starting in 1984, you may be able to receive retirement benefits with fewer credits than shown in Table 11-1. If you were 55 or older and an employee of the organization on January 1, 1984, you will need only the number of credits shown in Table 11-2. The credits must be earned after January 1, 1984. This special rule does not apply if you declined Social Security coverage when it was offered by your employer.

Table 11-2  EMPLOYEES 55 OR OLDER OF NONPROFIT ORGANIZATIONS

| Your age on January 1, 1984 | Credits you need |
|---|---|
| 55 or 56 | 20 |
| 57 | 16 |
| 58 | 12 |
| 59 | 8 |
| 60 or older | 6 |

Source: Social Security Administration

## Checking Your Earnings Record

Every 3 years you should verify that the Social Security Administration is maintaining your records properly. You can obtain a request for a statement of earnings form from your local Social Security office. You should fill out the form supplying your name, address, and Social Security number. You should then send the form to Social Security, which in turn will send you a record of your Social Security earnings.

The 3-year time frame is important because for periods over 3 years you may not be able to correct any errors in the Social Security records.

## Estimating Your Social Security Income

The Social Security Administration computes your retirement income based on a complex formula described in a booklet, *Estimating Your Social Security Check,* available free from your local Social Security office.

Your benefit is based on your actual earnings under Social Security, adjusted for inflation. The maximum earning credited for a particular year is indicated in Table 11-3. The credits you earn under Social Security are the basis for determining what your Social Security income will be when you retire.

When you approach retirement, you can ask the Social Security Administration to estimate your Social Security retirement income. You can request form SSA-7004 from a Social Security office. This form is a questionnaire that asks your name, Social Security number, birth date, previous earnings, estimated earnings for the current year, projected earnings, and when you plan to retire. You will receive an itemized list of estimated benefits about 4 to 6 weeks after you submit the form to Social Security.

The Social Security Administration has made some projections regarding the income you can expect from Social Security when you retire. These projections are shown in Table 11-4. They are based on the assumption that your future annual earnings will increase at the rate of 1 percent per year in addition to inflation increases, which is the national average.

The income shown in Table 11-4 is based on the assumption that you intend to work until age 65. You can elect early-retirement benefits when you are as young as 62. If you elect early retirement, your retirement benefits are reduced. For example, if you retired at 62, you would receive approximately 80 percent of the amount specified in Table 11-4.

The table indicates the amount that a worker and a nonworking spouse would receive at retirement age. If both parties worked under Social Security, the benefits would be higher, since each worker would be entitled to benefits based on his or her earnings under Social Security.

## Eligibility for Retirement Benefits

You are eligible to receive retirement benefits once you have reached age 62 and have earned sufficient credits to be fully insured. If you elect retirement benefits prior to age 65, however, your benefits will be reduced by approximately half a percent a month.

After you elect to receive benefits, you will receive a check once a

Table 11-3  MAXIMUM EARNINGS
CREDITED FOR COMPUTING
SOCIAL SECURITY INCOME

| Year | Earnings |
| --- | --- |
| 1989 | $48,000 |
| 1988 | 45,000 |
| 1987 | 43,800 |
| 1986 | 42,000 |
| 1985 | 39,600 |
| 1984 | 37,800 |
| 1983 | 35,700 |
| 1982 | 32,400 |
| 1981 | 29,700 |
| 1980 | 25,900 |
| 1979 | 22,900 |
| 1978 | 17,700 |
| 1977 | 16,500 |
| 1976 | 15,300 |
| 1975 | 14,100 |
| 1974 | 13,200 |
| 1973 | 10,800 |
| 1972 | 9,000 |
| 1968 to 1971 | 7,800 |
| 1966 to 1967 | 6,600 |
| 1959 to 1965 | 4,800 |
| 1955 to 1958 | 4,200 |
| 1951 to 1954 | 3,600 |

Source: Social Security Administration

month. You should apply to Social Security 3 months before you expect benefits. You must present a document that proves your date of birth, such as a birth certificate, hospital birth record, or baptismal certificate.

## Change in Retirement Age

If you were born in 1937 or earlier, you can retire at age 65 with full benefits. If you were born after 1937, you must be older than 65 to receive full benefits as indicated in Table 11-5.

Table 11-4  WHAT YOU CAN REALLY COUNT ON FROM SOCIAL SECURITY

These figures represent the approximate yearly income from Social Security benefits for a single person and, on the following line, for a worker and a nonworking spouse of the same age, when they become eligible for full Social Security benefits at age 65 to 67. All of the amounts in the table are Social Security Administration projections in 1988 dollars, based on continuous employment throughout an adult lifetime.

| Your age in 1988 | | Your Earnings in 1987 | | | | |
| --- | --- | --- | --- | --- | --- | --- |
| | | $20,000 | $25,000 | $30,000 | $35,000 | $45,000 or above |
| | | Annual Social Security Benefit | | | | |
| 25 | Individual | 11,796 | 13,548 | 14,568 | 15,600 | 17,652 |
| | Couple | 17,688 | 20,316 | 21,852 | 23,400 | 26,472 |
| 35 | Individual | 10,896 | 12,540 | 13,476 | 14,436 | 16,296 |
| | Couple | 16,344 | 18,804 | 20,208 | 21,648 | 24,444 |
| 45 | Individual | 9,972 | 11,496 | 12,360 | 13,104 | 14,412 |
| | Couple | 14,952 | 17,244 | 18,540 | 19,656 | 21,612 |
| 55 | Individual | 9,048 | 10,344 | 10,920 | 11,352 | 12,036 |
| | Couple | 13,572 | 15,516 | 16,380 | 17,028 | 18,048 |
| 65 | Individual | 8,100 | 9,216 | 9,564 | 9,792 | 14,412 |
| | Couple | 12,144 | 13,824 | 14,340 | 14,688 | 15,084 |

Source: Money Magazine

## Taxability of Social Security Benefits

Until 1984 benefits from Social Security were not taxable. Based on changes in the tax law, however, subsequent to 1984 part of your Social Security income—*up to* 50 percent—may be taxable based on your earnings and your tax filing status.

If you file jointly as a married couple, part of your Social Security income will be taxable if the sum of your adjusted gross income (AGI) —gross income minus allowable deductions such as business expenses and tax-deductible contributions to pension plans—income from municipal bonds, and half of your Social Security income exceeds $32,000.

Table 11-5   CHANGE IN RETIREMENT AGE

| If Born in | You Will Be Age 62 in | Your Age For Full Benefits Is |
|---|---|---|
| through 1937 | | 65 years |
| 1938 | 2000 | 65 years 2 months |
| 1939 | 2001 | 65 years 4 months |
| 1940 | 2002 | 65 years 6 months |
| 1941 | 2003 | 65 years 8 months |
| 1942 | 2004 | 65 years 10 months |
| 1943 to 1954 | 2005 to 2016 | 66 years |
| 1955 | 2017 | 66 years 2 months |
| 1956 | 2018 | 66 years 4 months |
| 1957 | 2019 | 66 years 6 months |
| 1958 | 2020 | 66 years 8 months |
| 1959 | 2021 | 66 years 10 months |
| 1960 or later | 2022 or later | 67 years |

Source: Social Security Administration

If you are single, the specified limit is $25,000. If you are married and file separate returns, then all of your income is taxable.

The amount of Social Security income that is taxable is the lower of (1) half of your Social Security income or (2) the difference between the three components (AGI, municipal bond income, half of Social Security income) and the specified limit ($32,000, $25,000, or $0.)

## SCENARIO

In 1989 you earn $45,000 in AGI; your municipal bond income is $5,000; your Social Security income is $12,000. You file a joint return.

| | |
|---|---|
| AGI | $45,000 |
| Municipal-Bond Income | 5,000 |
| Half of Social Security | 6,000 |
| Total | $56,000 |

Since the total of these three components exceeds $32,000, part of your Social Security income is taxable. The specific taxable amount is the lower of (1) $24,000 ($56,000 − $32,000) or $6,000. In this case, $6,000, half of your Social Security income, would be taxable.

## Benefits for Spouses

If both you and your spouse are entitled to Social Security benefits because of independent earnings, you will each receive independent benefits. A spouse who is a full-time homemaker is entitled to receive 50 percent of the amount of your benefits as long as you live and 75 percent of the amount of your benefits after your death.

## Losing Retirement Benefits by Working

You may lose some of your Social Security benefits if you earn more than a specified amount, which is updated and published periodically by Social Security. If you earn more than the specific limit, 50 percent of your earnings above these levels are deducted from your Social Security payments. In 1989 the limit for individuals 65 or over was $8,880; for individuals younger than 65, the limit was $6,480. Check with your Social Security office to determine the current limits.

## Survivor Benefits

If you are the widow or widower of an individual who earned Social Security credits, you may be eligible for survivor benefits. In some cases, survivor benefits can be paid if a worker has fewer credits than those required for retirement benefits.

If your spouse was born in 1929 or earlier, you are entitled to survivor benefits if your spouse had one credit for each year after 1950 and up to the year of his or her death.

If your spouse was born in 1930 or later, you are entitled to survivor benefits if your spouse had one credit for each year after the year he or she reached 21 and up to the year of his or her death.

Regardless of when you were born, monthly payments can be made to your surviving dependent children if you earn at least 6 credits in the 3 years before your death.

Your widower or widow also may be eligible for benefits if he or she is caring for children who are under 16 or disabled who are entitled to benefits based on your earnings.

## Disability Benefits

The number of credits needed depends on your age when you become disabled.

If you are disabled *before age 24*, you need 6 credits out of the 3-year period before you become disabled.

If disabled between 24 and 30, you need credits for half of the time between age 21 and the time you become disabled.

If you are disabled at 31 or over, you need the same number of credits that you would need for retirement benefits, just as if you had reached the retirement age at the time you became disabled. In addition, 20 of the credits must have been earned in the 10 years before you are disabled.

If you become disabled before age 21 and recover but become disabled again at 31 or older, you may not need 20 credits to be eligible for benefits. You will need credits for half of the time between age 21 and the second time you become disabled. However, the period you were previously disabled does not count.

A person disabled by blindness needs one credit for each year since 1950 that he or she was at least 21 up to the year he or she went blind. A minimum of 6 credits is needed.

## Medicare

Medicare is a health insurance program for individuals 65 and older and for disabled people under 65. It is a federal agency for administrative health care financing. Medicare has two parts: Part A is hospital insurance and Part B is medical insurance.

You will be eligible for Medicare hospital insurance at age 65 if:

- You are entitled to monthly Social Security or railroad retirement benefits, or
- You have worked long enough under Social Security or the railroad retirement system, or
- You have worked long enough in federal, state, or local government employment to be insured for Medicare purposes.

You may be eligible for hospital insurance before age 65 if you are disabled or have permanent kidney failure.

Medical insurance is a voluntary program, partly financed by the federal government and partly by individuals who sign up. Part B covers such things as medical supplies, doctor bills, and radiology treatments.

After you have paid a specified amount, Medicare will reimburse you for 80 percent of what it feels is the reasonable cost of a covered item.

Additional information regarding Medicare can be obtained from a free booklet, *Medicare,* available from your local Social Security office.

You cannot expect Medicare to pay all of your medical bills. Medicare does not cover all medical items, and it covers a maximum of 80 percent of covered items. Therefore, it is essential that you obtain supplementary health insurance to cover medical costs not covered by Medicare. It is likely that Medicare will cover less than 50 percent of your medical expenses.

## Supplemental Health Insurance Coverage

Before you retire, make sure you are aware of all health coverage options that are available to you. If you can, schedule a complete physical examination under your employer's health coverage prior to retirement, and undergo whatever treatment is necessary while you still have insurance coverage under that plan.

Medicare covers individuals who are 65 and over and those who are disabled or have permanent kidney failure. Thus, if you retire when you are younger than 65, or if your spouse is younger than 65, you will need other coverage. This coverage can come from an employer postretirement plan or from other supplementary coverage.

Medicare covers 80 percent of what it believes a bill should be. The bills of your physician, however, may be much higher than Medicare standards. Experts in the field have indicated that Medicare covers only 35 percent to 40 percent of the health care costs of individuals 65 and over.

### SCENARIO

You received a bill from your doctor for $200. You paid the required deductible amount of $75. Medicare indicates that the maximum payment is $150 according to their standards.

| | |
|---|---|
| Doctor's bill | $200 |
| Medicare's standard | 150 |
| Your reimbursement | 120 ($150 × 80%) |
| Amount not paid by Medicare | 80 |

After Medicare pays $120 based on its standard, you submit a claim of $80 to your supplemental carrier for the balance, enclosing a copy of the Medicare settlement. Many supplemental policies will reimburse you only for $30 (the 20 percent not paid by Medicare).

As indicated earlier, you will require health insurance to cover yourself and your spouse prior to age 65. If your employer offers you extended coverage at reasonable rates, you should take it by all means. If your employer does not offer you extended coverage, then you should obtain other supplementary coverage.

Although many insurance companies offer supplemental coverage, there are tremendous variations in the quality of coverage and the associated costs. Beware of any company that makes outlandish promises, such as offering to reimburse you for items covered by Medicare.

You should consider purchasing only those policies that have been reviewed and evaluated by an acceptable rating agency, such as a state consumer protection agency or by *Consumer Reports.* Policies that have received good ratings are sold by the American Association of Retired Persons (AARP) and by the National Council of Senior Citizens. AARP has been able to obtain attractive group rates because of its large membership.

## Social Security Taxes

You and your employer pay an equal share of Social Security taxes (FICA). If you are self-employed, you pay taxes for retirement, survivors, disability, and hospital insurance at a rate twice the employee rate.

Table 11-6 shows the Social Security tax rate effective for January 1988 through 1989 and for 1990 and later.

## Tax Credits

Self-employed people will receive a credit against the self-employment Social Security tax rate of 2 percent of self-employment income for 1986 through 1989.

After 1989 this credit will be replaced with deductions designed to treat the self-employed in much the same manner as employees and employers are treated for Social Security and income tax purposes under present law.

## When to Contact Social Security

You should contact a Social Security office for any of the following reasons:

- To obtain a Social Security number for you or a member of your family.

Table 11-6  SOCIAL SECURITY TAX RATES*

| | For You and Your Employer | | | |
|---|---|---|---|---|
| Years | Rate for Retirement, Survivors, and Disability Insurance | Rate for Hospital Insurance | Total Rate | Total Contribution (Both Employer and Employee Contribute at the Total Rate) |
| 1988–1989 | 6.06 | 1.45 | 7.51 | 15.02 |
| 1990 and later | 6.20 | 1.45 | 7.65 | 15.30 |

| | For Self-Employed People | | |
|---|---|---|---|
| Years | Rate for Retirement, Survivors, and Disability Insurance | Rate for Hospital Insurance | Total Rate (Total Contribution) |
| 1988–1989 | 12.12 | 2.90 | 15.02 |
| 1990 and later | 12.40 | 2.90 | 15.30 |

*Rates are percentages of covered earnings.

- To register a name change.
- To get a copy of a record of your earnings upon which Social Security taxes were paid and the amount of Social Security taxes (which you should do every 3 years).
- If you are unable to work because of an illness or injury that is expected to last a year or longer.
- If you are 62 or older and plan to retire.
- If you are within 3 months of 65, even if you do not plan to retire.
- If someone in your family dies.
- If someone you know has limited income and is 65 or older or blind or disabled; he or she should know about the federal SSI program. This is a program of supplemental security income paid for by general taxes, not Social Security taxes.
- If you require additional information regarding any Social Security programs. You can receive free brochures or get answers over the telephone.
- If you would like a Social Security expert to address a group you are associated with.

## Soundness of Social Security

Even though Social Security seems to have a sound financial base, you cannot assume that there will not be changes that may negatively affect you. For example, Social Security income is now indexed to inflation. There is no guarantee that Congress will not pass legislation that would partially or even completely change this feature. Social Security income is now partially taxable to single individuals earning $28,000 or more and married couples earning $32,000 or more. Congress can pass new legislation to make more of your Social Security income taxable.

Congress may pass legislation to reduce your after-tax retirement income. You should plan for such contingencies by assuring that you have other sources of income *that you can control* in the event that Congress does pass such laws.

# Employer Pension Plans

**U**nfortunately, most employees depend too much on their employers' pension plans (also called private plans) to meet their retirement needs. This is a mistake for several reasons. Even if your employer's pension plan seems attractive, there is no guarantee in most situations that the plan will not be terminated or adjusted in an unfavorable way for you. Companies can terminate nonunion pension plans at any time.

Federal law specifies certain requirements for corporations establishing a pension plan, but the law does not force a company to establish a plan, nor does it require the company to maintain the plan once established.

The law does establish vesting requirements, limits Social Security integration, and provides federal insurance to protect the employee's pension in the event that an employer defaults on a defined-benefit plan. These requirements will be reviewed in this chapter.

Unfortunately, many corporations are terminating their pension plans or modifying them in ways that are unfavorable to their employees. As an employee you have very little control over the actions of your employer in this regard. However, knowing that your employer may decide to terminate or modify your pension plan, you should realize that it is in your best interests to develop independent investment programs that you can control. This is also important if you are self-employed. Such independent plans include IRAs and Keogh plans for the self-employed. If your employer establishes the framework, you can also contribute to 401(k) plans and salary-deferral SEP plans. These plans are reviewed in Chapters 13 and 14.

## Inflation

In addition to the uncertain life span of private pension plans, there are other actual and potential problems. Inflation is a significant potential problem. Most private pension plans have no provision for inflation protection after you retire. Some companies have voluntarily made adjustments to the pensions of their retirees. However, corporations are under no legal obligation to do so unless a union contract requires it.

Most corporations today do not make voluntary inflation-based increases to their retirees' pensions. On the contrary, many corporations are terminating pension plans when they become overfunded in order to be able to extract the extra money.

A pension plan is overfunded when the value of the assets in the plan is more than adequate to meet the company's pension obligations to its employees. By discontinuing the plan the employer gains access to the surplus. If a company does terminate its pension plan, it may or may not initiate a new plan for its employees. Moreover, even if it does initiate a new plan, it may not be as favorable as the old plan.

Although an employer can discontinue a pension plan, it cannot take away benefits that you are credited with after you have worked for a specified minimum time. For example, if your employer's plan specifies that you earned permanent pension benefits after 5 years, these benefits cannot be taken away even if the company terminates its plan, if you have been employed for the 5-year minimum period.

You cannot expect that your employer will increase your pension benefits because of inflation. If your employer does provide you with extra benefits, splendid! But do not depend on it. You should depend on your own investment plans to counteract the problems associated with inflation.

## Social Security Integration

Many private pension plans are not as attractive as they seem on the surface because of what is called Social Security integration. Just as you contribute to Social Security, your employer contributes independently to Social Security on your behalf. Because of this contribution, the employer is permitted to subtract a portion of your expected Social Security benefit from your retirement benefit. This subtracted amount, called the Social Security offset, is limited by federal law and by the provisions of your employer's plan. The specific offset formula can vary by company, so you should determine exactly how the offset, if it is applicable to your plan, is computed.

---

### SCENARIO

Your pension is computed by multiplying your average salary of the last 3 years of your employment by the number of years you worked by 2 percent a year. Your pension is reduced by the Social Security offset of 2.5 percent a year, with a maximum reduction of 50 percent of your Social Security income.

Your average salary for the last three years is $50,000. You worked for your current employer for 20 years. You would be entitled to receive Social Security retirement benefits of $10,800 per year at retirement.

Social Security = $10,800/year

Pension = $50,000 × 20 years × 2% = $20,000 minus the offset

20 × 2.5% = 50

Offset = $10,800 × 50% (# of yrs × 2.5%) = $5,400

Pension = $20,000 − $5,400 = $14,600.

In this scenario a pension apparently of $20,000 a year is only $14,600 a year because of the Social Security offset.

---

Make sure you understand how your pension benefits are computed and whether there will be a Social Security offset. If there is an offset, your employer pension is the benefit you will actually receive after your employer subtracts the Social Security offset. If you accept early retirement from your employer, you may be eligible for an employer pension before you are eligible to receive Social Security benefits. You will not be eligible for Social Security income until you reach age 62. The Social Security offset will generally still be taken by your employer even though you are not eligible for Social Security benefits yet.

## Computing Your Employer Pension Benefits

There is no federal law that mandates how your pension benefits are computed. The law only specifies that your employer must provide you with the necessary data and formulas so that you can compute your estimated benefits. Most organizations publish such information in readable form. If you have not received such information, or you do not understand it, contact your personnel department. You cannot adequately plan for retirement if you do not understand the benefits you can expect from your employer's pension plan.

There are two basic types of pension plans—the defined-contribution plan and the defined-benefit plan.

## Defined-Contribution Plan

In a defined-contribution plan such as a money-purchase plan, the company contributes a specified amount, such as 10 percent of your gross salary, to your plan account. These funds are invested for you in various ways. In a defined-contribution plan, you have no way of knowing in advance what the value of your account will be when you retire, because you do not know how well the funds will be invested for you.

Some defined-contribution plans are flexible in that they give the employee several investment options. Many companies offer their employees options such as company common stock, a bond fund, a diversified common-stock fund, a money-market fund, or some combinations of these.

## Defined-Benefit Plan

In a defined-benefit plan the amount of your pension may be based on specific variables such as length of service and your average earnings over a specified time period. If you know which factors are applicable to your plan, you can precisely predict your pension benefits. The preceding scenario, in the Social Security Integration section of this chapter, includes an example of a defined-benefit plan.

## Federal Law on Pensions

The 1974 Employee Retirement Income Security Act (ERISA) provided a great deal of protection for employees. Although the law was not a cure-all, it did provide federal insurance for the first time for defined-benefit plans, and it did provide some standardization regarding vesting requirements.

Vesting refers to the minimum length of time you must work for an employer before you are guaranteed pension rights. The law also established regulatory reporting requirements and mandated that employers provide specific information to employees regarding eligibility, vesting, and computation of benefits.

Subsequent changes to the law mandated that if an employee is eligible to receive a lifetime annuity, then his or her spouse is entitled to a joint and survivor annuity. With a joint and survivor annuity option, the employee receives a permanently reduced income for life. After the death of the employee the surviving spouse receives a predetermined percentage of the initial annuity for the rest of his or her life. The percentage selected affects the amount of the initial annuity. For example, a 75 percent surviving spouse annuity would reduce the amount of the initial annuity by more than a 50 percent surviving spouse annuity. The amount of the initial annuity is also based on the difference in ages between the employee and his or her spouse. A large difference in ages will result in a smaller initial annuity.

The law specifies that if you *do not* want the joint and survivor annuity, then you must obtain the written consent of your spouse.

There were still inequities in the law, however, and the Retirement Equity Act of 1984 was passed. This law mandates that companies must provide survivor benefits to the spouse of an employee who had worked long enough to attain specific pension benefits. The act also reduced the age at which employers must allow employees to participate in pension plans. Other provisions give divorced spouses a share in pension benefits.

The Tax Reform Act of 1986 reduced the maximum time that an employee has to work to obtain permanent pension rights. For example, under one option an employee who previously had to work 10 years for pension rights would be vested—that is, would obtain permanent pension rights—after 5 years under the new law. This feature of the law became effective at the beginning of 1989.

It is very important that you clearly understand when you will become vested if you are not vested already. Review the latest literature issued by your company. If you still do not know when you will be vested, set up a meeting with your personnel representative to obtain this information.

In the following sections we will describe the major factors associated with private pensions with some specific references to federal law.

## Eligibility

Although there are some limits established by federal law, each employer can establish its own requirements regarding when you are eligible to receive a pension. Accordingly, when you start earning credits for retirement, you should make sure you understand how long you have to work to be eligible for a pension and how old you must be before you can collect benefits.

The Retirement Equity Act of 1984 imposed new eligibility rules on employers who establish pension plans. Specifically, the law cut the age at which a worker must be covered from 25 to 21.

The 1984 act also changed the rules regarding break in service. Under the new law, if an employee leaves a job and returns later, he or she must be credited for the earlier service unless the break in service was at least 5 years, or the number of years included in the employee's previous work record is greater than the break in service.

## Vesting

You become vested with an employer after you have worked for a specified minimum length of time that entitles you to specific pension benefits, which are irrevocable rights. Once you are vested, even if you resign or are terminated, you retain these pension rights.

Federal law specifies a limited number of options to employers regarding minimum vesting requirements. Make sure you understand the vesting requirements that have been established by your employer.

The Retirement Equity Act of 1984 and the Tax Reform Act of 1986 introduced some changes that affect vesting. The 1984 law specified that at age 18 employers must begin counting years of service for purposes of vesting. Previously the age was 22.

For example, an individual works 2 years, resigns, works for another organization for 4 years, and then returns to work for the original employer. He works an additional 9 years. Under the new law, that individual is credited with 11 years of service. He or she would be credited with the initial 2 years of service because the break in service was less than 5 years.

The 1986 act modified the available options regarding vesting requirements for employees. These provisions of the law went into effect at the beginning of 1989. For example, under one option the vesting requirements were shortened from 10 to 5 years. Thus, if you work for an employer whose plan initially specified a 10-year vesting period, the new law entitles you to be vested after 5 years. If you have not already been advised by your personnel department, you should contact the responsible party to determine if new vesting requirements have been introduced and if so what they are.

## Divorce

The Retirement Equity Act established that divorced individuals are entitled to spouses' pension benefits. Under the provisions of this act the courts can distribute a portion of an individual's pension to a former spouse as part of a divorce settlement. The court decides when the pension begins, the size of the payments, and how long the payments continue. If an individual does not elect early retirement but is eligible to do so, the divorced spouse may collect a share of the working employee's pension.

## Survivor Benefits

Federal law requires that a plan must provide the option of a joint and survivor benefit to be paid upon retirement. A joint and survivor benefit refers to payments made jointly to two or more parties, which are continued until the death of all parties. The law specifies that the only way to avoid the joint and survivor benefit is for both spouses to sign a waiver and elect an optional form of payment. The disadvantage of the joint and survivor option is that the monthly pension benefit is lower. This is to compensate for the possibility that if the employee's spouse outlives the employee, there will be more payments.

The 1984 act establishes that if you die before retiring but after you are vested, your spouse is entitled to your vested interest in the form of an annuity at the earliest age you could have elected to retire. The law also specifies that survivor benefits be paid in the form of an annuity for a specified period, usually the spouse's lifetime.

Even if you are married, you can consider a joint and survivor option with an individual other than your spouse. If you elect to use this option, however, you must obtain the written consent of your spouse. The actual annuity payment, as is the case with all joint and survivor annuity options, will be based on the age of both parties, you and the joint annuitant you select. If there is a large age differential, the amount of the annuity will be significantly reduced.

Other options are discussed in Chapter 17.

## Federal Insurance

Under the 1974 ERISA, defined-benefit plans are insured by the Pension Benefit Guarantee Corporation in Washington, D.C. If an employer terminates a defined-benefit pension plan that is insufficiently funded to provide you with a pension, the Pension Benefit Guarantee Corporation will insure part of the benefits you would be entitled to. The insurance will not, however, cover the complete amount. Thus, if a corporation did have to use its insurance protection, you would not receive the full amount of the pension you expected.

## Tax Status

If you elect 5- or 10-year averaging (see Chapter 16), you will receive preferential income tax treatment. If you have not made any contributions to your pension and you do not elect 5- or 10-year averaging, then all of your pension income is taxable at ordinary income tax rates. If you have made some contributions, which have already been taxed, then the pension you receive in excess of your contributions is taxed at ordinary income tax rates. For example, if your contribution is equal to 25 percent of the funds used to fund your pension, then 25 percent of your pension income is tax-free; 75 percent is taxable at ordinary rates.

# CHAPTER 13

# IRAs and Other
# Pension Plans

**W**e discuss a wide variety of pension plans in this chapter. The primary responsibility to initiate these plans is yours. In some cases not only you but also your employer may be able to contribute to your pension.

All the plans discussed in this chapter—401(k)s, 403(b)s, individual retirement accounts, and simplified employee pension plans (SEPs)—have significant advantages. These plans can be excellent vehicles for you to accumulate, significant tax-deferred assets during your working years.

There are some significant aspects of retirement that you have little control over—specifically, Social Security and employer-provided pension plans. There are pension plans, however, for which you may control both the amount of your contributions and the selection of investment vehicles. These investment plans can make the difference between a marginal standard of living during retirement and a pleasantly comfortable one. Accordingly, you should carefully examine all plans you are eligible for in order to determine how they can help you reach your financial goals.

After you reach retirement age, you will have several withdrawal options, which will be introduced here and explained thoroughly in subsequent chapters.

## 401(k) Plans

Cash or deferred arrangements (CODAs), also known as 401(k) plans, allow an employee to choose whether the employer will pay a certain amount of compensation directly to the employee in cash or as an alternative pay that amount to a qualified plan on the employee's behalf.

Although tax reform has eliminated or reduced many of the tax advantages of certain investments such as IRAs, 401(k) plans remain a very attractive instrument with tax advantages. However, your employer must set up the plan in order for you to take advantage of it.

## Tax Advantages

The allowable contribution to 401(k) investment plans for 1988 was $7,313. At this writing the allowable contribution for 1989 is not available; the upper limit changes every year, based on changes in the rate of inflation. The specific amount you can contribute depends on the formula established by your employer. Accordingly, you may not be able to contribute the full amount each year.

The amount that you contribute is deductible on your federal income tax return. All earnings on CODAs, whether interest income, dividends, or capital gains, are tax-deferred until you withdraw the funds. From a tax perspective there is no difference between contributions and earnings on contributions. When you withdraw funds from the plan, the amount you withdraw is taxed at the rates for ordinary income.

The two tax advantages—being able to contribute before-tax income and having earnings build up on a tax-deferred basis—provide an excellent tax shelter for you. Moreover, since contributions can go as high as $7,313 per year, the plan allows you to build up assets even faster than you could with IRA programs.

## Employer Contributions

Your employer may structure the 401(k) plan in order to make matching contributions on your behalf. The law does not require any employer contributions, however.

A typical matching plan might work as follows: You contribute up to 10 percent of your salary to your 401(k). Your employer matches your contribution up to 5 percent of your salary. If you contribute 5 percent, your employer contributes 5 percent. If you contribute 3 percent, your employer contributes 3 percent. The limit on contributions applies to the full amount, your contribution plus your employer's.

If your employer does match some or all of your contributions, it gives you an added incentive to participate. Your employer's contributions are treated for tax purposes in the same way your contributions are treated. The employer's contributions and earnings on these contributions are not taxable to you until you withdraw them from the plan.

## Investment Choice

Your selection of investments will be restricted to those offered by your employer. In most 401(k) plans, employers offer you only a few investment choices, such as common stocks, bonds, money-market instruments, and combinations thereof. Your investment choices should be based on your primary investment objectives.

## Withdrawal Options

You may withdraw funds from your plan when you reach age 59½, leave your job, become disabled, or undergo financial hardship. Unless you become disabled, however, you have to pay the IRS a 10 percent penalty plus income tax if you withdraw funds prior to age 59½. You don't have to pay this penalty if you leave your job on or after age 55 and accept a lifetime annuity or if you meet your plan's requirements for early retirement. The advantages and disadvantages of annuities are discussed in Chapter 17.

When you leave your job, you might not be able to leave your funds in the 401(k) plan. If the value of your account is less than $3,500, your employer may terminate the account even if you don't want to close it and withdraw the funds. You probably would want to terminate the account, however, and consider one of several distribution options. Each of the various distribution options open to you has different financial and tax implications. Options include a lifetime annuity, an IRA rollover, and possibly income averaging. The best choice for you will be based on personal considerations, such as how quickly you need access to the funds. Analysis and comparison of these alternatives can be quite complicated. These will be discussed in detail in Chapters 16 and 17. You must, however, begin withdrawal at age 70½.

When you leave your job, you have the option to withdraw all of your funds from the 401(k) and pay ordinary income tax on the whole distribution. There are no tax advantages; this is rarely the best alternative.

## The Loan Option

The law does give you the option to borrow money from your 401(k) plan, but this must be an allowable provision of the plan document. You may borrow the lesser of (a) $50,000 or (b) the greater of (1) half the value of your account or (2) $10,000. You have to repay the loan within 5 years, except for a loan for a personal residence. Consistent with the plan document, a residential loan can be repaid within 10 years. The interest you repay is not tax-deductible. The interest rate is set by your employer.

The only guidance the IRS provides is that the rate must be "reasonable." Do not be concerned if the rate seems high to you, since you are paying the interest to your own account.

If you leave your job while there is a 401(k) loan outstanding, you should repay the loan if you can. Otherwise the amount of the loan is treated as a distribution subject to ordinary income tax and a 10 percent penalty if you are younger than 59½.

### Federal Employees

Members of the Federal Employee Retirement System are eligible to participate in a 401(k) investment program, although it is not usually described as a 401(k) plan. Under this program employees can contribute up to 10 percent of their salary and the federal government matches up to 5 percent.

There are several investment options under FERS, including a special bond fund (Fund F), a long-term bond fund, and a common stock fund. Fund F is very attractive because it provides a relatively high rate of return with no downside risk.

### Summary of 401(k) Plans

If your employer has established the framework for a 401(k) plan, you should definitely participate if you can afford the contributions because of the potential for large tax-deferred contributions. This plan is especially attractive because the Tax Reform Act of 1986 has eliminated or reduced the tax advantages of many other investments.

## 403(b) Plans

If you work for a public institution that qualifies as a 501(c)3 organization, you may be eligible to participate in a 403(b) plan. The tax advantages are the same as those associated with 401(k) plans. Contributions are tax-deductible, and the earnings on contributions are tax-deferred. Withdrawals are taxable at ordinary income tax rates.

The upper limit of your contribution to a 403(b) plan is the lower of $9,500 or 20 percent of your salary. If you also contribute to a 401(k) plan, you must reduce the maximum amount of your 403(b) contribution by the amount you contributed to the 401(k).

You may have a choice of investments selected by the trustees of the plan. Before you select your investments, review the performance history of each of the options available and make your selection consistent with your financial objectives.

## Individual Retirement Accounts

An IRA is an account established for the purpose of contributing employment earnings that can increase in value in a tax-sheltered vehicle. Unfortunately, Congress cannot seem to make up its mind about whether it really wants workers to contribute to IRAs.

In 1981 Congress passed tax legislation that broadened eligibility requirements. From 1982 to 1986 workers were encouraged to make IRA contributions. During these years up to $2,000 per year could be invested in an IRA account with two advantages: (1) your contribution reduced your taxable income by the amount of your contribution, and (2) all earnings on your contribution were (and still are) tax-deferred until you withdraw the funds.

The passage of the Tax Reform Act of 1986 significantly changed the laws related to IRAs and reduced the advantages of the IRA account for the majority of employees. Under the new law, if neither you nor your spouse is covered by an employer-sponsored retirement plan, you can continue to contribute $2,000 to an IRA with the same tax advantages you had between 1982 and 1986.

If either you or your spouse is covered by an employer-sponsored retirement plan, the level of your earnings will determine whether you can make tax-deductible contributions to an IRA. For example, if you file a joint return with your spouse, you will be able to make tax-deductible IRA contributions only if your combined income is less than $50,000. This will be discussed in detail later.

Even if you cannot make tax-deductible contributions, you can make after-tax IRA contributions if you are earning money. The only tax advantage you have, however, is that the earnings on your contribution are tax-deferred. This advantage must be weighed against substantial disadvantages. The IRS has imposed complicated filing requirements for contributions and withdrawals of after-tax IRA funds. The most significant disadvantage is associated with withdrawals. You cannot simply withdraw your after-tax contributions without paying income tax. If you make a withdrawal, the IRS forces you to prorate your withdrawal based on the after-tax contribution and the earnings on it. If you deposited money at some time prior to the passing of the law, you must include this in your prorating and pay taxes based on this money as well as your earnings on it.

For example, assume you made $10,000 of tax-deductible contributions and $2,000 of after-tax contributions. You earned $8,000 on all your contributions, and the total value of your IRA is $20,000. If you withdrew $2,000, only 10 percent ($200) of your withdrawal would be tax-free; $1,800 would be taxable *even though you made $2,000 in after-tax contributions.*

In summary, if you can still make tax-deductible IRA contributions, continue to do so. If your IRA contributions can only be made with after-tax funds, you should be very cautious and make sure you understand the disadvantages, which may become apparent only when you start making withdrawals. After-tax IRA contributions are a potential nightmare for individuals who contributed to IRAs prior to 1987.

## Eligibility

Anyone who has compensation is eligible to establish an IRA. The IRS definition of compensation includes wages, salaries, commissions, tips, professional fees, bonuses, and any other money you receive for providing services; taxable alimony; and separate maintenance payments.

You may not make a contribution to an IRA during or after the year in which you reach age 70 1/2.

If both you and your spouse have compensation, you can each establish IRAs. Each IRA is established in the name of one individual, although beneficiaries can be specified.

## IRA Contributions and Deductibility

The maximum combined amount that you can contribute to IRAs from your earned income in one year is the lesser of 100 percent of your income or $2,000. Whether you can deduct your contribution is dependent on two factors: (1) whether or not you or your spouse is covered by an employer retirement plan, and (2) your income level in the applicable year.

## Contributions Not Covered by Employer Retirement Plan

If neither you nor your spouse is covered by an employer retirement plan and you have earned income during the year, each wage earner can contribute up to $2,000, or all of his or her earnings, whichever is less, on a tax-deductible basis, regardless of your income level. For example, if you earned $100,000 of taxable income in 1988 and neither you nor your spouse was covered by a retirement plan, you could make a $2,000 contribution, reducing your taxable income to $98,000.

If you are not sure whether you or your spouse is covered by an employer retirement plan, you should see your respective personnel departments. The W-2 (wage and tax statement) you receive from your employer at the end of the year should indicate whether you are covered by a retirement plan. If the pension plan box is checked, you are covered by a retirement plan for IRA eligibility purposes. If you are self-employed and establish a Keogh plan, you are covered by a retirement plan.

### Contributions Covered by Employer Retirement Plan

Even if you or your spouse is covered by an employer retirement plan, you may be able to make tax-deductible IRA contributions if your income is below established limits. The limits are established based on your filing status.

If you are married and file jointly, you may take your entire $2,000 per-wage-earner deduction only if your adjusted gross income (AGI) is $40,000 or less. If your AGI is $50,000 or greater, none of your contribution is tax-deductible. If your AGI is between $40,000 and $50,000, you are entitled to a partial deduction. For example, if your AGI is $45,000, you are entitled to a $1,000 deduction; if your AGI is $47,500, you are entitled to a $500 deduction.

If your filing status is single or head of household, a different AGI limit applies. If your AGI is $35,000 or more, you are not entitled to a deduction. If your AGI is $25,000 or less, you are entitled to the full deduction, $2,000. If your AGI is between $25,000 and $35,000, you are entitled to a partial deduction, prorated in the same manner as if married, filing jointly.

If your filing status is married, filing separately, you are not entitled to a deduction if your AGI is higher than $10,000. If your AGI is lower than $10,000, you are entitled to a partial deduction on a prorated basis.

### Advantages

There are two possible advantages to making IRA contributions.

- Your contribution may be deductible from your taxable income.
- All earnings on your contributions are tax-deferred until you make withdrawals.

In the previous section, we discussed eligibility requirements for making tax-deductible contributions. If you are eligible to make this type of

IRA contribution, you should make every effort to do so, because it is such a powerful way to save money and have it grow tax-deferred.

Individuals who are eligible to make only after-tax IRA contributions have only one advantage—the tax deferral of earnings on IRA contributions. This can be a considerable advantage, but it must be weighed against the disadvantages: (1) You cannot withdraw after-tax contributions without incurring some tax liability. (2) You must maintain meticulous records to avoid an administrative nightmare at tax preparation time. Further information is provided later in this chapter.

Whether you make tax-deductible IRA contributions or after-tax contributions, you have a wide variety of investment options. The only type of investment that is not allowed for IRA contributions is investment in collectibles such as art objects and precious metals.

## SCENARIO

Dora Kaufman earns a salary of $40,000 in 1988, and she is not covered by an employer retirement plan. She is eligible to make a $2,000 tax-deductible contribution because she is not covered by a retirement plan. She is in the 28 percent tax bracket in 1989 and accordingly would immediately save $560 in taxes.

Assume she invests the $2,000 in a certificate of deposit and earns 10 percent, or $200, on her investment in 1989. Since her investment is in an IRA, she owes no tax on this $200 interest.

In subsequent years her IRA grows even faster because she is compounding her earnings, that is, earning interest on interest.

### Nonworking Spouse Contribution

Even if your spouse does not work, you are allowed to establish an independent IRA for him or her if you are not covered by an employer-sponsored plan, or if your income is less than $40,000. The maximum amount you are allowed to contribute to the two independent IRAs is $2,250, $250 more than the maximum contribution for one IRA. You and your spouse must file a joint return.

The minimum amount that can be contributed to either IRA is $250. Other than this limitation the $2,250 can be split in any way. The proportion can be varied from year to year.

### SCENARIO

Sue Fleming earns $20,000, and her husband Martin does not work. The Flemings can contribute $2,250 to two IRAs. They choose to split the $2,250 in half and contribute $1,125 to each IRA. These are separate IRAs, not one joint account. Each IRA must be established in the name of one individual.

If Mr. Fleming starts earning income, he can make a full $2,000 contribution to his account, and Mrs. Fleming can also make a $2,000 contribution if she continues to work.

When you consider how to apportion nonworking spouse contributions, you should consider the age of each spouse. If you allocate a higher percentage to the older spouse, for example, you will have access to the funds earlier without penalty, since IRA funds cannot be withdrawn without penalty until age 59½.

### Disadvantages

There are some disadvantages associated with IRA investments. The most important disadvantage is the lack of flexibility regarding fund withdrawals prior to age 59½ and after age 70½.

#### Penalty for Early Withdrawal

Once you make a contribution to an IRA plan, you cannot withdraw funds prior to age 59½ without incurring a 10 percent penalty and paying income tax on the amount of your withdrawal. You can withdraw funds for up to 60 days without penalty. After 60 days you incur the 10 percent penalty.

There are a few exceptions to the early-withdrawal penalty: disability, death, and accepting a distribution after age 55 in the form of an annuity, or regular periodic payments. This latter option will be explored subsequently in this chapter.

Assume you have $12,000 in your IRA when you are 50 years old. You need to withdraw $10,000. If you withdraw $10,000 and do not put the funds back into an IRA within 60 days, you incur a 10 percent penalty. In this case your penalty is $1,000 (10% × $10,000 — the amount you withdraw). If all your contributions are tax-deductible, you also have to report the $10,000 as ordinary income when you file your federal income tax return for that year. If you make both after-tax and tax-deductible contributions, the amount of income you report has to be determined pro rata. Some specific examples are given in the withdrawal section of this chapter.

### Withdrawals after Age 70½

Once you reach age 59½, you have complete flexibility regarding fund withdrawals; i.e., you can withdraw some or all or none of your IRA funds without penalty. If you did not make nondeductible contributions, all of your withdrawals are subject to ordinary income tax.

After you reach age 70½, however, you have less flexibility. You *must* make minimum withdrawals based on your life expectancy. You have until April 1 of the year following the year you turn 70½ to initiate these minimum withdrawals.

---

**SCENARIO**

Assume that when you reach age 70½, you have $45,000 in your IRA, and the IRS tables at that time indicate that your life expectancy is 15 years. Your minimum withdrawal per year is $45,000 ÷ 15, or $3,000 per year. If you do not make at least a $3,000 withdrawal, you are subject to a *50 percent penalty* on the difference between what you withdraw and the minimum amount the IRS indicated you should withdraw.

If you withdrew only $2,000 in one year, the penalty is $500 (50 percent of $1,000), because you withdrew $1,000 less than the $3,000 minimum. Obviously, once you reach age 70½, you should withdraw at least the minimum required by the IRS. The penalty is too severe not to do so.

---

The reason for this penalty is that the IRS does not want to wait too long for you to pay income tax on your IRA. All your withdrawals are taxed at ordinary income tax rates.

Because of the forced withdrawal requirement after age 70½, you must give it some forethought when you are between ages 59½ and 70½. If your income fluctuates during that time frame, you should consider making withdrawals from your IRA during years when your other income is lower. This strategy has two advantages: (1) Your income is more stable. (2) You make IRA withdrawals when your income tax rate is lower.

### Income Tax Rates

Many financial institutions promote IRAs by suggesting that you will be at a lower tax rate when you withdraw IRA funds than you were when you made your contributions. *Do not believe this.* You may be in a *higher* tax bracket because it is likely that tax rates will increase and because your taxable income may be close to or higher in retirement than it was when you were working. This does not mean that you should avoid IRAs, however. The advantages of making after-tax contributions and having these funds grow tax-deferred far outweigh the possibility that you will be in a high tax bracket during retirement. You should not be deluded, however, into thinking that your IRA withdrawals will be taxed at a low rate. When you are preparing your long-term plan, you should assume that tax rates will increase over time. In this way you will avoid a rude shock during your retirement.

### Short-Term Investment

You are significantly penalized if you withdraw funds prior to age $59\frac{1}{2}$. You incur a penalty that is 10 percent of the amount of your withdrawal. Accordingly, you should not put funds into an IRA unless you are reasonably sure that you will not have to withdraw these funds on a short-term basis. If you are reasonably sure that you can keep the funds invested for at least 10 years, the advantages of tax deferral will likely outweigh the 10 percent penalty. Obviously, you want to avoid the penalty except in an emergency.

## Pros and Cons of After-Tax Contributions

There is no question that you should make tax-deductible IRA contributions if you are eligible and if you can afford to do so. The argument for making after-tax IRA contributions is not so persuasive. There is only one advantage to this — tax deferral of the earnings on your contributions.

This advantage must be weighed against the disadvantages of after-tax IRA contributions. There are two significant disadvantages: (1) You cannot make withdrawals of after-tax contributions without incurring some tax liability. (2) You will be forced to maintain meticulous records or face an administrative nightmare at tax time.

---

### SCENARIO

Assume you have been making tax-deductible IRA contributions for five years, and now you are no longer eligible to do so. You make after-tax contributions for a few years, and then you retire. Let us review what happens when you start making withdrawals.

| | |
|---|---:|
| Tax-deductible contributions: | $10,000 |
| After-tax contributions: | 6,000 |
| Earnings on all contributions: | 4,000 |
| Total value of IRA: | $20,000 |

You would like to withdraw $6,000. Since you have made a contribution of $6,000 from after-tax earnings, you might think you could withdraw $6,000 without incurring any tax liability. This is not true. You have to compute the ratio of the portion of the IRA that has not been taxed to the total value of the IRA. In this example the untaxed amount is $14,000 ($20,000 − $6,000), and the total value is $20,000. The ratio is 70 percent. You have to report 70 percent of the $6,000 withdrawal, or $4,200, as taxable income.

Moreover, you have to maintain records of each withdrawal. For example, the after-tax contribution remaining in your IRA is now $4200 ($6000 − (30% × $6000)). If you expect your accountant to keep these records for you, it may cost you more in accounting fees than the value of your tax deferment.

---

Overall, the administrative headaches of after-tax contributions make the advantages look feeble. As an alternative, look carefully at personal investments in municipal bonds before you decide to make after-tax IRA contributions.

Many individuals in retirement have taxable income, especially now that part of Social Security is taxable. Funds you invest in municipal bonds rather than after-tax IRAs will be available to you completely tax-free in retirement. At least part of your IRA withdrawals will be taxable. Thus, if you build up a substantial investment in municipal bonds rather than after-tax IRA contributions, you will have more control over your tax situation.

### Required Distributions for IRAs and Other Qualified Plans

The law specifies that you must begin taking distributions from an IRA or other qualified plan no later than April 1 of the year following the year you reach age 70½. A qualified plan is one that meets the rules and regulations of the Internal Revenue Service.

Minimum withdrawals must be made annually based on life expectancy tables published by the IRS. Your options include the following:

- Your life span
- The life span of yourself and your designated beneficiary
- A period not exceeding your life expectancy
- A period not exceeding the joint life expectancy of you and your designated beneficiary

## Annuity Distributions

As one of your IRA distribution options, you can elect to receive a lifetime annuity for either yourself or for both yourself and your designated beneficiary. In order to meet IRS requirements, payments must be substantially equal and they should be made at least annually.

### Installment Payments

After age 59½ you can elect to have a distribution made in equal installments if you prefer. You can make such an arrangement with an insurance company and receive a fixed monthly or quarterly income for life.

As an alternative you can consider an installment distribution plan with a mutual fund.

Some mutual funds, such as Scudder, have retirement planning specialists who can assist you in establishing an installment distribution plan. Most mutual funds have toll-free telephone numbers. You can contact the funds you are interested in and inquire whether they offer installment distribution plans and whether they have retirement planning specialists who can assist you.

In this way you have more flexibility regarding your selection of investments. Your investment results will vary each year, however, and the amount of the annual distribution you receive will be based on the performance of the fund you select. If you did not make any nondeductible contributions, all income you receive in installment form is taxable at ordinary income-tax rates: the tax treatment is the same—no better and no worse—than that for any other distribution method. The portion of your income that is derived from nondeductible contributions is not taxable.

## IRA Rollover

After you reach age 59½ or leave your job, or after your pension or profit-sharing plan is terminated, you can roll over or transfer all or part (over half) of your lump-sum distribution into the IRA of your choice. There are several advantages.

The primary advantage of the rollover is that you incur income-tax liability only when you withdraw funds from your IRA. If you do not need access to your funds right away, this is an important advantage.

A second advantage of a rollover is that you continue to earn tax-deferred interest on the funds left in your IRA. In contrast, if you elect averaging, you no longer have that tax deferral.

In Chapter 16 eligibility for rollovers is discussed in detail.

If you wish, you can roll over part of your lump-sum distribution into an IRA as long as the amount you roll over is at least 50 percent of the amount of your distribution. This option is beneficial if you need some of the distribution immediately.

## Beneficiaries

You may select anyone you wish as the beneficiary of your IRA. However, a surviving spouse is the only beneficiary who is eligible to roll over an inherited IRA account into his or her own IRA. Obviously, this is only one factor for your consideration when you decide who to select as the beneficiary of your IRA. A detailed discussion of beneficiary options and other aspects of estate planning is discussed in Chapter 21.

## IRA Investments

The Tax Reform Act of 1986 allows you to invest your IRA funds in anything other than collectibles, such as art objects, gems, stamps, and coins. According to the act, gold and silver coins minted in the United States and acquired after December 31, 1986, are not collectibles. Chapter 15 provides some guidelines for IRA investing.

## Simplified Employee Pension Plans

A simplified employee pension plan (SEP) is an individual retirement account that is established and maintained by an employee and to which an employer contributes. This also applies to self-employed individuals. The SEP is similar in concept to a regular IRA. The primary difference is that with a SEP the employer makes the contribution rather than the employee. Contributions made to a SEP by an employer on behalf of an employee are excluded from the gross income of the employee. Some employers established SEPs because they are much simpler than qualified pension plans, which have more stringent reporting requirements.

The maximum deductible contribution to a SEP is higher than the limit for an IRA. The limit is 15 percent of compensation, with an upper limit of $30,000 per year. If you are self-employed, the limit is the same as it is for a Keogh plan. (See Chapter 16.)

The law allows you to make voluntary contributions to an IRA established under SEP if your employer has 25 or fewer employees and other conditions are satisfied. The limit of the voluntary contributions is $7,313 per year. The total of your contribution and your employer's contribution cannot exceed the lesser of $30,000 or 25 percent of your annual salary. If you also contribute to a 401(k) plan, the combined limits are still $7,313 and $30,000.

### SCENARIO

Mr. West earns $100,000. His employer, who has established a SEP, contributes $20,000 to Mr. West's SEP IRA. There are 20 employees in the firm. Accordingly, Mr. West is eligible to make $5,000 in voluntary contributions to his SEP IRA, since 25 percent of $100,000 is $25,000, the maximum contribution under existing law.

## Summary of Withdrawal Options

All of the plans reviewed in this chapter have some tax advantages. In many cases your contributions are tax-deductible, and in all cases earnings are tax-deferred. When you start making withdrawals from these plans, most or all will be fully taxable. It is to be hoped that you will have built up a sizable amount of money using these plans. If so, the decisions you make regarding fund withdrawal are very important. Fortunately, you have more than one option, and you can select the option or options that most productively fit your needs.

The options that you may be eligible for are income averaging, IRA rollovers, and annuities. Chapter 16 compares IRA rollovers with income averaging and annuities. Chapter 17 discusses annuities in detail.

### Income Averaging

Income averaging is a special tax break that IRS allows you to use if you withdraw the total amount from a profit-sharing plan or a pension plan in a single lump sum. Averaging provides you with a tax advantage because you are allowed to pay tax on the distribution separately from your other income; your tax is computed as if you received the income over a longer period—either 5 or 10 years. This tax treatment saves you money, since you pay taxes in a lower tax bracket. However, you have to report this income in the year you received the income. If you received the distribution in 1989, for example, you would have to report all of the income on your 1989 tax return.

There are two options, 5-year and 10-year averaging. To be eligible for 5-year averaging, you have to be 59½ or older when the distribution is made or age 50 before 1986. An individual who reached age 59½ before 1986 is eligible for 10-year averaging, which is generally more favorable. Specific situations will be discussed in Chapter 16.

The primary advantages of electing averaging are that you have access to the complete distribution immediately and that you do get some income tax savings. The disadvantage is that you have to pay income tax on the whole distribution in one tax year. If you do not need all the funds immediately, other options may be more attractive.

## IRA Rollover

In general, if you expect to keep the majority of your funds from your distribution invested for longer than 10 years, the IRA is probably better for you than averaging.

## Annuity

Your third option is to accept a lifetime fixed annuity, either a joint annuity for yourself and your spouse or an annuity for yourself alone. There are a few advantages and some disadvantages.

The primary advantage of an annuity is that you are guaranteed a specified income for life. Depending on the size of the income, of course, that can be quite attractive.

A second advantage is related to your age. If you are younger than 59½, you cannot make withdrawals from an IRA without incurring a 10 percent tax penalty. However, if you have reached age 55 and if the term of the annuity is 60 months or longer, you can elect an annuity and receive monthly or quarterly payments immediately and without penalty.

The major disadvantage of the annuity is inflexibility. Once you accept the annuity, your payment is fixed. If there is a great deal of inflation during your retirement, the purchasing power of your annuity will be significantly reduced.

Another disadvantage is that you have given your lump-sum distribution to an insurance company in exchange for the annuity. You will not be able to leave that capital to your heirs.

### Ordinary Income Tax

Your last alternative is to pay ordinary income tax on the complete distribution. This is obviously a poor alternative, and it is not recommended. One of the other alternatives will definitely be better for you.

# Keogh Plans

In 1962 Congress introduced Keogh plans to allow self-employed individuals to establish and fund retirement plans. Since 1962 several items of pension legislation have been enacted to provide for parity between corporate and self-employed retirement plans. The tax advantages of Keogh plans were essentially the same as those of IRAs prior to tax reform—contributions are tax-deductible and earnings on contributions are tax-deferred. Tax reform in 1986 did not reduce the tax advantages of Keogh plans.

## Eligibility

You are eligible to establish a Keogh plan if you have any income from self-employment. You are eligible whether you are a sole proprietor or a member of a partnership. Full-time self-employed individuals such as doctors, lawyers, and merchants can establish Keogh plans. In addition, you are eligible if you engage in consulting, teaching, or free-lance work, part time or otherwise. Contributing to an IRA account does not exclude you from establishing a Keogh plan. However, the deductibility of the IRA may be reduced or eliminated.

## Advantages

There are two primary advantages to a Keogh plan: Your contributions are tax-deductible, and earnings on your contributions are tax-deferred. You will not incur a tax liability until you withdraw funds. Depending on your income level, Keogh plans can have an additional advantage over IRAs: You can contribute up to $30,000 per year rather than the $2,000 maximum associated with IRAs.

## Disadvantages

Keogh plans have the same disadvantages that IRAs have. You cannot withdraw funds until age 59½, and early withdrawals are subject to a 10 percent penalty.

If you are an employer, there is another disadvantage. You cannot establish a Keogh for yourself and exclude your employees. If you start a Keogh account for yourself, you must also open one for each of your employees. Moreover, you cannot establish a plan that discriminates against any employee or group of employees. Accordingly, it may be too expensive for you to have a Keogh account, in which case you could open an IRA for yourself.

## Types of Plans

There are two types of Keogh plans, defined-contribution and defined-benefit. As you would expect, with a defined-contribution plan, your contribution is based on your income level. With a defined-benefit plan, the amount of your contribution is based on your projected benefit at retirement.

### Defined-Contribution Plans

The defined-contribution plan is by far the more common type of Keogh plan. There are two categories of this type—profit-sharing plans and money-purchase plans.

With a profit-sharing plan, which is quite flexible, you may contribute up to 15 percent of your gross self-employment income minus your contribution. Your maximum contribution is $30,000. Effectively, this means that you can contribute 13.043 percent of your gross income. For example, if your gross income is $50,000, you can contribute up to $6,522 for that year.

With a money-purchase plan, you must contribute a fixed percentage of your income. You can contribute the lesser of $30,000 or 25 percent of your gross income minus the contribution. This means you can contribute 20 percent of your gross income from self-employment up to $30,000. For example, if you earn $50,000, you can contribute $10,000 to your plan.

You can combine a money-purchase plan with a profit-sharing plan. In this way you can increase the limits of your contribution but maintain flexibility regarding the amount you can contribute. Your combined contribution cannot exceed $30,000.

### Defined-Benefit Plans

A defined-benefit plan is much more complicated than a defined-contribution plan. An actuary or professionally trained individual whose primary functions include establishing rates and determining reserves required to fund future liabilities, is required to establish and maintain this type of plan, and, accordingly, it can be expensive.

You may not have to hire an actuary personally. Financial institutions that offer defined-benefit plans either have actuaries on their staff or contract for their services.

You should establish a defined-benefit plan only if you want to contribute more than you could with a defined-contribution plan. Defined-benefit plans are generally suitable only for individuals with substantial earned income who can make larger contributions than they could to a defined-contribution plan.

The allowable amount of contribution is based on the specific benefit you want to receive at retirement. Your benefit at retirement cannot exceed the smaller of $90,000 per year or 100 percent of your average earnings for the 3 consecutive years in which your earnings are the highest. You may not, however, contribute in one year more than your income for that year.

For example, your earnings for the last 3 years were $50,000, $60,000, and $70,000. You want to contribute enough to fund a maximum benefit at retirement of $60,000 per year. The specific amount of the contribution must be determined by an actuary based on when you plan to retire, preretirement and postretirement actuarial assumptions, actuarial funding method, and past contributions' investing performance.

## Your Investment Choice

There are very few restrictions regarding eligible investment choices for Keogh plan contributions. The same restrictions that apply to IRAs apply to Keogh plans. You cannot invest Keogh monies in certain collectibles without losing the tax advantages. Chapter 15 contains a discussion of appropriate investments.

Fewer financial institutions are willing to act as trustees for Keogh plans than for IRAs. However, many major banks and brokerage firms are willing to act as trustees. Most mutual funds have an established trustee relationship with a financial institution to administer Keogh plans. If you choose, you may serve as your own trustee, although it is not usually worth the effort, since trustee charges are generally nominal. If you do serve as your own trustee, however, you will have more flexibility in your investments.

## Timing

In order to contribute to a Keogh, the plan must have been established by December 31 in the applicable tax year. However, you do not have to fund the plan until the due date of your tax return in the following year. If you miss the December 31 deadline, you can establish a simplified employee pension plan (See Chapter 13.)

## Plan Termination

When you stop working, you may wish to terminate your Keogh plan. You have the option to roll over the funds in your Keogh into an IRA and continue to defer taxes on all income from the monies. Rollovers are discussed in more detail in Chapter 16.

## Establishing a Plan

A plan may be established by

1. Requesting a determination letter or special forms issued by the IRS, or
2. Using an IRS-approved master or prototype plan prepared and sponsored by another organization such as a bank, an insurance company, or a mutual fund.

# Selecting Your IRA and Keogh Investments

**E**verything in this chapter that refers to IRAs is also true of Keogh plans.

The existing law allows you to invest your IRA in almost any manner. The only category specifically excluded is collectibles, or art, rugs, antiques, metals, gems, stamps, and coins. You can, however, invest in gold or silver coins minted by the Treasury Department. If you feel strongly about investing in precious metals, you can buy individual gold-mining common stocks or mutual funds specializing in precious metals. These are acceptable IRA investments.

Because you have practically the whole universe of investment products available to you, the advantages and disadvantages of specific IRA products are essentially the same as they are outside of an IRA. However, some special factors that pertain to IRAs can affect the type of investment you select. These factors include special fees, costs, and flexibility. These factors and the advantages and disadvantages of different IRA products are discussed below. At the end of the chapter we will review each major financial objective from the perspective of available IRA investments.

## Sellers and Trustees of IRAs

Because of the restrictions on IRAs in the Tax Reform Act of 1986, you will find that many financial service organizations are not giving as much attention to IRA accounts as they used to. Accordingly, you should make sure that your trustee (in some cases the financial service organization hires an independent trustee) will give your IRA adequate attention. All

IRA accounts must have an IRS-approved trustee. The trustee can be a bank, credit union, savings and loan association, or any other corporation or person who has specific IRS approval. You are not restricted to the use of one IRA account or one trustee. You may open as many IRA accounts as you wish with as many trustees as you wish. If you have a very large IRA account, as you may have if you roll over a large lump-sum distribution, consider using different forms of investments with different trustees.

You may want to consider the use of a self-directed trustee. With this type of trustee you can select any form of investment you wish. This gives you the most flexibility. The IRAs offered by most brokerage firms should also provide you with a great deal of flexibility.

Organizations still actively marketing IRAs include mutual funds, banks, credit unions, savings and loan institutions, brokerage firms, and insurance companies. When you select an organization that markets IRAs, make sure you understand the investments that are being offered. You do not want to use a selling organization that is not willing or able to provide the type of investment you want.

## Special Fees

Many trustees charge fees for opening an IRA as well as an annual fee for maintaining your account. These fees may seem small, but you should review them from the perspective of the effect of the fee on your investment return.

### SCENARIO

You plan to establish an IRA with a $2,000 investment. You expect a 10 percent rate of return, that is, earnings of $200 a year. If you pay a $50 fee to the trustee for the first year, your net rate of return for the first year is 7.5 percent, not 10 percent. If you contribute only $1,000, your net return is 5 percent.

You should consider the trustee fee as an earnings drain. Not all trustees charge fees or charge the same fee. Accordingly, you should not open an IRA if you have to pay a large fee unless you are convinced that your net rate of return will be higher even with the fee.

Most financial institutions do not charge fees when you purchase certificates of deposit. Most trustees for mutual funds charge nominal fees, such as $10 a year; some charge no fee at all. For example, the trustee of the Scudder family of funds, which manages many funds with above-average performance histories, does not charge a fee. Many insurance company IRA investments have substantial fees, both initial and recurring. Make sure you know what these fees are before you consider investing in an insurance IRA or any other investment.

If there is a fee for the IRA you are investing in, pay it separately if you can rather than having the fee deducted from your contribution. You want to have as much in your IRA as possible. If you subtract a fee from your $2,000 contribution, you will not have $2,000 invested. The fee can be deducted as a miscellaneous item if you pay it separately, if you itemize your deductions on your tax return, and if your deductions exceed 2 percent of your adjusted gross income.

## Sales Commission

Some IRA investments carry no sales commission, while others have sales commissions ranging from nominal to high. Although a sales commission should not be the most important factor when you are selecting an IRA, it should be considered to some extent because it can be a significant percentage of your investment.

Certificates of deposit are generally sold with no sales commission. Mutual funds can be sold either no-load (no sales commission) or load (up to 8 percent commission). Brokerage firms set their own commission structures. Since most IRA transactions involve relatively small investments, you should determine the commission structure of a broker before opening an account. You want to avoid a broker whose minimum commissions are too high for the transaction you expect to be executing. For example, if you expect to invest $1,000 in common stocks, you should ask what the commission is. You may find that with some brokers the commission structure inhibits small accounts, and you may be better off with a different broker or conceivably with a different form of investment.

Many investments offered by insurance companies have relatively high front-end sales commissions. Other insurance company products do not have a front-end commission, but you incur charges if you do not hold the investment for a minimum time. Accordingly you lose a great deal of flexibility. Make sure you understand all the sales commissions and fees associated with any insurance company investment before you buy.

Technically life insurance is not an allowable IRA investment; however, it may be included as part of a qualified plan. Life insurance premiums are not tax-deductible. For example, if you paid $2,000 for a package that included $500 worth of life insurance, your maximum deduction would be $1,500. It is best to avoid buying life insurance as part of an IRA program.

## Safety of Principal

If your primary investment objective is protecting your principal, consider the following acceptable IRA instruments: certificates of deposit, Treasury bills, money-market accounts, and money-market funds. You will not obtain the highest yield on these types of investment, but your principal will be protected.

## Flexibility

Some forms of IRA provide you with a great deal of flexibility, while other vehicles are not flexible at all.

Investment in a mutual fund that manages several funds, commonly called a family of funds, provides you with a great deal of flexibility. You can switch investments from one fund to another by making a telephone call, generally toll-free. Moreover, with most funds your transfer will be free, although some funds charge nominal fees for switches from one fund to another.

For example, if you originally contributed $2,000 to a money-market fund and you wanted to switch $1,000 to a common stock fund in the same mutual fund family, you could execute the transaction with one phone call. The change in investment would be made at the end of the same day at the prices in effect then.

Most brokerage firms also offer you a great deal of flexibility in changing investments. Although you have much flexibility with a brokerage-based IRA, you may incur substantial sales commission costs if you have too many transactions, especially if your transactions are small.

Many insurance company investments have limited flexibility. Other offerings may provide you with flexibility through a variety of options. Beware of charges if you change investments, however. If you must pay a fee to change investments, you lose much of your flexibility.

If you purchase a long-term CD, you lose some flexibility. You must wait until the CD matures before you can withdraw funds without penalty. Moreover, a financial institution is under no obligation to release funds to you prior to maturity. The vast majority of institutions, however, will release funds after subtracting an early-withdrawal penalty.

## Income

Some excellent sources of high income are intermediate- and long-term bonds, long-term CDs, and common stocks of corporations noted for high earnings and generous payout ratios.

Do not purchase municipal bonds for an IRA or Keogh, because all withdrawals are taxed as ordinary income. Thus, the advantage of the tax-free (federal) income is lost.

## Capital Growth

Some excellent choices for capital growth are common stocks in emerging and growing industries, mutual funds specializing in growth, and zero-coupon bonds.

Zero-coupon bonds are an extremely good vehicle because you know with certainty what your rate of return will be for the term of the investment, and you can select the maturity you wish. (See Chapter 10.)

Major full-service brokerage firms can advise you regarding the selection of appropriate common stocks and zero-coupon bonds.

# Alternatives for Lump-Sum Distributions

**A** lump-sum distribution is the payment an employee receives from an employer's qualified pension or profit-sharing plan. To qualify as a lump sum, a distribution must be made within one tax year.

A lump-sum distribution in this context refers to the tax code definition. It does not mean that an individual who receives such a distribution has to accept it in a lump sum. In this chapter we will examine the major ways to pay such a distribution.

The distribution must be made for one of the following reasons:

- Death of employee
- Employee reaches 59½
- Termination of employment
- Self-employed individual becomes disabled
- Termination of plan

If you receive a lump-sum distribution, you will be eligible for one or more of the following alternatives:

- Rollover into an IRA
- Ten-year averaging
- Five-year averaging
- Purchase of annuity

If you receive a lump-sum distribution from a pension plan or profit-sharing plan, you will have to make a decision that will profoundly affect your financial future. After you receive the distribution, you will only have 60 days to select certain alternatives. Accordingly, before you receive your distribution, you should make sure you understand your alternatives.

You should also address the question of when you will need or want to use the funds.

In this chapter we will review the major options—IRA rollovers, averaging, and lifetime annuities—for accepting lump-sum distributions. No one option is best for everyone. The best choice for you will depend on several factors, such as tax considerations, early-withdrawal penalties, accessibility to the funds, and whether guaranteed income is important to you.

## IRA Rollovers

A rollover is a tax-free transfer of cash or other assets from one retirement plan to another. Rollover contributions must be made within 60 days after you receive your distribution. There are two types of rollover contributions to an IRA: (1) from one IRA to another IRA and (2) from a qualified employer benefit plan to an IRA. Rollovers are not restricted to any maximum dollar amount.

SEP, 401(k), 403(b), and Keogh plans, discussed in Chapters 13 and 14, are examples of plans from which you will receive a lump-sum distribution when you terminate employment. If you choose, you will be able to make an IRA rollover.

## IRA-to-IRA Rollovers

Once you have established an IRA, you may roll over your assets only once a year. It is important for you to understand the difference between a rollover and a change in trustee. With a rollover you yourself have access to the funds. When you ask the trustee of your IRA funds to transfer the assets to another trustee, it is *not* a rollover. Transferral of IRA funds from trustee to trustee is not subject to the once-a-year restriction. There is no legal limit to the number of times you can transfer IRA assets from one trustee to another as long as you never receive the funds directly.

## Inherited IRAs

When you establish an IRA, you have the opportunity to designate a beneficiary. Your decision, and that of your spouse if he or she establishes an IRA, has implications regarding future rollover options. Only a spouse can roll over an inherited IRA. By designating your spouse as the beneficiary of your IRA, you give him or her the flexibility to roll over the inherited IRA or to elect another option.

If a surviving spouse elects the rollover, the new IRA is subject to the same legal and tax considerations as any other IRA.

For example, if a 55-year old spouse inherits an IRA and decides to roll it over, withdrawals cannot be made until age $59\frac{1}{2}$ without a 10 percent early-withdrawal penalty. Funds withdrawn from an inherited IRA are subject to ordinary income taxes, just like those from a regular IRA.

## Advantages of Rollovers

There are three primary advantages to the rollover. First, you incur no reduction in principal and no immediate tax liability. The total amount of the distribution at the time you receive it can be invested in your IRA.

The second advantage is that earnings on your IRA investments are tax-deferred until you withdraw the funds from your IRA.

The third advantage is that you retain complete investment flexibility within the IRA. You can change trustees and your mix of investments and still have no tax liability until you decide to make withdrawals.

If you decide to roll over your lump-sum distribution, it is important that you place these funds in an independent IRA, separate from any other IRA accounts. This action will enable you, if you choose and if it is consistent with your subsequent employer's plan, to transfer these funds to a new employer's pension or profit-sharing plan. This will give you more flexibility in the future because it may allow you to use more options, such as averaging, which can reduce your subsequent income tax liability.

The principal disadvantage of the IRA rollover relative to other available alternatives is that you receive no favorable tax treatment when you withdraw the funds. All withdrawals are taxed at ordinary income tax rates. If you are not yet $59\frac{1}{2}$ when you roll over the distribution, you have an additional disadvantage: You may not withdraw the funds before age $59\frac{1}{2}$ without incurring a 10 percent early-withdrawal penalty.

One additional disadvantage is that after age $70\frac{1}{2}$ you have to make minimum withdrawals based on your life expectancy as established by the IRS. This is not a major consideration, however, since you have complete flexibility between ages $59\frac{1}{2}$ and $70\frac{1}{2}$ regarding the amount of withdrawals you can make.

You do not have to roll over the entire lump sum, but you must roll over at least half of it. The portion that you do not roll over is subject to ordinary income tax. If you are younger than 59½, you also incur a 10 percent penalty tax on the amount you withdraw.

## Five-Year and Ten-Year Averaging

Some individuals who receive a lump-sum distribution are eligible for either 5-year or 10-year averaging. If you are eligible and elect averaging, you are subject to income taxes in the tax year you receive the distribution. For example, if you received a lump-sum distribution in 1989 and elected averaging, you would have to report the amount of the distribution on your 1989 tax return. If you elect averaging, you receive special tax treatment, and you have immediate access to the distribution.

Five-year averaging reduces your income-tax bill because even though you pay the full tax in the year you receive the distribution, the tax is calculated as if you received the money annually over 5 years. For example, if you received a $50,000 distribution, you would compute your tax on it as if you received a $10,000 distribution and, as if that were the only income you received in that tax year. Then you would multiply that tax liability by 5 to determine your total tax liability for that distribution.

To be eligible for 5-year averaging, you have to be a participant in a qualified plan for 5 years and be at least 59½ years old. You may elect 5-year averaging only once.

If you were at least 50 years old on January 1, 1986, you qualify for 10-year averaging. If you elect 10-year averaging, your tax is computed as if you had received the money annually over 10 years and as if it were your only income. For example, if you receive a $50,000 distribution, your tax liability is the income tax on a $5,000 distribution multiplied by 10. If you elect 10-year averaging, you must use the tax rates that were in effect in 1986. Once you elect 10-year averaging, you may never again use either 5-year averaging or 10-year averaging.

## Five-Year versus Ten-Year Averaging

If you are eligible for both 5- and 10-year averaging, you will find that based on 1988 tax rates, you should elect 10-year averaging for lump-sum distributions below $420,000. For distributions above $420,000, you should use 5-year averaging.

If a portion of your distribution was accumulated prior to 1974, part of your distribution may be taxable at lower capital gains rates. If this is the case, you should review the situation with your tax adviser before you choose any option.

In summary, the advantage of using either 5-year or 10-year averaging is that you receive favorable tax treatment without restrictions on the use of the proceeds of the distribution. You have immediate access to the funds and you can spend or invest the funds in any manner you wish.

There are two primary disadvantages. First, you have less capital, since you have a tax liability in the year that you receive the distribution. Second, you receive no tax deferral on earnings derived from the distribution. All subsequent earnings are taxable.

## IRA Rollover versus Averaging

Whether rollover or averaging is better for you depends on how soon you expect to withdraw the funds. If you expect to use these funds over 10 years or more, the IRA will prove to be a superior alternative. The longer the time you can postpone withdrawing funds, the more your capital will increase.

If you intend to withdraw the funds in 3 years or less, averaging will be better for you.

### SCENARIO 1A:

You expect a $100,000 distribution, which you do not expect to use for at least 10 years. If you elect 5-year averaging, after you pay taxes you will have approximately $85,500 to invest. If you invest the $85,500 and receive a return of 6.5 percent after taxes, the value of your investment will be approximately $160,500.

If you roll the distribution into an IRA, receiving a return of 9 percent for 10 years, the value of your investment comes to approximately $236,700. After paying taxes of 28 percent, the value of your investment is $170,400. Accordingly, the IRA rollover is a better choice for you at current tax rates if you do not plan to use the distribution for 10 years. The longer you wait to withdraw the funds beyond the 10 years, the better the rollover becomes.

### SCENARIO 1B:

If you plan to use your $100,000 distribution within a 3-year period, the results are different. If you elect 5-year averaging, the value of your distribution grows from $85,500 to $103,300 at 6.5 percent after taxes. If you roll over your distribution into an IRA and obtain a

9 percent return, the value of your IRA is $129,500 after 3 years. After you pay taxes of 28 percent, the value of your investment is $93,240. Clearly, forward averaging is better in this case.

---

If your timing lies between 3 and 10 years, it may be worth your while to make some assumptions as accurately as possible and run some computations to determine which alternative provides more income for you after taxes. To do this computation, make some assumptions regarding your withdrawal rate and the return you expect on your funds. Since this calculation can be complicated, you may want to use the services of an accountant or tax adviser.

## Annuities

Another alternative is to withdraw the money in the form of a lifetime annuity. Your annual income from the annuity is fixed and based on your life expectancy, or if you so elect, the life expectancy of you and your spouse or another dependent. Insurance companies maintain up-to-date life-expectancy tables to compute annuity income according to your age and if applicable the age of your spouse.

### SCENARIO

Marie Jones, a widow, expects to receive a $100,000 lump-sum distribution in 1989, when she retires. All of the distribution will be taxable. She has two children, both of whom are financially independent. She does not intend to leave any of her assets to her children or other relatives. She does not want to manage the distribution herself. She talked with many insurance agents and was surprised to find a wide variance among annuity products. The best proposal she received, from a well-established company, offered her approximately $1,000 per month for as long as she lives. She intends to accept this proposal.

---

The annuity is advantageous for individuals who do not want the responsibility for managing their own funds and who want the security of a fixed income.

Another advantage of an annuity is that individuals younger than 59½ can elect a lifetime annuity without incurring an early-withdrawal penalty tax as they would with an IRA. Thus, an individual who needs retirement income prior to age 59½ but does not want to incur a penalty can consider an annuity.

In contrast to averaging, an annuity is advantageous in that you pay income tax on annuity income as you receive it rather than at the time of the distribution.

Income from an annuity is taxable at ordinary income rates in the tax year you receive the funds.

For example, if you receive $24,000 a year, your taxable income is $24,000 a year unless you made nondeductible contributions to the retirement plan. If you made nondeductible contributions, part of each payment is nontaxable based on the proportion of contributions you made. If your annuity principal contains 25 percent taxable contributions and 75 percent nontaxable contributions, 25 percent of your annuity income is tax-free.

There are a few disadvantages associated with fixed annuities. The most significant disadvantage is that you are restricted to a fixed income for life. In a period of rising inflation this disadvantage can be significant.

A second disadvantage, related to the first, is that you do not have flexibility in investment choices. Once you turn your assets over to an insurance company, you are turning the responsibility for investing these funds over to them. Regardless of how the funds are invested, your income is fixed.

A third disadvantage is that once you purchase a fixed annuity, you cannot leave the principal to your heirs. Chapter 17 contains a more detailed discussion of annuities.

## Annuities versus Rollovers

Some individuals may be comfortable with the idea of a fixed annuity income. For these individuals the annuity has a possible advantage over the uncertainty inherent in managing one's own IRA funds.

Another advantage of the annuity over the IRA rollover is that as long as the term of the annuity is at least 60 months, individuals under 59½ can receive the income without incurring an early-withdrawal penalty.

Overall, however, the IRA rollover is more attractive for most individuals. The IRA provides much more flexibility because it allows you to make investment decisions and possibly protect yourself against inflation. If you select an IRA rollover, you still retain the option of selecting an annuity later. The reverse is not true. Purchase of an annuity is irrevocable. The guaranteed fixed income is not much of an advantage because you can probably produce income close to that of an annuity with a conservatively invested IRA while still conserving assets to leave to your heirs.

# Annuities

There are two basic types of annuities, *immediate and deferred.*

The immediate annuity is the traditional form, in which you give a specific sum of money to an insurance company, for which the insurance company provides you with a fixed income for life or for a specified period. Other options are available; in one the insurance company guarantees that either you or both you and your beneficiary receive a variable return with a minimum dollar amount.

For example, at age 65 you purchase an annuity from an insurance company for $100,000. The insurance company guarantees you a fixed income, at today's rates perhaps $8,000 per year, for the rest of your life. The income varies among companies and at any company is based on prevailing interest rates.

With the deferred annuity you provide a life insurance company with either a lump sum or several payments over time. The insurance company invests your funds on your behalf for a period called the accumulation phase.

Deferred annuities are offered with two main variants, fixed and variable. The fixed annuity pays a fixed rate of return for a specific period; after that the rate is adjusted annually. With a variable annuity the rate of return varies with the value of the securities in the portfolio of the insurance company. Most variable and fixed annuities are guaranteed not to fall below a specified income level. With the deferred annuity at some point you elect one of two options: (1) Withdraw the funds that have been accumulated in your behalf or (2) purchase an immediate annuity that will provide income to you for the rest of your life.

This chapter will explore the general advantages and disadvantages of annuities. You will be presented with some guidelines so that you can select, if appropriate, the best annuity and associated life insurance company to suit your needs. Deferred annuities will be discussed first, since you may want to use a deferred annuity prior to converting to an immediate annuity.

## Advantages of Deferred Annuities

The principal advantage of a deferred annuity is that the earnings on the funds you provide to the insurance company are tax-deferred until you start withdrawing funds. Thus, an insurance company that invests your funds properly should be able to provide a higher after-tax return on your investment than alternative conservative investments with no tax advantages. For example, investments in CDs or money-market instruments have no tax advantage.

There are no upper limits established by law regarding the amount of money that you can invest in deferred annuities. In contrast, you are limited to contributions of $2,000 a year as nondeductible IRA contributions. Deferred annuities and nondeductible IRA contributions have the same tax advantage. Initial investments are not tax-deductible, but earnings on these investments are tax-deferred until the funds are withdrawn.

## Disadvantages of Deferred Annuities

There are many disadvantages associated with deferred annuities. The most important disadvantage is that it is very difficult to compare competing deferred annuities, for consumers and financial professionals alike. Many variables, including the following factors, will be discussed more fully in this chapter: surrender charges, partial withdrawals, minimum rates of return, different rates of return depending on whether a customer decides to convert a deferred annuity into an immediate annuity, and administrative charges. There are significant differences among the insurance companies in terms of these variables. Therefore, it is extremely difficult to evaluate deferred annuities and to compare those of competing companies.

In addition to the difficulty of evaluating deferred annuities, there are other disadvantages. If you withdraw funds from your deferred annuity within a few years after you made your initial contributions, you will generally incur surrender charges, or early-withdrawal fees.

You cannot borrow against any accumulated value in your deferred annuity, an option you have with cash-value life insurance. In short, deferred annuities are not very liquid, and administrative costs may be considerable, especially for small accounts.

### Surrender Charges

Surrender charges are fees the insurance company charges you if you fail to leave your investment with the insurance company a minimum length of time. In effect the surrender charge is the vehicle used by the company to ensure that it can make a profit and pay a sales commission. Generally surrender charges are high in the first few years after your initial purchase but decrease over time. Usually after 7 or 8 years there are no surrender charges. You should not be misled by a sales pitch that promises a 3- or 5-year rate of return without taking into consideration surrender charges.

Surrender charges are generally expressed as a percentage of the accumulation value. Some surrender charges are computed as a percentage of the premium you pay. Generally a surrender charge based on your premium will result in a smaller penalty.

### Administration Charges

Many contracts specify administrative charges, generally $10 to $30 a year for small accounts. Beware of the annual administrative cost and its effect on your rate of return. For example, a $25 fee on a $10,000 investment would reduce a 6 percent rate of return to 5.75 percent.

Do not be misled if a salesperson indicates that his or her company does not charge any administrative expenses. You may find that the company offers lower interest rates—which will affect you basically the same way.

### Partial Withdrawals

You may be able to withdraw some of your funds from your annuity without having to pay a surrender charge. You may, however, incur a service charge of $25 or more. In addition there will be limits regarding the amount and number of withdrawals.

Your contract will specify the percentage of accumulated value that you can withdraw without incurring a surrender charge. This is generally 10 percent. You should be aware of the many variations among companies. For example, some companies allow withdrawals limited to 10 percent of your premiums, a smaller amount—substantially smaller after you have been investing for several years.

If you are under age 59½ when you make a withdrawal, there will be a 10 percent early-withdrawal penalty on the total amount. Moreover, some policies specify that if your withdrawal exceeds 10 percent, you incur surrender charges on the whole withdrawal, not just the portion that exceeds 10 percent.

For example, assume you have $20,000 in accumulated values. If your withdrawal is $3,000, which exceeds the 10 percent allowable, you may incur a surrender charge on $3,000, not $1,000.

Another feature you should be aware of is restrictions regarding the number of free withdrawals you can take per year, even if the combined value is less than 10 percent. The contract may specify that only the first withdrawal is exempt from surrender charges and that subsequent withdrawals incur charges.

## Safety

Most annuities have been safe investments, although some insurance companies, namely Baldwin-United and Charter Security, have run into financial difficulties.

Before you purchase an annuity, whether it be deferred or immediate, you should verify that the insurance company selling it is financially stable. The best source for reviewing the financial health of an insurance company is A.M. Best & Co., which publishes *Best's Insurance Reports*. This publication rates the financial health of insurance companies that have at least 5 years of experience. Most major public libraries subscribe to this service.

Most states have guarantee associations that live up to the promises of insurance companies that become insolvent. The guarantee associations assess companies that sell insurance in the state. If you plan to purchase an annuity or insurance in a state that does not have a guarantee association, you should be especially careful to select a company with Best's higher ratings of A or A+. These states do not have guarantee associations: Alaska, Arkansas, California, Colorado, Louisiana, Missouri, New Jersey, Ohio, South Dakota, Tennessee, and Wyoming.

## Key Questions

Before you purchase a deferred annuity, make sure that you know the answers to the following questions:

1. What are the guaranteed monthly annuity payments per $1,000 of accumulated value?
2. What is the rate currently being paid to owners of annuities?
3. What is the guaranteed minimum rate at which funds accumulate?
4. What percentage of the initial investment is being taken as a sales commission?
5. What is the surrender cost of redemption?
6. What restrictions and penalties apply to partial withdrawals?
7. What is the rating of the selling insurance company?
8. Does your state tax annuities?

## Advantages of Immediate Annuities

The principal advantage of the immediate annuity is that the insurance company guarantees you a specific monthly payment for as long as you live. You do not have to be concerned as to how the funds are invested.

When you purchase the annuity, you are essentially turning investment responsibility over to the insurance company for your lifetime. Regardless of how long you live, the insurance company will continue to pay you a monthly income for your lifetime.

At your option you can get a joint annuity either with your spouse or with anyone else you choose. Although your income will be lower if you elect a joint annuity, you are providing some protection to your dependents with this option. If your spouse outlives you, for example, he or she still receives a lifetime annuity. This option and others will be explained in this chapter.

## Disadvantages of Immediate Annuities

There are three primary disadvantages associated with the immediate annuity. Although the insurance company guarantees you a lifetime annuity at a fixed level, you are not provided with protection from inflation. For example, with an inflation rate of 6 percent, prices double in 12 years; with an inflation rate of 8 percent, prices double in 9 years. Thus, before you decide on an immediate annuity, you should review your other sources of income to ensure that you have some protection against inflation during your retirement.

The second disadvantage is related to flexibility. Once you purchase an annuity, you have effectively given up the power to manage the value of the distribution. The insurance company manages your money. You cannot retrieve this money in order to invest it yourself.

The third disadvantage of immediate annuities is associated with your estate. The assets that you provide to the insurance company cannot be left to your beneficiaries. The assets become the property of the insurance company, and the income stops with the death of the covered person. Essentially, when you purchase an annuity, you are giving up the option of giving those assets to your beneficiaries in return for a guaranteed and perhaps higher level of income than you would obtain on your own.

## Annuity Payment Options

There are many options available to you when you are ready to select an annuity. The major options and their advantages and disadvantages will be described below.

### Lifetime Annuity with One Annuitant

With this option you receive payments for the rest of your life. This option is desirable if you do not have a spouse or if your surviving spouse would not require this annuity income. For example, if you have a great deal of life insurance and your spouse is the beneficiary, you can buy an annuity knowing that the life insurance proceeds will provide your spouse with an adequate income after your death.

### Uniform Joint and Survivor Annuities

You receive payments for the rest of your life, and the same payment is received by the other annuitant if he or she survives you. This type of annuity is useful if you are concerned with providing income to another party such as your spouse. The annuity paid is based on the combined life expectancies of both parties. Say you are 50. If your spouse is much younger than you are, the amount of the annuity is less than it would be if he or she were older than you. Before you select this type of option, consider whether the annuitant, the person receiving the annuity, will need the annuity after you die. If your life insurance and other assets are of sufficient size, you may not need this type of annuity.

### Limited Time Annuities

You receive payment until your death or until the end of a specified period, whichever comes first. Consider this type of annuity if you are less concerned with income after a certain time. For example, if you know that in 10 years you will receive a large sum of money, you may wish to buy a 10-year annuity to maximize your income in the meantime.

### Annuity with Stepped-up Payments

You receive a small payment for a specified number of years, after which you receive larger payments. Use this type of annuity when you expect a reduction in other income at a certain time or if you want some protection from inflation.

### Annuity with Stepped-down Payments

You receive large payments for a specified number of years, after which you receive smaller payments. Use this type of annuity when you antici-pate other income or a lump-sum distribution in the future. Normally this type of plan is used if an individual retires early and expects Social Security or other pension payments in the future.

### Joint Annuity with Lower Survivor Payments

Payment is at one level while both annuitants are alive. When one of the annuitants dies, the survivor receives a smaller payment for the rest of his or her life. This type of annuity should be considered in association with an in-surance program if the survivor otherwise would not have sufficient income.

---

## Taxability of Annuity Income

The taxability of your annuity is based on the amount of your contributions. If you did not make any after-tax contributions, all of your annuity income is taxable. If you made some after-tax contributions, nontaxable income will be prorated according to the amount of your contributions.

To compute the part of your annuity that is tax-free, multiply the exclusion ratio by the amount of the annuity you receive. To figure the exclusion ratio, divide your investment in the annuity by the amount you can expect to receive from the annuity over your lifetime according to the life expectancy tables.

### SCENARIO

You contributed $10,000 in after-tax salary toward the purchase of a lifetime annuity. Based on your age, your agent indicates that you can expect to receive $100,000 from your annuity. The exclusion ratio is 10 percent ($100,000 ÷ $10,000). Thus, 90 percent of your annuity income is taxable.

## Lump-Sum Distributions

If you are eligible to receive a lump-sum distribution, one of the options you can elect is to receive a lifetime annuity. If you choose an annuity, you will be able to roll over your distribution into an IRA, and you may be eligible for either 5- or 10-year averaging. These options are reviewed in Chapter 16. You should review these options before you make a final choice. Selecting a lifetime annuity is a very important decision, and you should make sure that it is the best available option for you.

## Sources of Ratings

Reliable sources such as *Consumer Reports* and *Money* magazine do periodic in-depth reviews of specific types of annuities. You can contact these publications to determine when they have most recently reviewed annuities:

> *Consumer Reports*
> P.O. Box 53029
> Boulder, Colorado 80322-3016
>
> *Money*
> Rockefeller Center
> New York, NY 10020

## Summary

For both deferred annuities and immediate annuities, there are significant differences among the offerings. Before you purchase any annuity, satisfy yourself that you have reviewed comparative annuities and that you are obtaining the one that best accommodates your objectives.

# Credit

**M**any aspects of financial planning are directly related to an understanding of existing credit laws that protect the consumer and encourage the proper use of credit. This is especially important now because of complex mortgage instruments such as adjustable rate mortgages (ARMs) and home equity mortgages. Another major factor is the strong competition for consumer credit in the form of credit cards and revolving credit lines among others. It is essential for consumers to understand their rights in light of the wide variety of available credit.

Five federal laws provide protection to you regarding consumer credit:

- Truth in Lending Act
- Equal Credit Opportunity Act
- Fair Credit Reporting Act
- Fair Credit Billing Act
- Fair Debt Collection Practices Act

These laws will be reviewed in this chapter so you will know their major protection features and what actions you can take to obtain their full benefit.

## Truth in Lending Act

The Truth in Lending Act requires creditors to provide certain basic information about the cost of buying on credit or taking out a loan. These disclosures help you shop around and compare costs. The law also limits your risk on lost or stolen credit cards.

The Truth in Lending Act requires creditors to provide you with accurate and complete credit costs and terms. These credit terms must be disclosed to you in a clear and conspicuous manner and in writing.

The creditor must specify the finance charge and the annual percentage rate (APR) for each credit transaction. The finance charge is the cost of the credit to you, and it must be expressed as a dollar amount. The APR is the cost of credit expressed as an annual rate. The APR is considered accurate according to federal law if it is no more than 0.125 percent above or below the actual rate.

If you request a loan with a fixed term, a creditor must specify the following information:

- Dollar amount financed
- Payment schedule
- Total dollar amount of payments
- Total sale price, including down payment
- Property the creditor can take if you do not pay on time
- Other terms and conditions of the loan

Before you use a credit card or charge account, a creditor must tell you:

- The cost of credit as a monthly or daily rate
- When and how interest will be charged to the account
- Service charge or annual fee if applicable
- Property the creditor can take if you do not pay on time
- Statement of your billing rights
- Other terms and conditions

The creditor must send you statements of all credit accounts that have a debit balance (amount you owe) or credit balance (amount owed to you) at the end of the billing cycle. These statements must include

- Prior balance
- Credits and debits in that billing cycle
- Periodic rate and corresponding APR
- Finance charges imposed during that billing cycle
- New balance
- Explanation of how new balance was computed

If the creditor increases the APR or changes any other terms of a credit account, you must be notified at least 15 days before the effective date of these changes.

If an advertisement for credit contains specific terms such as down payment, monthly payment, and so on, the advertisement must state:

- Only those terms a typical consumer could actually receive
- Other important information to avoid misleading you

If you use your home as security in a credit transaction:

- The creditor must notify you in writing that you have a right to cancel.
- You have 3 business days to cancel the transaction.
- During those 3 business days, no money can be paid and no services can be performed.
- If you cancel the agreement, the creditor must release the security interest and return all money or property received.

The right of cancellation does not apply to a first mortgage to finance the purchase of your home.

## Equal Credit Opportunity Act

Under the provisions of the Equal Credit Opportunity Act, a creditor is prohibited from discriminating against you on the basis of:

- Age
- Sex
- Marital status
- Race, color, religion, or natural origin
- Reliance on income from a public assistance program

Moreover, a creditor cannot discourage you from applying for credit if you are a reasonable applicant.

A credit application form must ask only for information permitted by law. With the exception of monitoring purposes in real estate credit, a creditor cannot ask:

- Your sex
- Your race, color, religion, or natural origin
- Your birth control practices
- Your marital status in applications for unsecured individual credit
- Information about a spouse or former spouse except in specific situations

Creditors, in evaluating your credit application:

- Cannot automatically deny credit because of your age
- Cannot ignore income derived from a public assistance program, retirement income, or part-time employment

- Must consider credit history of accounts that you have used or are liable for, if they normally review credit histories

If a creditor denies you credit, you must be notified within 30 days and provided with:

- A statement of reasons for the denial of credit or of your right to receive such a statement
- An explanation of the Equal Credit Opportunity Act
- The name and address of the agency that enforces the act

If a creditor grants you credit, the creditor:

- Must allow you credit in your own name
- Cannot require a spouse to cosign the note
- Must for joint accounts keep joint records showing that both spouses use credit or have cosigned the note

## The Fair Credit Reporting Act

The Fair Credit Reporting Act allows you to check the information in your file at a credit agency and to correct entries that are inaccurate. This act establishes penalties for disclosing information to anyone not authorized to receive it.

Whenever you are denied consumer credit because of information in a credit report, in accordance with the Equal Credit Opportunity Act, you must be given:

- The name, address, and phone number of the credit bureau that provided the information, and
- The reason for denial, or
- Information on your right to request the reason for denial

If you have been denied credit because of information in your credit report, you should contact the applicable credit bureau and request your credit report. You can receive the report at no cost.

If you contact the credit bureau, it must:

- Provide you with your credit report
- Inform you of its sources of information
- Provide you with the names of employers, creditors, and others who have recently received copies of its report
- Reinvestigate within a reasonable time any information you dispute

If the credit bureau finds its information is inaccurate, or if it cannot verify it, it must correct or delete it. If the information is accurate, the bureau must allow you to write a brief statement of dispute, which it must include in all subsequent reports.

If any deletion or notation is made, you may request that the new information be sent to any employer who has received information during the past 2 years, or anyone else who has received a report during the past 6 months. Credit bureaus can provide information only to:

- Creditors who are considering granting you credit or who have already done so
- Potential employers
- Potential insurers
- Government agencies reviewing your financial status in connection with issuing a license
- Anyone else with a legitimate business reason for needing the information

The credit bureau must withhold information on a bankruptcy over 10 years old and any other adverse information over 7 years old. These rules do not apply to loan applications that exceed $50,000, underwriting over $50,000 of insurance, or employment decisions when the annual salary exceeds $20,000.

## The Fair Credit Billing Act

The Fair Credit Billing Act establishes a procedure for promptly correcting billing errors without damage to your credit rating. It establishes circumstances under which you may withhold payment on any damaged goods or poor-quality services purchased with a credit card.

You have the right to dispute a bill, and the creditor must:

- Acknowledge your written complaint within 30 days
- Investigate and notify you of the action taken within two billing cycles or 90 days, whichever is shorter

You cannot be billed or forced to pay the disputed amount until the creditor has finished its investigation. The creditor must indicate on your statement that you need not pay any amount in dispute. If it is determined that you do owe the amount, you must be given the usual time to pay. If there was an error in your bill, you do not have to pay any finance charges on the disputed amount. If it is determined that there was no error, you must pay the finance charges.

Your credit history is protected during the dispute process. A creditor may not report you to a credit bureau as delinquent while the error is being investigated. If it is determined that there was no error and you disagree with the finding, the creditor *can* report you as delinquent, but must also report that the item is in dispute. When the matter is settled, the creditor must report the outcome to the credit bureau and to anyone else who received reports of the dispute.

A credit balance in your account must be refunded promptly—within 7 business days—if you make a request in writing. If a credit balance remains in your account for more than 6 months, the creditor must refund it by cash, check, or money order.

## Your Credit Card Rights

Special rules protect you when you receive and use a credit card. A creditor cannot send you a card you have not requested. If your credit card is lost or stolen:

- You pay nothing on unauthorized charges if you notify the creditor before any charges are made.
- You must pay the first $50 charged if you fail to notify the creditor before the charges are made.
- The creditor may send a replacement or renewal card.
- You have no liability if you haven't "accepted" the credit card.

You may withhold payment of any balance due on defective merchandise or services purchased with a credit card provided you have made a good-faith effort to return the goods or resolve the problem with the merchant from whom you made the purchase.

If you use a third-party credit card such as VISA or MasterCard, your right to withhold payment applies only if:

- The original amount of the purchase exceeded $50, and
- The sale took place in your home state or within 100 miles of your current address.

Even if you have enough cash to cover the cost of a major purchase, you should consider using a third-party credit card in order to protect yourself from merchandise or services that may be defective. Many times you do not immediately know whether merchandise or services you purchased are satisfactory. If you paid cash, it may be difficult or impossible to recover your costs. By charging the item, you have effectively bought time to test the merchandise. As indicated above, you have the protection of the federal law only if you purchased the merchandise or services in your home state or within 100 miles of your current address.

## The Fair Debt Collection Practices Act

The Fair Debt Collection Practices Act protects you from debt collectors who engage in abusive, deceptive, or unfair practices. It allows you to obtain written verification of a debt. The Fair Debt Collection Practices Act protects consumers from debt collectors who engage in abusive, deceptive, or unfair practices.

The act applies only to third-party debt collectors, people in the business of collecting debts owed to someone else. Creditors who collect their own debts are not covered by the act.

A debt collector who contacts you must send you written notice informing you of:

- The amount of the debt
- The name of the creditor
- Your right to dispute the debt and an explanation of what will happen if you do

If you dispute the debt, the debt collector must provide you with written evidence of the debt before trying to collect it.

A debt collector who is trying to find a debtor cannot:

- Tell another person that he or she is a debt collector unless asked
- Use a postcard or indicate on the envelope that he or she is a debt collector
- Contact a person other than the debtor more than once to learn the debtor's whereabouts
- Contact a person at an unusual time (generally between 9 p.m. and 8 a.m.)
- Make continuous or anonymous phone calls with the intent to harass
- Contact a person at his or her place of work if the employer forbids such communication during working hours
- Use profanity or other abusive language
- Threaten you with violence, such as cementing your feet and throwing you into the river, or other criminal means to harm your person, reputation, or property

- Impersonate a police officer or government official
- Misrepresent the legal status of a debt
- Threaten imprisonment or other action the debt collector or creditor could not legally take
- Make other false or misleading statements

You can write to the debt collector saying you refuse to pay or you want him or her to cease communications. The debt collector must stop contacting you except to advise you of any legal action the collector or the creditor intends to take.

## Federal Enforcement Agencies

If you believe that your rights have not been protected, you should contact the following agencies and request that they investigate on your behalf. The agency is listed below the type of financial institution it regulates.

**National banks**
Comptroller of the Currency
Washington, DC 20219

**State-chartered banks that are members of the Federal Reserve System**
The Federal Reserve bank serving the state bank's district

**Other state-chartered banks**
Federal Deposit Insurance Corporation
Washington, DC 20429

**Savings institutions**
Federal Home Loan Bank Board
Washington, DC 20552

**Credit unions**
National Credit Union Administration
Washington, DC 20456

**Credit reporting agencies and debt collection agencies**
Farm Credit Administration
Washington, DC 20578

**Federal land banks and production credit associations**
Farm Credit Administration
Washington, DC 20578

Other creditors, including department stores, consumer finance companies,
and nonbank credit card issuers
Federal Trade Commission
Washington, DC 20580

A number of these enforcement agencies have regional offices serving
the area in which the creditor or other institution is located. If you need
help in reporting a problem relating to credit, contact your nearest Federal
Reserve bank for referral to the appropriate agency.

## Shopping for Credit

Although the federal laws do offer you protection, no federal agency can
tell you which is the best credit or credit card for you. The laws require
creditors to provide you with information essential to make sound decisions.
The laws do not require that creditors provide standard rates or terms.
Thus it is up to you to do comparison shopping.

You will find a great deal of variation among creditors for creditor cards
and other forms of credit. Before you accept any credit, you should make
comparisons, taking into consideration the following factors:

- APR
- Annual fees
- Number of days (if any) in billing cycle without incurring finance
  charge
- Late payment fees
- Other fees
- Special features such as collision insurance and free air travel
  insurance
- Rebates

No one credit card or creditor is best for everyone. Therefore, you have
to review the most important factors that affect you and make your
decision based on your own needs.

For example, an individual who does not pay his credit card balance in
full each payment cycle should be concerned about the APR (interest rate)
charged. An individual who always pays in full should look for an issuer
that charges no fees and offers a period, such as 28 or 30 days, in which
there are no service charges if the bill is paid in full. An individual who
charges thousands of dollars a month should consider a creditor who pays
a 1 percent rebate, even if an annual fee is charged. A 1 percent rebate on

$24,000 per year, for example, is $240, which far outweighs a $50 annual charge for the card.

An individual who rents cars frequently and is not covered for it by his car insurance policy should use a credit card that covers collision insurance. For example, the Chase Manhattan VISA card provides this feature.

In short, look at the features and decide which ones are most important to you. Then you can make a logical choice regarding the creditors and credit cards that are best for you.

## Credit and Tax Deductions

The Tax Reform Act of 1986 greatly reduced the deductibility of most forms of consumer interest. With the exception of real estate interest expenses, interest deductions for most forms of credit are being phased out. Table 18-1 shows the allowable interest deductions for consumer debt.

Table 18-1  TAX DEDUCTIONS FOR INTEREST
ON CONSUMER DEBT

| Year | Allowable Percentage Deduction |
| --- | --- |
| 1989 | 20 |
| 1990 | 10 |
| 1991 and later | 0 |

As this table shows, indiscriminate use of credit can be very costly to you. The federal government is no longer willing to subsidize your interest payments for consumer credit. Accordingly, it is even more important for you to shop for credit carefully and to avoid consumer debt as much as possible.

# Life Insurance

**L**ife insurance is a contract in which an insurer agrees to pay a beneficiary selected by the policyholder a specified amount when the insured party dies. In effect, life insurance lets you protect your family and others against the risk that there will be less income when you die.

Before you purchase any life insurance, you should be able to answer the following questions:

- Do you in fact need any life insurance?
- How much coverage do you need?
- For what periods do you need coverage?
- Where should you purchase it?

In this chapter we will cover the basics of life insurance so that you will be able to answer these questions.

As you grow older, your need for life insurance will change and may diminish. In fact, you may find that you do not need any life insurance. On the other hand, you may find that even though you have significant assets, you need life insurance in order to provide liquidity for your estate so that assets you own will not have to be sold to satisfy the creditors of your estate.

## How to Compute Needs

In order to determine your life insurance needs, project the required expenditures of your dependent beneficiaries and compare those with the income that can be produced from your financial assets and other income that your beneficiaries would have. If there is a gap, you can compute the amount of life insurance required to fill that gap.

In general you can make the assumption that your dependents will need 70 percent of your current after-tax income. Of course, each situation is different and you should take your own circumstances into account.

### SCENARIO

Assume that a family now earns $3,000 per month in after-tax income. Seventy percent of $3,000 is $2,100 per month, which will be our initial target. (See Table 19-1.)

### Table 19-1   CALCULATION OF LIFE INSURANCE NEEDS

#### Assumptions

| | |
|---|---|
| Minimum income requirement | $ 2,100 per month |
| Present financial assets | 50,000 |
| Existing life insurance coverage | 40,000 |
| Interest rate used to compute earnings on investment | 10% |

#### Expected Sources of Income

| | |
|---|---|
| Earnings on $50,000 | $    417 per month |
| Other family income | 500 |
| Social Security income | 500 |
| Earnings on life insurance $40,000 × 0.1 ÷ 12 | 333 |
| Expected Income | 1,750 per month |

#### Shortfall

| | |
|---|---|
| $2,100 − $1,750 | (350) per month |

#### Additional insurance requirement

| | |
|---|---|
| $350 × 12 ÷ 0.1 | $42,000 |

As indicated in Table 19-1, $50,000 in available assets can produce $417 per month in earnings. The family has other income of $500 a month and Social Security income of $500 per month. There is also an outstanding life insurance policy for $40,000, which can produce additional earnings of $333 per month.

There is still a gap of $350 a month in earnings. The next question is how much additional life insurance is required to produce $350 a month. Assuming a rate of return of 10 percent, additional life insurance of $42,000 is required.

Thus, without a very sophisticated analysis, this family arrived at a reasonable figure for additional life insurance. The family decided to buy an additional $45,000 of life insurance on the breadwinner in order to maintain essentially the same standard of living after that person's death.

Some of your sources of income, such as Social Security, will be indexed to inflation. Others may not. Accordingly, when you do project your future income needs, taking inflation into consideration, you should also review each source of income to determine whether it will increase consistent with expected inflation. You will probably find that at least some of your sources of income do not increase as much as inflation. In this situation you should adjust your insurance requirements accordingly.

## What Kind of Insurance You Should Buy

Although many new and complicated forms of life insurance policies are being offered today, there are still only two basic ones—term and cash-value.

### Term Life Insurance

Term insurance is the purest form of insurance that you can buy. You pay a fixed premium for a specified time. If you die during that time, your beneficiaries receive the face value of the policy. If you are alive at the end of the policy, the policy terminates unless you have the option to renew at a new premium and decide to do so.

There are advantages and disadvantages associated with term insurance. The most important advantage is that the premiums are low for young purchasers. Because the premiums are low, individuals can purchase a large amount of insurance for a relatively small premium. For example, a 30-year-old female nonsmoker can purchase a $50,000 5-year term policy from a New York savings bank for $63 a year. An equivalent amount of whole life insurance, which will be discussed below, would cost $377 a year.

There are some disadvantages, however. The premium does increase with age. If a 60-year-old woman purchased a $50,000 term policy from the same carrier, the premium would be $472 a year. Another disadvantage is that after a certain age you may not be able to purchase term insurance. Most companies will sell term insurance up to age 65. Others will sell up to age 70. Some insurance spokesmen say that another disadvantage is that term insurance does not build up any cash value.

It is true that term insurance does not build up cash value, but that is a disadvantage only if saving money for yourself is one of your objectives in purchasing life insurance.

There are four major categories of term insurance — guaranteed renewable term, convertible term, decreasing term, and level term.

Guaranteed renewable term insurance is renewable *regardless of your physical health.* You should insist on this feature. For example, if you purchased 5-year renewable term insurance, you would have the option to renew the policy for another 5 years at the end of the first period. The premium would be higher, since you are 5 years older and in a different risk category. If you purchase renewable insurance, the insurance company cannot refuse the renewal, even if your health has deteriorated during the 5-year period. The policy is renewable up to a specified age, stated in your policy.

Convertible term insurance allows you to convert to a whole life policy until you reach a specified age, regardless of your health. This is an important feature, and you should insist upon it. You may not feel that you need it, but you should request it when you purchase your policy because you will not be able to add it to an existing policy at your option. This feature can be attractive if you have a continued need for life insurance when you become older and would like to fix the amount of premium that you pay.

In level term insurance the benefit and the premium are fixed for the term. The term may be any interval at the option of the insurance company issuing the policy. Standard terms are 1, 3, and 5 years.

Decreasing term insurance is a type in which the premium is fixed for the term of the policy, although your coverage decreases over the term. This type of policy is inexpensive relative to level term insurance because the coverage decreases each year.

The normal use for decreasing term insurance is mortgage protection. For example, assume you have a 15-year $50,000 mortgage on your home. You can protect your beneficiaries by taking out a $50,000 decreasing term policy for 15 years. The amount of your insurance coverage will be approximately the same as the amount of your outstanding mortgage at any time. Then your beneficiary has the option of paying off the mortgage or investing the proceeds of the policy. It is important to point out that you want your family member, not the mortgage holder, to be the beneficiary of the policy. If the interest rate on the mortgage is low, the beneficiary will not want to pay it off early.

Although decreasing term policies are generally used for mortgage protection, they can be used for any purpose you wish. For example, if you are sending a child to college, you may consider a 5-year decreasing term policy to cover the collegiate years.

### Cash-Value Life Insurance

The term *cash-value life insurance* refers to the class of life insurance policies in which you are making an investment in addition to purchasing life insurance. You can look at your premium as being apportioned in two segments—an insurance portion and an investment portion. Over time your investment accumulates cash value. Cash value is the amount you can get for your policy if you cash it in. You can also use the cash value by taking out a policy loan.

It is important for you to realize that the cash value of a policy is *not* added to the face value of your policy. For example, assume you have a $10,000 life insurance policy, and when you die, the cash value of the policy is $1,000. Your beneficiary will receive $10,000, not $11,000.

The cash value that accumulates in your policy is used by the insurance company to pay your beneficiary. In this example you are paying for $9,000 worth of insurance, since you could terminate your policy and receive $1,000. If your cash value increased to $5,000 in a $10,000 policy, your premium is purchasing $5,000 worth of insurance.

The increased cash value in your policy allows the insurance company to fix your premium because you are getting less insurance coverage each year. As a further illustration, assume you do not wish to cancel your policy, but you would like to borrow against your cash value. Insurance companies allow you to borrow from your cash value at rates specified in your policy. The policy will specify how fast cash values increase per $1,000 in face value.

Assume you have $1,000 in cash value on your $10,000 policy and you borrow $1,000. If you die with the $1,000 outstanding, your beneficiary will receive $9,000, the $10,000 face value minus the loan.

Thus, you should look at your premium as purchasing an amount of insurance that is the difference between the face value of the policy and the cash value. As your cash value approaches this face value, you are not buying very much insurance.

This is a very important concept for you to understand. Many insurance salesmen inform their customers that one of the advantages of cash-value over term insurance is that the premium is fixed. The premium *is* fixed, but you are also purchasing less insurance each year. You are not a better risk for the insurance industry because you buy cash-value life insurance. The insurance companies can fix the premium only because you are subsidizing the face value of your policy with your cash value. The true cost of insurance is identical whether you buy term or cash-value life insurance.

There are several forms of cash-value life insurance. The most common type is whole life insurance.

### Whole Life Insurance

There are two basic types of whole life insurance—straight life and limited-payment life. With a straight life policy, you pay the same premium each year as long as you live or until you cash the policy in.

With a limited-payment life insurance policy, you pay premiums only for a specified time. Then you no longer have to pay premiums to keep the policy in force. For example, assume an individual of 35 wanted a $50,000 policy but did not want to pay premiums after retirement at age 60. A 25-year limited-payment policy might be appropriate. The premiums are higher for a limited payment policy than for a straight life policy. However, after age 60, no additional premiums will be made, and the beneficiaries will receive the $50,000 face value upon the death of the policyholder.

There are advantages and disadvantages associated with whole life insurance in comparison with term insurance. One of the most important advantages is that the policy functions as a forced savings account in which the earnings grow on a tax-deferred basis. You can get access to these earnings, known as your cash value, by terminating the policy, or you can borrow up to the cash value in your policy at a predetermined rate specified in your policy.

A second advantage is that the premium is fixed for your life. No matter how old you are, you continue to pay the premium that you paid in the first year you purchased the policy.

Another advantage is continuous insurance. Regardless of your age or health, you will have coverage as long as you continue to pay your premiums. At a certain age, generally after 65 or 70, you will not be able to purchase term insurance.

One of the disadvantages of whole life insurance is that the amount of the premium when you are young is higher than if you purchased an equivalent amount of term insurance. This can be a serious disadvantage if the breadwinner in the family is underinsured because of the decision to purchase whole life insurance with a fixed insurance budget.

For example, a 25-year-old man who does not want to spend more than $200 a year on life insurance can purchase whole life insurance for himself for approximately $20,000 (according to savings bank life insurance (SBLI) rates in New York for a male nonsmoker). For a $64.50 annual premium, a male nonsmoker could purchase $50,000 worth of 5-year renewable term insurance. If his family needed more than $20,000 in life insurance coverage, he would be underinsured because he purchased whole life insurance rather than term insurance.

A second disadvantage of whole life insurance is a relatively low return on investment. The actual return on the savings portion of your premium will vary among various policies. In general, however, the rate of return on most whole life policies is not attractive relative to that of other investments. Moreover, it is not usually easy to determine what rate of return you can expect, since most whole life policies are not sold on the basis of rate of return. It would be better for you if they were. If your insurance salesman recommends that you purchase whole life, you should ask him what rate of return you can expect on your investment. If you do not get a straight answer, you should purchase your insurance elsewhere.

Insurance salesmen generally earn a much higher sales commission on whole life insurance than they do on term insurance. Accordingly, you should beware of any possible bias in the sales approach.

## Summary—Term versus Whole Life

Most individuals would be better off purchasing term insurance and developing an independent investment program. Individuals who are disciplined enough to do this will generally build up assets faster with even conservative investments than they would using whole life policies. As assets grow in value, there is less need for life insurance. At retirement age there should be very little or no need for life insurance if a disciplined investment system is used.

As indicated in Chapter 21, you may need some life insurance payable to the estate to ensure that there are sufficient liquid assets to cover any outstanding liabilities and administrative expenses associated with the settlement of the estate.

For individuals who have more trouble saving money, the use of whole life policies can be advantageous. As long as individuals keep paying premiums, cash values will increase. Even if the policy is subsequently canceled, that is, surrendered, the policy will have some value.

You must decide whether you want life insurance to provide pure insurance or whether you want a forced-savings vehicle also. Since whole life insurance is not normally sold according to rates of return, you should be careful to find out what interest rate you will be receiving.

## Universal Life Insurance

In the early 1980s, astute investors were aware of the low borrowing rates available in their cash policies and borrowed as much as they could from them. These funds, often invested in money-market instruments, were essentially taken out of the insurance companies, that is, borrowed at low interest rates. In order to counteract this trend, the insurance companies introduced new products to compete with other financial institutions. One of the first of these new products was universal life insurance.

Universal life insurance was truly innovative. For the first time there was a distinction between the concepts of insurance and investment from the point of view of the policyholder. Universal life insurance offers the following features:

- The policy owner selects a specific death benefit.
- Premiums can be paid either regularly or irregularly.
- The insurance company takes a sufficient amount from the premium to cover the cost of insurance and associated administrative costs.
- The amount of premium remaining after the insurance and administrative costs are subtracted is invested in a separate account.

The universal life policy is a combination term policy and money-market account. You can't invest in the money-market account unless you buy a minimum amount of insurance. Interest earned on the investment account is tax-deferred. The tax deferral is one advantage of the insurance industry over other financial institutions.

Universal life insurance is much more attractive than standard whole life insurance. It offers higher rates of return and provides much more flexibility; and perhaps most important, insurance companies provide a separate statement of investment performance.

There are many variations among policies. There is no standard universal policy. There is a great deal of flexibility regarding premium payments. After the first policy year, the insurance buyer can vary the amount, the payment date, or the frequency of subsequent premium payments. As long as there is sufficient cash value to pay for the insurance costs and administrative costs, the policy remains in force.

There is no standardization regarding how interest rates are determined. Some insurance companies base these rates on a specific external index such as the Treasury bill rate, but many companies use internal criteria, making it difficult for an insurance buyer to evaluate various policies.

Because of the lack of standardization, you cannot simply select any company offering the product. When you compare policies, use the same criteria as much as possible. For example, you can specify the amount of insurance coverage you want and the amount of your initial and subsequent investments. You can ask each agent to compute what the value of your investment would be if you had purchased a particular policy at a particular time, such as 5 years ago. In order to make a fair comparison, be careful to provide each agent with identical specifications.

Even the best universal life policy may not outperform investments you can make independently in traditional investments. Sometimes insurance companies quote their rates *after* administrative and sales expenses are subtracted. A rate of return computed in this way does not offer a fair comparison with rates of return on certificates of deposit, money-market accounts, and money-market funds, which are true returns because they are based on your actual investment. Beware of attractive-sounding rates of return that do not include costs.

## Variable Life Insurance

Variable life insurance combines insurance and investment options. Conceptually it is similar to whole life insurance. The significant difference is that variable life insurance gives you a choice of investments. Your choice is limited to the options offered by your insurance company, which may include common stocks, bonds, or a mixed portfolio. Essentially you are given a possibly limited set of alternatives to choose from. You can switch from one form of investment to another at predetermined intervals.

One of the disadvantages of variable life is that the cash value of your policy is variable. This is in contrast to whole life policies, with which you always know what the value of your policy will be. The face value of the life insurance portion of your variable life policy is fixed, however.

As with all insurance products, make sure you understand all the sales commissions charges and administrative expenses. Even with the tax deferral of the variable life policy, it is unlikely that you can obtain a better overall return with a variable life policy than you can get with more conventional investment alternatives.

## Adjustable Life Insurance

Adjustable life insurance allows you to switch from term insurance to cash-value insurance and vice versa. You can also allocate portions of your premium dollars periodically between the two basic forms of insurance according to your needs. You have the flexibility to change both the type of coverage and the amount of coverage. One attractive feature of this type of insurance is that you can decrease the amount of coverage without canceling the policy.

This form of insurance is advantageous to relatively young individuals who need flexibility and who require large amounts of insurance but cannot afford large premiums. The net cost of adjustable life insurance is higher than that of pure term insurance, however, because there is a price to be paid for the flexibility that this type of insurance offers.

## Single-Premium Life Insurance

The Tax Reform Act of 1986 placed restrictions on popular tax-sheltered investments such as IRAs and 401(k) plans. The legislation was much kinder to insurance in general and single-premium life insurance in particular. Congress is being pressured by powerful lobbies outside the insurance industry to make investment in single-premium life insurance less attractive from a tax standpoint. Therefore, it is very important for you to understand what options the applicable life insurance company is offering you in the event of changes in tax law. Investments in this product are attractive primarily because of the tax advantages. This is why it is critical that you know what the company policy is in the event of changes in legislation. If your sales agent simply dismisses your concern with a comment such as, "The tax laws won't change," you should find another insurance agent.

Single-premium life insurance is an investment product more than an insurance product. Life insurance is sold as part of the package in order to maintain tax advantages. When you purchase single-premium life insurance, you provide a lump sum, generally $5,000 or more. There is no upper limit imposed by law. The insurance company provides you with a specified amount of life insurance plus the prevailing rate of interest on your investment, which is tax-deferred. Generally a specific rate of return will be guaranteed for only a limited time.

You may borrow some of your investment without penalties at a predetermined interest rate, generally 8 percent or lower. There is almost always a penalty if you withdraw funds in the first year or so. Usually these early-withdrawal penalties are on a sliding scale. For example, the penalty may be 8 percent in the first year, 7 percent in the second year, and so on.

In summary, single-premium life insurance offers you a tax-deferred vehicle for investing your funds. You should consider it only if you are willing to commit your funds long enough to avoid early-withdrawal penalties. Make sure you understand the penalties and know what the guaranteed interest rate is and how long it is guaranteed.

Before you commit any money to single-premium life insurance, you should review other alternatives that provide tax-deferred savings at lower sales and administrative costs. For example, you can consider a non-deductible 401(k) plan if your employer offers it, and a nondeductible IRA—if you have earned income—for up to a limit of $2,000 per year. These investment options are reviewed in depth in Chapter 13.

## Participating Policies

A participating life insurance policy can be either whole life or term. It pays dividends on excess investment earnings left after the insurance company pays the benefits and expenses for the current year.

As an owner of participating life insurance, you have seven dividend options from which you can select. Regardless of which option you select, the dividend is not taxable because it is considered by the IRS to be a return of principal. The options:

1. Receive the dividend in cash.
2. Use the dividend to reduce your premium.
3. Purchase paid-up additional insurance of the same type. This is an attractive option if you need additional insurance because no sales commission is charged and no physical examination is required.
4. Leave your dividend with the insurance company to earn interest for you. The interest earned is taxable to you in the year you earn it even if you do not withdraw the interest. If you consider this option, make sure that you receive a rate of return comparable with what you could obtain on your own.
5. Purchase one-year term insurance. The minimum is based on your age at that time. This option is also attractive if you need additional insurance because no sales commissions are charged. Insurance

companies generally put an upper limit on how much term insurance you can purchase using dividends. If your dividends exceed these limits, you can use other dividend options.

6. Pay off the policy earlier.
7. Use some combination of the first six options.

Nonparticipating policies do not pay dividends. The premiums for participating policies are generally higher than for nonparticipating policies because of the dividend factor. Thus, in order to compare the two types of policy, you have to consider the historical pattern of dividends paid on a participating policy. Insurance companies do not guarantee a specific dividend, but you can get a pretty good idea of what to expect by reviewing the history of the participating policies of a particular company. You can get the history from your insurance agent.

Neither type of policy is inherently better. The primary advantage of the nonparticipating policy is that initially its premium is lower than that of a participating policy. Participating policies, however, allow you to benefit from any favorable experience. Accordingly, their long-term costs may be lower.

## The Interest-Adjusted Method of Cost Comparison

One of the major problems you will have in purchasing life insurance is to determine which policy is the cheapest. Premiums can and do vary significantly among companies. Unfortunately, you cannot compare prices based on premiums alone, because of variations in other factors such as dividends and accumulation of cash values.

In order to compare insurance costs on the same basis, you need to use an index that takes these variables into consideration. The interest-adjusted method of computing costs has been developed to take into consideration three basic variables—premium, dividends, and cash value. This method also takes into consideration the time value of money. A common interest rate is applied to these three variables over time to produce a single cost index that allows comparison between policies.

The index must be applied to the same type of policy—for example, a $10,000 whole life policy for a 45-year-old nonsmoking female.

For New York Savings Bank Life Insurance, the index per $1,000 for policies of $50,000 for a 5-year renewable term for a female nonsmoker age 45 was $4.94. If you were considering another insurer, ask the salesperson for the index for the identical policy. A higher index means a higher overall cost to you.

Unfortunately, there are no federal or state laws that force an insurance agent to provide such information. If a company has a very good index, you can expect the salesperson to have the information available. Otherwise you may get a blank stare from an agent when you ask how that index compares to indexes of other insurance companies.

If the agent does not have such information, request the required data, explaining that you do not intend to purchase any policy without that information. If the agent cannot or will not provide the data, find a new agent.

There are a number of sources available for you to obtain cost-index information. This type of information is published regularly by A.M. Best & Company, Inc., Oldwick, New Jersey 08858. The insurance department of your state government should have this information. Periodically such information is published in *Consumers Guide* and *Money* magazines.

## Group Rates

You can usually obtain better insurance rates as a member of a group than you can as an individual because there are fewer administrative costs for the insurance company. For example, one payment covering thousands of employees is much cheaper to process than thousands of separate checks, and the cost savings can be passed on to you. Thus, before purchasing any individual insurance, determine whether you are eligible to purchase insurance through a group affiliation.

Group life insurance is generally available through the American Association of Retired Persons, employer groups, professional societies, trade associations, military organizations, labor unions, and other organizations. Group coverage is generally different from coverage under an individual policy in the following ways:

- You are eligible for insurance because you are a member of a specific group. Generally no medical examination is required.
- Separate policies are not issued. A single policy for the whole group is issued, and each group member receives a booklet explaining the benefits.
- The cost is generally low because the coverage is term insurance and because of the lower administrative costs.
- The premium is based on the composition of the group. If a group is composed of primarily older members, the cost will be higher.
- When your group affiliation ends, you usually have the right for a limited time only to convert to an individual life insurance policy.

This conversion privilege, however, may be to only a specific type of policy. For example, you may be able to purchase only a whole life policy, even if the group policy was a term policy.

The cost of this insurance is based on your age at that time. Accordingly, you may find the cost prohibitive. For this reason if you expect to need life insurance coverage after your group affiliation ends, you should consider obtaining independent coverage to supplement your group coverage.

You should not assume that every group policy is cheaper than an individual policy you can purchase. For example, if you are a nonsmoker, you can obtain cheaper individual rates than a smoker. Some individual rates are very attractive and are less expensive than some group rates. For example, residents of states that sell savings bank life insurance often secure lower rates.

Before you terminate a group policy for an individual policy, make sure that you understand whether you are eligible to reenter the group plan. If you cannot rejoin the group without a physical examination, it is generally in your best interests to remain covered by the group policy. Sometimes an individual policy is cheaper only for a specific time, and when the individual term policy ends, the group policy becomes cheaper.

## Riders

The rider is an optional feature usually offered when a policy is issued. These options are generally cheaper if you purchase them at issuance rather than adding them later. Some of these options:

- *Waiver of premium*—ensures that the policy will remain in effect without premium payment if you become disabled before a specific age.
- *Disability income*—provides monthly income following total disability. Income is provided after a period specified in the policy.
- *Accidental death benefit*—provides a multiple, usually two or three, of the face amount of the policy in the event of an accidental death prior to a specified age.
- *Decreasing term rider*—allows you to purchase decreasing term insurance as a rider rather than in a separate policy.
- *Guaranteed insurability*—allows you to purchase an additional specific amount of insurance at predetermined intervals up to a maximum age without medical examination. This is an excellent feature if health deteriorates as well as a good inflation hedge.

- *Cost-of-living rider*—permits you to purchase additional insurance each year to offset increasing insurance needs due to inflation.
- *Level-term rider*—allows you to purchase term insurance for a specified time as a rider to a cash-value policy. This feature can be useful during a period when you have special economic obligations such as the need to educate your children or grandchildren.

Make sure that you understand the riders included in the policy before you enter into any insurance contract. If some riders seem important to you, discuss them with your agent to determine if paying the cost of adding them to your policy is worthwhile.

## Naming a Beneficiary

Your selection of a beneficiary for your life insurance policy should be based on your overall estate plan, which is discussed in detail in Chapter 21. Your selection of a beneficiary can have a significant impact on the amount of federal estate taxes due from your estate.

If you own an insurance policy—that is, if you have an incidence of ownership in a policy—the face amount of the policy will be included in your gross estate regardless of who the beneficiary is. Incidence of ownership includes having the right to cancel the policy, change beneficiaries, change ownership, or convert the policy to another form of insurance. If your spouse is the beneficiary of such a policy, the proceeds will be available to him or her free of federal estate-tax liability. If the total amount of your estate, excluding what you leave your spouse, exceeds $600,000, your estate is taxable.

On the surface, then, it appears that you should always name your spouse as a beneficiary. This is a simplification, however, and before you decide, you should read Chapter 21 and discuss your options with your attorney.

## Ownership of Policy

In some circumstances it may be to your family's benefit for a policy on your life to be owned by someone other than yourself. If you own the policy, the face amount of it will be included in your taxable estate after you die. If the beneficiary is not your spouse, there may be federal estate taxes due.

If the size of your taxable estate will exceed $600,000, consider giving up ownership of your policies to another party. For example, if your life insurance policy is owned by your son or daughter, the value of the policy will not be included in your estate because it is not your property.

There are some disadvantages to renouncing ownership. The new owner of the policy, not you, makes any decisions regarding change in beneficiary. You no longer have access to the cash value of a policy. Moreover, if you give the policy away within 3 years of your death, the IRS still counts it as part of your estate. The IRS will not honor a change in ownership unless the new owner pays the premiums. Review this option with your attorney before you renounce ownership of your policies.

## Borrowing on Your Cash Value

One of the advantages of cash-value life insurance is that you can borrow on the equity in the policy. Your policy will specify the amount of cash value you have built up based on the number of years the policy has been in force and on the face amount of the policy. The policy also specifies the amount you can borrow, which can be as much as the cash value.

The policy also states the interest rate you will pay for the loan. For older policies the rate could be as low as 5 percent or 6 percent. The rates for newer policies are somewhat higher, such as 8 percent, and are sometimes tied to a popular financial index such as the prime rate.

With most policies you do not have to repay the principal unless you choose to; only the interest payments are mandatory. The interest is tax-deductible on the same basis as other consumer interest. In 1989 only 20 percent of the interest will be deductible; after 1991, no interest paid will be deductible.

You should not borrow on your life insurance policy if your dependents need the full face amount in the event of your death. Your beneficiary will receive the face amount of your policy minus any loans outstanding. Thus, if you have a $10,000 policy with a $2,000 loan, your beneficiary will receive only $8,000. On the other hand, if your beneficiaries are in the fortunate position of not requiring the life insurance proceeds, then borrow by all means. It is unlikely that you can find another such inexpensive source of funds.

If your beneficiaries do not need the proceeds of your policy, you may wish to cash in, or surrender, your policy. Using this option you have permanent possession of the cash value of your policy and you do not have to pay any interest. You should not exercise that option, however, unless you are convinced your beneficiaries will not require the proceeds of your policy and that you will never want to exercise other options available in the policy. If you are uncertain and can afford the interest payments, you may as well use the loan option. You can cancel the policy later if you wish. Once you cancel the policy, however, you cannot reactivate it.

## Selecting a Company

Regardless of the type of insurance policy you select, you should make sure that the insurance company is in sound financial condition. One of the best sources to check the financial status of an insurance company is *Best's Insurance Reports,* published annually, which evaluates major insurance companies and is available at most libraries.

You should also verify that the company is licensed to sell insurance in your state. This is important because life insurance is regulated by state law, not federal law. If you have a problem with your policy, your state insurance agency can be helpful to you if the insurance company is licensed in your state.

Some state insurance agencies provide basic consumer insurance information such as cost comparisons, glossaries, and checklists. Contact your state agency to determine whether they have such information available to the general public.

## Tax Information

Income tax, federal estate tax, state estate tax, inheritance tax, and gift tax are associated with life insurance.

### Income Tax

Premiums you pay for life insurance are generally not tax-deductible except possibly as alimony. That is a special situation you can review with a tax specialist or the IRS.

Dividends from participating policies are not taxable income. They are treated as a partial return of your premium. If you leave your dividends on deposit with the insurance company to accumulate interest, that interest is taxable. If you use the dividends to purchase additional insurance, there is no tax liability.

If you surrender a policy and receive more than you paid in premiums, the difference is taxable. For example, if you paid premiums of $4,000 for a policy and cashed it in for $5,000, the difference of $1,000 is taxable.

The beneficiary of a life insurance policy does not incur any income-tax liability on the proceeds. If the funds are left with the insurance company to accumulate interest, however, all interest accumulated is taxable.

### Federal Estate Tax

When an estate is valued, any life insurance policies on the person who died are included. The value of the policy is its face amount minus any outstanding loans.

If the decedent owned a policy on someone else's life, the value of this policy is also included in the decedent's estate. The value of this policy is its cash surrender value.

If the decedent was insured but the policies were owned by another party for at least 3 years, the policies are not included in the estate for tax purposes. This is the case only when the decedent had no *incidence of ownership* in the policy. If the decedent did have incidence of ownership, the value is included in the estate for tax purposes.

Note that having insurance included in one's estate does not mean that it incurs a federal estate tax. This subject is covered in detail in Chapter 21.

### State Estate and Inheritance Tax

There is no uniformity among the states regarding estate tax. States generally use the same criteria that the federal government uses regarding what and how much is included in the taxable estate. However, some states exempt all insurance proceeds from taxation.

In some states benefits that are inherited by individuals are subject to an inheritance tax. However, in many states insurance proceeds payable to certain relatives specified by the state or to trusts are not taxable. Each state limits the amount of the exemption for both estate and inheritance taxes.

### Gift Tax

If you give, or assign, your policy to someone else, you may incur a gift tax. Gift tax and estate tax are combined into a unified tax explained in detail in Chapter 21. Gift tax applies only to cash-value policies. The cash value at the time you assign the policy to someone else is the value of the policy for tax purposes.

Under existing tax law, you can give any individual up to $10,000 per year, or a joint donors gift of $20,000 per year, and not be subject to the gift tax.

# Impact of
# Tax Reform

The Tax Reform Act of 1986 has had a significant impact on most United States taxpayers. This chapter examines aspects of the Tax Reform Act that can affect the financial planning process. Changes in tax rates, personal exemptions, standard deductions, interest deductions, medical expenses, miscellaneous deductions, capital gains taxes, and children's taxes are specifically addressed.

You will find that marginal tax rates, or tax rates paid for any additional income earned, have been reduced and that personal deductions have been increased. These changes are beneficial to you. However, almost all of the other changes are unfavorable. In general, if you do not itemize or take nominal deductions, you will probably find your taxes reduced. On the other hand, if the amount of your itemized deductions has been high, you will probably find that your taxes are now higher. It is important for you to understand the major changes because in some situations you may be able to reduce your tax liability. For example, some types of interest deductions are treated much more favorably than others. This topic is important and will be examined in detail in this chapter.

## Tax Rates

For the tax years 1989 and beyond, there are two regular tax brackets, 15 percent and 28 percent. Table 20-1 illustrates how the tax rates apply, based on your filing status. As indicated in the table, if your taxable income exceeds a specific level, you incur a 5 percent surcharge.

For example, if you file a joint return in 1989, any taxable income you earn over $74,850 up to $155,320 is subject to a 5 percent surtax. If your taxable income for the year is $84,850, you have to pay an additional $500 in taxes. In effect the 5 percent surtax increases your marginal tax bracket to 33 percent for earned income that falls within the range the surtax applies to. All earned income above the maximum level in the range is taxed at 28 percent. No surcharge is applicable.

Thus, although on the surface it appears that the maximum marginal tax rate has been cut to 28 percent, the maximum marginal rate is 33 percent. Moreover, because many deductions have been eliminated, many people pay more taxes despite the cut in rates.

## Personal Exemptions and the Standard Deduction

Personal exemptions have been increased from $1,950 in 1988 to $2,000 in 1989, and the amount will be adjusted for inflation in subsequent years. The standard deductions for 1989 are listed in Table 20-2.

These rates will continue to be adjusted for inflation.

## Interest Deductions

The Tax Reform Act of 1986 has drastically changed the way in which interest can be deducted on your return. Prior to tax reform, all interest was essentially deductible. Now that the laws are different, you have to make distinctions among the following types of interest:

- Mortgage
- Home-equity mortgage
- Personal
- Investment
- Business
- Passive activity

### Mortgage Interest

Homeowners have survived tax reform at least temporarily. You may still deduct all mortgage interest for both your primary residence and one other home. For mortgages originated after October 13, 1987, interest up to a total of $1 million covering one or two homes can be deducted. You should recognize, however, that that interest deduction is worth less to you because you are now in a lower tax bracket.

## Table 20-1   INCOME TAX RATES

| Taxable Income | Rate |
| --- | --- |
| **Married, Filing Joint Returns and Surviving Spouses** | |
| Up to $29,750 | 15% |
| $29,751 to $74,850 | 28 |
| $74,851 to $155,320 | 33 |
| Above $155,320 | 28 |
| **Heads of Households** | |
| Up to $24,850 | 15 |
| $24,851 to $64,200 | 28 |
| $64,201 to $128,810 | 33 |
| Above $128,810 | 28 |
| **Single** | |
| Up to $18,550 | 15 |
| $18,551 to $44,900 | 28 |
| $44,901 to $93,130 | 33 |
| Above $93,130 | 28 |
| **Married, Filing Separately** | |
| Up to $14,875 | 15 |
| $14,876 to $37,425 | 28 |
| $37,426 to $117,895 | 33 |
| Above $117,895 | 28 |

NOTE: These are 1989 rates. They will be adjusted for inflation in subsequent years.

## SCENARIO

You are paying $5,000 in mortgage interest each year. Prior to tax reform, your marginal tax bracket was 40 percent, and now it is 28 percent. When you were in the 40 percent tax bracket, the $5,000 deduction was worth $2,000 to you after taxes. Now the deduction is worth $1,400 to you.

Table 20-2   STANDARD DEDUCTIONS
FOR 1989

| Filing Status | Deduction |
|---|---|
| Married, filing jointly | $5,200 |
| Head of household | 4,500 |
| Single | 3,100 |
| Married, filing separately | 2,600 |

Because your interest deduction is worth less to you in after-tax dollars, you should reexamine whether it is to your advantage to prepay some of your outstanding mortgage if you can.

### SCENARIO

You are currently paying 10 percent interest on your mortgage. Because you are in the 28 percent tax bracket, 28 percent of your interest payment is tax-deductible, and the other 72 percent is not. So the after-tax cost to you of the loan is 7.2 percent (10 percent × 72 percent). Accordingly, if you are earning less than 7.2 percent after taxes on other assets, you may wish to consider repaying some of your mortgage early. Before you do this, however, you have to consider the loss of liquidity you incur. Once you repay part of the mortgage, you cannot easily recover those assets without either refinancing or selling your home.

### Home Equity Mortgages

A home equity mortgage is a loan backed by a homeowner's equity in the house. Equity is the difference between the market value of the house and the remaining principal amount owed on it. The loan is secured by the property.

Some financial institutions offer lines of credit against the equity in the borrower's home. A home equity line of credit is a type of mortgage in which the lender sets an upper limit, and the borrower borrows money as needed up to that limit.

Terms of repayment vary widely and are set by the offering financial institution. The financial institution specifies an upper limit of the loan based on the equity in the property of the homeowner. Normally a financial institution will lend you between 70 percent and 75 percent of your equity in the property.

As a result of tax reform, home equity loans are favorable relative to other types of consumer loans. For mortgages incurred after October 13, 1987, interest may be deducted on home equity loans up to $100,000 regardless of the purpose of the borrowing. Interest deductions on mortgages incurred before October 14, 1987, on one or two homes are fully deductible.

In addition to the tax advantage, another significant advantage is the low interest rate in comparison with that of other types of consumer loans. Thus, home equity loans provide two advantages over consumer loans — more deductions under the tax law and lower interest rates. Accordingly, home equity loans have become very popular.

Interest rates on loans of this type vary based on some index such as the prime rate. A typical rate is prime plus 1.5 percent or prime plus 2 percent. Since the prime rate can increase quickly in inflationary periods, you must be especially careful of borrowing large sums of money in this way.

You will find that fees and closing costs for this type of loan vary widely. In some areas of the country, you can obtain such loans with no application fees or closing costs, or at least with low ones. In other areas you may find that obtaining a home equity mortgage is as expensive as obtaining an original one. You must comparison-shop, since there are tremendous variations.

Although the home equity loan has many advantages, you must be aware of the disadvantages. Your property is collateral, and if you cannot make your payments, you can lose your home.

In a period of high interest rates, the interest rate on your loan can increase dramatically. Most home equity rates are tied to a volatile interest rate such as the Treasury bill rate. This rate can go up 3 percent or 4 percent in a few years. If this happens, your interest costs can increase dramatically.

The home equity line of credit is almost too easy to use. You must avoid the trap of using it to purchase items that will provide you short-term satisfaction but will take many years to pay for.

In short, although the home equity line of credit has significant advantages, you must be very careful to use it properly, keeping your debt under control and closely monitoring the index that determines your interest rate.

## SCENARIO

You purchased a home for $100,000 in 1986. The value is now $150,000. You owe $50,000 now, so you have $100,000 in equity in the property. Your bank is willing to lend you 70 percent of your equity, or $70,000, at the prime rate plus 1.75 percent. The rate is to be updated monthly.

Do not obtain a home equity loan without carefully examining the advantages and disadvantages. You certainly do not want to jeopardize your home by borrowing too much. Make sure you understand all of the costs of a home equity loan before you apply, and make sure you understand how the interest rate is computed. Ask your lender for a history of the index the rate is based on. From your perspective a stable index is better than a volatile one. Another important factor is flexibility, both in terms of withdrawing funds and repaying the loan. The optimum situation is one in which you can withdraw any amount you choose and prepay the mortgage whenever you choose to.

Avoid any agreement in which there are fees whether you borrow on your line of credit or not. Some banks will charge you anyway. Another fee to avoid is for prepaying a mortgage.

### Personal Interest

Prior to tax reform, interest on personal loans was fully tax-deductible. These interest deductions are now being phased out, as illustrated in Table 20-3. Personal loans encompass loans you make for automobiles, student loans, revolving credit, vacations, and so forth. The only loans that do not fall into this category are mortgage loans, business loans, and investment-related loans.

Thus it is to your advantage to reduce the amount of personal loans outstanding wherever possible, since the tax advantages to you are rapidly disappearing.

You may not want to prepay certain outstanding loans, such as student loans, obtained at attractive rates. However, if you have substantial assets earning less than 10 percent, you should certainly consider using these assets to reduce any personal loans on which you are paying interest rates of 10 percent or more. Of course, this principle works the same way at any interest rate.

| Table 20-3   PERSONAL INTEREST | |
| --- | --- |
| Year | Deductible Amount |
| 1989 | 20% |
| 1990 | 10 |
| After 1990 | 0 |

## Investment Interest

Investment interest is paid on debt incurred to purchase investment property other than your principal and secondary residence. Also excluded from this category are any interest payments associated with passive activity, which is discussed later in this chapter. Investment interest is what you pay on loans used to purchase common stock, corporate, or government (not municipal) bonds. Tax law limits the deduction for investment interest you pay to the amount of net investment income for the year. Net investment income is defined as the excess of investment income over investment expense. If you pay more investment interest than you receive in interest income, the excess must be treated as personal interest. (See Table 20-3.)

### SCENARIO

You borrowed $50,000 from your broker in a margin account, a type in which your broker lends you money to purchase securities. In one year the interest you incur on your loan is $5,000. In the same year you receive investment income of $4,000. You are entitled to deduct interest expense up to the amount of investment income—$4,000. The $1,000 by which your interest expense exceeds your interest income is reported on your tax return as personal interest. (See Table 20-3.)

Any investment interest expense not deductible because it exceeds your investment income can be carried forward with no time limit until you generate enough investment income to match it.

## SCENARIO

In 1989 your interest expense exceeds your investment income by $1,000. You can deduct 20 percent of $1,000, or $200 of the interest, as a personal interest deduction. Thus, you incurred $800 in nondeductible interest expense.

If your investment income in 1990 or any subsequent year exceeds your interest by $800, you can deduct the $800 interest expense you carried forward from 1989. The burden of proof is on you to maintain proper records so you can back up your deductions based on prior-year interest payments and copies of your tax returns.

Investment income includes not only dividend and interest income but also any profits from the sale of your securities. Thus, if you purchase common stock and hold it for a gain of $1,000, this $1,000 is part of your total investment income for that tax year.

It is very important for you to maintain separate accounts associated with loans you obtain for investment purposes. The burden of proof is on you to maintain separate accounts in order to justify the tax deduction for investment interest. If you use the proceeds of a loan for both investment purposes and other purposes, it is likely that the IRS will disallow your deduction.

### Passive Activity Interest

As part of tax reform, Congress has introduced the concept of passive activity. Passive activity refers to business interests such as limited partnerships, in which you do not materially participate. If you do not participate in the business on a regular, continuous, and substantial basis, the IRS categorizes your role in the business as a passive activity. An example of passive activity is investing in a limited partnership but not participating in management of the business.

Interest expense associated with passive activity is treated similarly to that of investment interest. Passive activity interest is deductible only to the extent that you can offset the interest against passive activity income. If your passive activity interest expense exceeds your passive activity income in a tax year, you can deduct the excess as personal interest. In the same manner as with investment interest expense, you can carry passive activity interest expense forward indefinitely.

There is one significant difference, however. When you dispose of your passive investment, you can deduct passive activity interest that you were not able to deduct in prior years regardless of whether the investment was profitable or not.

---

### SCENARIO

You invested in a limited partnership for $10,000, and you borrowed money to finance your investment. Five years later you sold your investment for $11,000. During the interim 5-year period, you have carried forward $2,000 in passive activity interest expense. In the tax year you disposed of the limited partnership, you could deduct the $2,000 in interest expense that you have carried forward.

---

## Business Interest

Interest expense that you incur to operate your business is still completely tax-deductible. Tax reform did not affect the treatment of business interest expense.

---

## Medical Expenses

Tax reform has made it very difficult to deduct medical expenses. Current law specifies that you may deduct only medical expenses that exceed 7.5 percent of your adjusted gross income. This does not include insurance reimbursements. These deductions are available to you only if you itemize.

For the majority of working people as well as many retirees, this limitation will preclude you from deducting any of your medical expenses. When you compute the total amount of your allowable medical deductions, you should include transportation expenses. The cost of transportation to and from medical facilities is tax-deductible regardless of the method of transportation you select. Check the latest IRS mileage allowance if you travel by automobile, since it is updated periodically.

Transportation expenses that you incur when you visit members of your immediate family who are ill should be included with your other transportation-related medical expenses.

If you require any special equipment for medical reasons, the associated expenses are tax-deductible. For example, a physician may prescribe the installation and maintenance of air conditioning equipment to treat an allergy. The associated initial expenditure and recurring costs are tax-deductible.

At the beginning of a tax year, you will not know whether your total medical expenses will exceed 7.5 percent of your adjusted gross income. You should maintain records on the assumption that your expenses will exceed the 7.5 percent minimum. You should maintain a daily log of all your visits to a medical facility. You should also record all of your medical expenses and retain receipts. Try to avoid cash payments so that you will have credit card receipts and canceled checks. You will find it much easier to prepare your taxes if you maintain tax records continuously, for medical and all other deductions, rather than searching for receipts and other documents at filing time.

## State and Local Taxes

The Tax Reform Act of 1986 eliminated state sales tax as an allowable itemized deduction. Other state and local taxes such as income taxes, real property taxes, and personal property taxes are still deductible.

In some tax years, you may find that the amount of state tax withheld is insufficient, and you may have to pay a state income tax in addition to what has been withheld. Be sure to deduct this payment when you file your taxes the next year.

In some tax years, you may be fortunate enough to receive a refund from your state for overpayment of state income taxes. This income has to be reported on your federal return the following year if you itemize your deductions. It is not reportable income, however, if you do not itemize.

Your state may impose state transfer taxes on the sales of securities. The law allows you to deduct taxes if they are ordinary and necessary expenses of producing income. Thus, if you do itemize, be sure to include state transfer taxes or any other state tax that falls under this category.

## Miscellaneous Deductions

Miscellaneous deductions are itemized deductions that do not fall under any of the following categories:

- Charitable contributions
- Medical expenses
- State and local taxes
- Casualty losses
- Interest expenses

Some examples are expenses for professional journals, union dues, fees for IRA and other retirement accounts, financial advice, career counseling, education, business subscriptions, and work clothes.

Tax reform has significantly reduced the advantages of miscellaneous deductions. Under prior tax law, all miscellaneous deductions were 100 percent deductible for individuals who itemized their deductions. Now, only deductions that exceed 2 percent of your adjusted gross income are deductible.

For example, let's say you have an AGI of $80,000. Only miscellaneous expenses that exceed $1,600 are tax deductible. For most taxpayers the 2 percent threshold essentially eliminates the deduction. You may have known perhaps you would not exceed the 2 percent threshold in 1988, so perhaps you postponed some miscellaneous expenses until the next year, when your miscellaneous expenses might exceed 2 percent. You should try to minimize and when feasible avoid miscellaneous expenses altogether since their tax value is now marginal at best.

## Children's Income

Under the old tax laws, income that was earned under a child's Social Security number was taxed at the child's tax rate. Since the child was generally in a lower tax bracket than his parents, there was a tax advantage in transferring income to a child.

The Tax Reform Act of 1986 changed that. After 1986 income greater than $1,000 earned by a child under 14 became taxable at the parents' tax rate.

The impact of the tax law is that there is still an advantage to transfer income up to $1,000 per year to a child, but when the income exceeds $1,000, there is no advantage, since the income is taxed at the parents' rate. The law has essentially eliminated the advantages of income-shifting techniques such as Clifford trusts.

## Elimination of Capital Gains Tax

Tax reform repealed the advantages of the capital gains tax. Under the old law, if you held a capital asset longer than 6 months, you had to only report 40 percent of the gain as income.

Under existing law, regardless of the holding period, all gains are taxable at ordinary income tax rates. Accordingly, there is no longer any reason to hold any asset for 6 months in order to reduce the tax on gains.

# Estate Planning

**U**nfortunately, many people postpone doing any estate planning. There is no logical reason for you not to develop a well-thought-out estate plan. If you do, your assets will go to the intended parties. Also, federal and state estate taxes will be minimized and there will be no unnecessary and burdensome administrative problems.

There is no point in spending a lifetime building assets unless you take the proper steps to ensure that your assets go where you want them to go and to minimize estate tax liability.

## Identifying Your Estate Assets

A useful first step you should take is to identify the assets that will be part of your estate. You should list all of your existing assets and all of the assets that will subsequently be part of your estate. (See Table 21-1.) For example, the face value of all of the insurance policies you own should be listed as assets that will be part of your estate.

You should identify the specific ownership of each asset. Some may be owned by you outright. Others may be owned jointly, with right of survivorship with your spouse; that is, your spouse owns the property if you die first. Other property may be owned jointly with other parties. Identify the co-owners and beneficiaries of all assets.

This information is critical to you and your attorney in many ways. It is essential in order to ensure that each major asset has been identified, that the value of your estate can be estimated, that estate taxes can be

Table 21-1   STATEMENT OF ASSETS AND LIABILITIES

|  | Husband | Wife | Joint |
|---|---|---|---|
| **Present Assets** | | | |
| Liquid | | | |
| Checking accounts | | | $ 1,000 |
| Savings accounts | $     2,000 | $3,000 | |
| Stocks | 100,000 | | |
| Bonds | 55,000 | | |
| Subtotal | 157,000 | 3,000 | 1,000 |
| Nonliquid | | | |
| Residence | 150,000 | | |
| Other real estate | 100,000 | | 50,000 |
| Tangible personal property | 20,000 | | |
| Life insurance (cash value) | 5,000 | 2,000 | |
| Subtotal | 275,000 | 2,000 | 50,000 |
| Gross present assets | 432,000 | 5,000 | 51,000 |
| Less liabilities | | | |
| Mortgages | (100,000) | | (30,000) |
| Net present assets | 332,000 | 5,000 | 21,000 |
| **Deferred Assets** | | | |
| Retirement income plan | | | |
| Vested | 80,000 | | |
| Nonvested | 20,000 | | |
| Subtotal | 100,000 | | |
| Assets at death | | | |
| Personal life insurance as of 12/31/89 | 200,000 | | |
| Total net assets | $632,000 | $5,000 | $21,000 |

computed, that tax strategies can be formulated, and that logical decisions can be made regarding the disposition of all your assets.

## Disposition of Assets

You must decide how you wish to dispose of your assets. In a well-designed estate plan, each major asset is identified and a decision is made as to its disposition. Many factors should be taken into consideration, such as the needs of your dependents, your personal wishes, tax factors, and state law. You should list all of your significant assets and think about whom you would like to leave them to before you meet with your attorney.

You should also consider disposing of some of your assets during your life, based on personal considerations as well as tax considerations. You can discuss this option with your attorney to determine if it is applicable to your situation.

You can decide to transfer property by means of a will, which will go into effect after your death. However, some property can be passed by contract or law. Assets that pass by contract or law are nonprobate property.

## Nonprobate Property by Contract

Property that passes to a named beneficiary upon your death does so by contract. For example, life insurance passes by contract rather than by will if you have named a beneficiary other than your estate or a trust created in your will. If you specify a beneficiary, the assets from your life insurance policy will not be assessed for estate taxes or other estate settlement purposes. Even if you do specify a beneficiary, however, the face value of the life insurance policy, minus any loans outstanding, will be included in your estate for federal tax purposes. If you are the owner of the policy, the value of the policy will be included in your estate. The advantages and disadvantages of transferring ownership of life insurance policies are explored later in this chapter.

Assets other than life insurance can pass by contract because of beneficiary designation. These include corporate benefits such as pension plans and profit-sharing plans, IRA and Keogh accounts, and United States savings bonds.

Trust agreements are regulated by the terms of the contract. The associated assets are not subject to probate. As will be explored later in this chapter, a trust can be established either during your lifetime or upon your death. In either case the assets are not probate assets.

Another example of assets passing by contract is through a business partnership agreement. One partner can designate a beneficiary for his or her share of the business. Assets pass according to the terms of the agreement.

## Nonprobate Property by Law

When property is jointly owned, it passes by law. There are two common types of joint ownership: (1) joint tenancy with right of survivorship and (2) tenancy in common. In either case the assets are not subject to probate.

In joint tenancy two or more individuals own a share in property with the agreement that when one individual dies, the survivors obtain the decedent's share.

With tenancy in common, each co-owner retains control over his or her share of the property. This share can be sold or transferred during the lifetime of each co-owner, or passed by will. Thus, it is important to know whether property is held in common or in joint tenancy. Tenancy in common is generally used for business relationships.

## Probate Property

Probate property includes all property that is not transferred by a substitute for a will such as contract or law. The provisions of a will pertain only to probate property. Probate is the process by which property is transferred at death either by will or by intestacy. Dying without a will is called dying intestate.

The executor of an estate is entitled to a commission on probate property only. An executor is a person or institution appointed by the testator, or person making the will, to carry out its terms. No property that is transferred through a substitute for a will is subject to commission. Other estate settlement costs are generally fixed.

Individuals take steps to avoid probate so that assets will change hands more quickly. However, there can be many delays associated with transferring assets even if probate is avoided. For example, transfer agents, brokerage firms, insurance companies, and financial institutions cannot legally release large amounts of money or assets when property is held jointly or is payable because of beneficiary designation. Documentation must be obtained and clearance provided from the required tax authorities. Paperwork is similar whether the assets are probate or nonprobate property. A testamentary (pertaining to a will) substitute should not be selected only to avoid probate. Your selection should be based on other factors such as tax considerations. You should make such selections only with proper legal advice.

## Wills

The major function of a will is to control the disposition of your assets. You should have an attorney prepare your will, and it should reflect the assets you now have as well as additional assets that will go into your estate at your death. The will should take into consideration your present family situation and be broad enough to accommodate contingency planning.

A fiduciary is an individual invested with rights and powers to be used for the benefit of another. You can designate a trust company, a bank, or a person as a fiduciary if your beneficiary may need help managing the assets. For example, if your spouse, whom you intend to be your primary beneficiary, is inexperienced in financial matters, consider the use of an experienced fiduciary to manage the assets your spouse will inherit from you. If you use a fiduciary, give instructions and powers to the fiduciary so that any problems after your death can be dealt with quickly. Your will should be signed under the supervision of an attorney.

Before you meet with your attorney, prepare a personal balance sheet. Also make sure you understand the present form of ownership of all your assets. A competent attorney will discuss the advantages and disadvantages of changing the form of ownership of your assets with you and your spouse. Before you meet with your attorney, you should also decide which of the following are your primary objectives:

- Financial support of spouse
- Financial support of other dependents
- Establishing guardians for children
- Minimizing federal or state taxes
- Management of specific assets
- Making charitable contributions
- Special needs and concerns

You should consider having a will drawn up for your spouse at the same time. The cost will probably be lower, and you will ensure consistency between the two wills. It will be easier for your attorney to give you sound advice for the family as a whole if the assets and wills of both spouses are reviewed at the same time.

The major function of your will is to specify how you would like to distribute your probate assets. You may decide to leave all of your probate assets to your surviving spouse. As will be shown later in this chapter, the size of your estate and the associated federal estate tax laws may have an impact on your decision. Your decision as to how to dispose of your assets should be based primarily on your personal wishes, but you should be aware of the implications for federal tax on your estate as well as on your spouse's estate.

## Dying Intestate

If you do not have a will, you should have your attorney draw one up as soon as possible. If you die without a will—that is, intestate—the laws of the state you reside in will control the disposition of your probate assets. It is unlikely that you want state law to dictate disposal of your assets.

State laws vary. In some states a surviving spouse receives a third to half of the property, and children receive the balance. If you allow the state to determine the recipients of your assets, some persons may receive less than you intend.

A simple will is not an expensive document. A straightforward will can cost less than $200. Discuss fees with your attorney first. If you don't have one, ask your bank, your friends, or business associates to recommend one. As your circumstances change, you can have your will updated inexpensively.

## Unified Tax

The Tax Reform Act of 1986 combined the federal gift and estate taxes. Under this law an individual is allowed a lifetime estate tax allowance (exemption), which can be applied against his or her tax liabilities. For tax years after 1987, this exemption is fixed at $600,000. Your estate will not incur a federal tax liability unless your taxable estate exceeds $600,000. If so, your estate will be taxed progressively as indicated in Table 21-2. The incremental tax rate increased from 18 percent for estates of $600,000 to $610,000 up to 50 percent for estates over $3.1 million. For example, the tax on an $3.1 million estate is $1.025 million.

When you review your own taxable estate, you may be both pleasantly surprised and concerned—surprised because your estate is larger than you expected and concerned because of large federal estate tax that may have to be paid.

Every individual has an initial lifetime exemption of $600,000. This can be reduced, however, if you make large gifts during your lifetime. Under existing tax law, you can make gifts up to $10,000 per person or party per year to as many parties as you want without incurring a gift tax liability and without reducing your $600,000 lifetime exemption. If your spouse concurs, you can make joint gifts of up to $20,000 per

Table 21-2  ESTATE AND GIFT TAXES, 1989

| Your taxable estate | | Tax owed | Plus | on amount over |
|---|---|---|---|---|
| $      0- | 10,000 | $          0 | 18% | $          0 |
| 10,000- | 20,000 | 1,800 | 20 | 10,000 |
| 20,000- | 40,000 | 3,800 | 22 | 20,000 |
| 40,000- | 60,000 | 8,200 | 24 | 40,000 |
| 60,000- | 80,000 | 13,000 | 26 | 60,000 |
| 80,000- | 100,000 | 18,200 | 28 | 80,000 |
| 100,000- | 150,000 | 23,800 | 30 | 100,000 |
| 150,000- | 250,000 | 38,800 | 32 | 150,000 |
| 250,000- | 500,000 | 70,800 | 34 | 250,000 |
| 500,000- | 750,000 | 155,800 | 37 | 500,000 |
| 750,000- | 1,000,000 | 248,300 | 39 | 750,000 |
| 1,000,000- | 1,250,000 | 345,800 | 41 | 1,000,000 |
| 1,250,000- | 1,500,000 | 448,300 | 43 | 1,250,000 |
| 1,500,000- | 2,000,000 | 555,800 | 45 | 1,500,000 |
| 2,000,000- | 2,500,000 | 780,800 | 49 | 2,000,000 |
| 2,500,000 and up | | 1,025,800 | 50 | 2,500,000 |

person per year without reducing your exemption. This technique is called gift splitting.

However, you reduce your lifetime exemption if you make any gift that exceeds the $10,000 limit to an individual in one year. For example, if you gave your son $110,000 in one year, you would have to file a special form with the IRS revealing the size of the gift. Your lifetime exemption would be reduced from $600,000 to $500,000. If you made this gift, your estate would have a tax liability if its value exceeded $500,000.

### SCENARIO

The value of your taxable estate is $600,000, but your lifetime exemption has been reduced to $500,000. The federal estate tax liability is $23,800. (See Table 21-2.)

The use of gifts of $10,000 or less per year can reduce or eliminate future estate tax liability.

## SCENARIO

Mrs. Smith, a widow, expects to have a taxable estate of $850,000. Estate tax will be incurred on the amount that exceeds $600,000, in this case $250,000. The tax due on $250,000 is $70,800 according to Table 21-2. If Mrs. Smith gives away $250,000 before she dies, there will be no federal estate tax due. If she gives away $100,000, estate tax will be reduced by 32 percent, or $32,000. There may be gift tax implications. Accordingly, Mrs. Smith should discuss her gift giving with her attorney.

You should not give away assets you expect to use during your lifetime. However, if you are in the fortunate position of having some assets that you do not need, you can consider giving some of these assets during your lifetime to those family members, friends, or charities that could most use it. This reduces your estate tax liability and lets your beneficiaries have the benefit of your gift while you are alive to enjoy seeing the results of your gift. Moreover, if you keep all your assets and a beneficiary dies before you do, he or she will never see the money.

## The Marital Deduction

Under existing law you can leave an unlimited amount of assets to your surviving spouse without incurring any federal estate tax liability. On the surface, then, it seems logical to leave all your assets to your surviving spouse. However, this strategy is not always appropriate for several reasons.

First of all, avoiding estate taxes should not be your sole objective in estate planning. You may want to give certain assets to specific parties or organizations even if there will be estate taxes owed. You should develop your plan based primarily on how you want your assets distributed. Ideally this can be done with little or no estate tax liability. But the avoidance of taxes should not be your sole criterion.

If the value of your taxable estate is lower than $600,000, you will not incur federal estate tax liability. This is true regardless of who your beneficiaries are. In this situation the marital deduction does not offer any tax advantage, and you should distribute your assets based on your wishes and the needs of your beneficiaries. In fact, as you will see from the next example, if your spouse already has substantial assets, leaving him or her most or all of your estate can subject your spouse's estate to unnecessary taxes.

As indicated already, you can leave unlimited assets to your spouse, free of federal estate taxes. If a spouse does not remarry, however, he or she may be unable to avoid estate taxes when his or her estate is settled. Table 21-2 illustrates the current federal estate tax rates. If an unmarried surviving spouse dies with a taxable estate of $1 million, the federal estate tax is $345,800. Thus, the assets that escaped taxes in the first estate are taxed in the surviving spouse's estate. For that reason it is very important for you to understand your options. You will find that there are approaches you can use to achieve your estate planning objectives, meet your beneficiaries' needs, and minimize or eliminate estate tax liabilities.

## Trusts

Many of the tax-saving options available to you involve trusts. The concept of the trust is simple: It is an agreement in which the trustor, or establisher of the trust, gives property to a trustee to invest and manage for the advantage of a beneficiary. You can use a trust to keep partial control over assets during your lifetime as well as after your death. There are four parties associated with a trust: the donor, or trustor, or grantor; the trustee; the beneficiary; and the remainderman. The individual who establishes the trust is the donor. The manager of the assets is the trustee. The individual who receives income is the beneficiary. The party who receives the residue of the assets when the trust is terminated is the remainderman. An individual can serve in more than one of these functions.

The primary objective of a trust is to provide proper management of assets. You would select a trustee because you are confident that this person has more investment expertise than the beneficiaries. The trustee manages the assets and distributes income based on the objectives established by the donor.

When you establish a trust, you determine the degree of flexibility that the trustee will have. You can give the trustee broad responsibilities and the right to decide how much income to distribute, whether principal can be used, and to which of the beneficiaries funds are to be disbursed.

## Revocable Trusts

A trust that takes effect during your lifetime is called a living trust or *inter vivos* trust. You can set up a trust so that you can change the conditions. If you retain the right to change the provisions, the trust is called revocable.

A revocable trust has no tax advantages. You are subject to income taxes on any earnings of the trust assets. When you die, the assets of the trust will be part of your estate for tax purposes.

The primary advantages of a revocable trust are providing some benefits to your beneficiaries while you are alive and relieving you of the responsibility of managing the assets and distributing income. Moreover, trust assets are not subject to probate.

If your primary objective in establishing a trust is to save money on taxes, consider an irrevocable trust. (See next section.)

## Irrevocable Trusts

A trust that cannot be changed by the donor is irrevocable. A trust established in a will is irrevocable. All revocable trusts become irrevocable when the donor dies.

Irrevocable trusts can have tax advantages. For example, if you are in a high tax bracket, you can contribute income to the trust to be distributed to beneficiaries in a lower tax bracket. This provides a net saving in taxes because of the lower rate paid by the beneficiary. There may be gift tax implications, however, depending on the size of your contribution to the trust within one year. If your contribution within a year exceeds $10,000, your lifetime exemption of $600,000 is reduced by the amount of your contribution over $10,000. You can establish a trust for each of several different individuals and contribute $10,000 to each trust.

Irrevocable trusts can also minimize estate taxes. For example, a woman expects her taxable estate to exceed $600,000. Rather than make outright gifts of $10,000 per year to an individual, she may prefer to make a periodic gift into an irrevocable trust and leave the interest in the trust. By using this technique, the donor is minimizing the estate tax because the assets in the irrevocable trust are not part of her estate. Interest on assets in the trust are taxable to the trust, but generally the trust is taxed at a lower rate than that of an individual in a high tax bracket. Thus, in this example there are savings in both estate tax and income tax. Eventually the trust income will go to the beneficiaries based on the conditions specified in the trust agreement.

There are many different forms of irrevocable trust. After you compile the required financial information and establish your estate planning objectives, your attorney should be able to advise you as to whether the use of trusts can be beneficial to you. In the following sections, examples of specific types of trusts are presented. These examples are not intended, however, to encompass the complete universe of available trusts.

### Power of Attorney

Power of attorney is a written document that allows an individual to designate another person to act on the first individual's behalf. In a trust agreement, the use of power of attorney is a way to maintain flexibility because it allows the donor to review the trust to determine whether disposition of the assets should be changed. For example, executing this option would be reasonable if there were significant changes in the economic wellbeing of the beneficiaries.

Power can be general or specific. A general power of attorney allows the holder to direct that trust assets be distributed to anyone, including himself or herself. The undistributed portion of the trust assets are taxable in the estate of the person with the power of attorney.

A limited power of attorney is almost as flexible as a general power of attorney. It can be as broad or as narrow as you dictate. The only restriction is that the power cannot be exercised for the benefit of the individual holding the power. A limited power is not taxable for estate purposes to the person who holds it.

You can exercise a great deal of flexibility with power of attorney. You can give limited power to anyone, with the constraints you specify, exercisable during your lifetime and after your death. You can specify that trusts be continued for your children or other beneficiaries and assign general power of attorney to them.

### Marital Deductions and Residuary Trusts

If your estate exceeds $600,000 and you are married, a very attractive option is the use of the marital deduction and the residuary trust. The residuary trust is established in a flexible way so that the beneficiaries are your spouse, your children, or anyone else you name.

The concept is fairly simple and genuinely practical. The IRS allows you to leave an estate up to $600,000 tax-free to anyone you wish. By leaving any amount up to $600,000 in the residuary trust, you are ensuring that those funds are never subject to estate tax. The amount that you leave your spouse is not taxed regardless of the amount. Thus, you maintain flexibility and limit tax exposure.

The funds in the residuary trust can be made available to anyone you select, including your spouse and children. You can and should arrange with your lawyer that the terms and conditions of the residuary trust are very flexible. If you want your spouse to have ready access to the funds in the residuary trust, you can specify that in the trust agreement. By establishing a flexible trust agreement and a marital deduction, you have reduced the size of your spouse's estate and the estate tax associated with it.

We will look at two scenarios to illustrate the power of residuary trusts.

---

### SCENARIO 1A

Mr. Smith establishes a residuary trust in which he leaves $600,000, the maximum he can offset against his lifetime limitation. The beneficiaries are his wife and children. He leaves the remainder of his estate to his spouse as a marital trust. Mr. Smith dies in 1989. This is what he leaves:

| | |
|---|---:|
| Gross estate | $960,000 |
| Less nontaxable items: | |
| Expenses and liabilities | 60,000 |
| Net estate | 900,000 |
| Marital trust | 300,000 |
| Residuary trust | 600,000 |
| Net taxable estate | $ 0 |

---

In this scenario Mr. Smith leaves the maximum amount possible in the residuary trust without incurring any estate tax. The $300,000 he left his spouse through a marital trust was not taxable either.

---

### SCENARIO 1B

After her husband's death, Mrs. Smith has access to both her own assets and the assets placed in the residuary trust established by her husband. The children of Mr. and Mrs. Smith would also have access to the assets of the residuary trust, based on the terms of the trust agreement. Assume Mrs. Smith dies in 1995 with a gross estate of $840,000.

| | |
|---|---|
| Gross estate | $840,000 |
| Less: | |
| Expenses and liabilities | (40,000) |
| Net Estate | 800,000 |
| Allowable exemption | (600,000) |
| Taxable estate | $200,000 |
| Approximate tax | $ 54,800 |

When Mrs. Smith dies, there is a $54,800 tax on her estate. During widowhood Mrs. Smith receives interest income each year from the residuary trust but does not withdraw any of the capital. Thus the value of the residuary trust remains at $600,000, and it is not taxable.

## SCENARIO 2A

Mr. Robbins has the same amount of assets as Mr. Smith, but he does not establish a residuary trust. He leaves all of his estate to his wife. Assume he dies in 1990.

| | |
|---|---|
| Gross estate | $960,000 |
| Less expenses and liabilities | (60,000) |
| Amount left to spouse | $900,000 |
| Tax liability | $ 0 |

There is no estate tax incurred because he leaves his entire estate to his wife, using the marital deduction.

## SCENARIO 2B

Assume Mrs. Robbins dies in 1995. Although she maintains the same standard of living as Mrs. Smith, her estate is $600,000 larger because Mr. Robbins did not establish a residuary trust.

| | |
|---|---|
| Gross estate | $1,440,000 |
| Less expenses and liabilities | (40,000) |
| Net Estate | 1,400,000 |
| Allowable exemption | (600,000) |
| Taxable estate | $ 800,000 |
| Approximate tax | $ 267,800 |

The estate of Mrs. Robbins incurred a tax of $267,800, $213,000 more than on the estate of Mrs. Smith. The difference in tax liability is due solely to the lack of a residuary trust.

A residuary trust is a very powerful tool if used properly. If you expect that the size of your spouse's estate will exceed $600,000, you should review with your attorney the applicability of a residuary trust in your estate plan.

## QTIP Trusts

A qualified terminable interest property (QTIP) is a trust that is useful for second marriages when you want to protect children from first marriages. The QTIP is similar in concept to the residuary trust described above. The trust helps you to minimize overall estate taxes, while the assets from the trust can provide income to your spouse. When your spouse dies, the property goes to your children or whoever else you designate. The value of the property is included in your spouse's estate, however.

If you have children from a first marriage that you would like to benefit from your estate, discuss this option with your attorney.

If you are the owner of life insurance policies in your name, the face value of the policies will be included in your estate regardless of who the beneficiary is. A significant liability may be incurred, depending on the size of your taxable estate, the face value of the policy, and your relationship to your beneficiaries.

It may be to your advantage to have your policies owned by someone other than yourself in order to minimize estate taxes. Any individual who plans on leaving an estate worth over $600,000 to someone other than his or her own spouse may want to consider alternate life insurance ownership options.

---

### SCENARIO

Mr. Jones, a widower, plans on leaving his entire estate, valued at $600,000 (not counting insurance) to his son and daughter. He has a $100,000 cash-value life insurance policy and he has named his daughter as the beneficiary. If Mr. Jones continues to own this policy, it will be included in his estate when he dies. Then the value of his estate will be $700,000. The additional $100,000 will result in a $23,800 tax liability.

Mr. Jones can reduce the size of his taxable estate by transferring ownership of the policy to his daughter or to someone else. In order for his daughter to own the policy, she has to pay the premiums, and Mr. Jones has to renounce all ownership rights, including the right to change beneficiaries. Mr. Jones may not want to do that, since he would lose some flexibility, including the rights to cash in the policy and take out a loan on its cash value.

If the cash value of the policy were $10,000 or less, Mr. Jones could make a gift of the policy to his daughter without incurring any gift tax. If the cash value (not the face value) of the policy is greater than $10,000, Mr. Jones loses part of his lifetime exemption of $600,000. (See the gift section in this chapter.)

If the policy were a term policy, which has no cash value, there would be no gift tax.

---

If your spouse is the beneficiary of your policy, there is no advantage in transferring the policy to him or her. As indicated earlier, you can leave an unlimited amount of assets to your spouse without incurring any tax liability.

If your spouse has sufficient assets, however, you should reconsider whether or not your spouse should be the beneficiary. If your spouse does not need the funds from your policy, it may be more beneficial to consider other options. If the size of your estate, other than what you are leaving your spouse, is smaller than $600,000, you can consider a different beneficiary. Another option is to change the beneficiary—instead of your spouse, make the beneficiary one of your children and transfer ownership of the policy.

If you do decide to change ownership, do not procrastinate. The IRS will not recognize a change in ownership if it occurs within 3 years of the original owner's death.

## Summary

Effective estate planning is not simple. As your estate increases, it becomes very important that you take steps to ensure that your assets are going to your chosen beneficiaries and that you have set up the proper vehicles to ensure that you have minimized your estate taxes, consistent with your overall objectives.

If you have not developed an estate plan or had a will drawn up, do so as soon as possible. As your financial situation changes, review your new status with your attorney and make whatever changes are necessary.

# CHAPTER 22

# Selecting
# Financial
# Specialists

**A** number of specialists can help you develop and maintain your financial plan. You may find that you require none or all of these specialists, based on your own situation and the complexity of your requirements. In this chapter we will review the most commonly used financial specialists and identify the circumstances in which you could use their services. These specialists include financial planners, accountants, lawyers, brokers, insurance agents, stockbrokers, and representatives of financial institutions.

## Selecting Your Specialist

There are no surefire rules for selecting a specialist, whether it be a financial planner, attorney, or anyone else, but here are some guidelines. Ask your respected business acquaintances and friends for their recommendations. They are generally unlikely to recommend anyone with whom they are dissatisfied. Ask any advisers you are considering about their qualifications, including education, special training, and the number of years of experience they have. Ask about their fee structures. Make sure you understand precisely how you are expected to compensate them for their services. Always ask for references from individuals who have been clients of the adviser for quite some time. Ask the local Chamber of Commerce or Better Business Bureau if there have been any complaints about anyone you are thinking of engaging.

## Financial Planning

After you finish this book, you may still feel that you do not have the competence or the time to be your own financial planner. If you would like someone with a broad spectrum of knowledge and background to assist you in establishing a plan, consider the use of a financial planner.

There is no accepted standard regarding the qualifications of financial planners. Planners who have earned a Certified Financial Planner designation or a degree in financial planning (College of Financial Planning, 9725 East Hampden Ave., Suite 200, Denver, CO 80231) have demonstrated they have broad-based qualifications. Unfortunately, in most states an individual can advertise as a financial planner with no real qualifications at all. This is why it is essential that you ascertain the background and qualifications of anyone you are considering to be your financial planner.

Make sure that the individual planner or planning organization you consider is registered with the Securities and Exchange Commission (SEC) as an investment adviser. The SEC requires that registered investment advisers provide their clients with a description of fees, investment specialties, education, background, and industry affiliations.

The compensation of financial planners can be categorized in three ways: (1) fee-based, (2) commission-based, (3) a combination of fee and commission. It is important for you to understand the distinction.

A fee-based planner charges you a fee for his or her services. That fee may be fixed or hourly. Obviously, you should not engage any planner until you know his or her pay basis. The advantage of using a fee-based planner is that he or she will not be influenced to recommend investments with high sales commissions.

The disadvantage of using this type of planner is that you have to pay a fee to have your plan developed. This is not a significant disadvantage, however, since you will have to pay one way or the other. You can be somewhat confident that your plan does not contain products that carry unnecessary sales costs. For example, a fee-based planner is more likely than a commission-only planner to recommend a good no-load mutual fund.

A commission-only planner will generally develop a plan for you for "free." You may find, however, that many of the recommended products have unnecessary or too-high sales commissions. For example, assume you invest $10,000 in a fund with an 8 percent load (sales commission). You pay $800 in fees, part of which goes to the planner. If there are well-managed no-load funds of the same quality, you could have avoided the $800 commission. In this situation the free plan is not so free.

If you do decide to use the services of a commission-only planner, make sure that the planner explains the fees and commissions completely before you initiate any transactions.

Many planners earn income from both fees and commissions. If you hire such a one, your initial fee may be smaller than if you engage a fee-only planner, since he or she expects to earn some income via sales commissions.

The most important factor is not whether a planner is fee- or commission-based but whether he or she is good for you. No planner is an expert in every phase of financial planning. Accordingly, it is important for you to recognize what aspects are most important to you and look for a planner whose strengths match your needs. Before you engage a planner, make sure you understand what his or her areas of expertise are. Avoid a planner who has one area of expertise, such as insurance, if that is not the sort of investment you are looking for.

## Accountants

Generally accountants are not well-rounded enough to offer you broad-based financial planning advice, although there are exceptions. Accountants can be very useful, however, in preparation of your income tax returns and offering tax planning advice. Generally, the more complicated your tax return, the more useful an accountant can be.

In most states anyone can legally prepare tax returns, so you must be especially careful to review qualifications before you hire anyone. Anyone who has earned the designation certified public accountant (CPA) has passed a rigorous set of examinations and has established his or her qualifications.

## Lawyers

When you do your estate planning (see Chapter 21), you should use an attorney both for advice and for structuring your will and any applicable trust agreements. Estate planning is very important, and the financial implications are considerable. Accordingly, you do not want to rely on nonprofessionals for advice in this field.

If your estate plans are very basic, your attorney should be able to give you competent advice and develop a will at relatively little cost to you— probably less than $200. If your needs are complex, however, you may find that your attorney is not sufficiently experienced to satisfy your requirements. Be direct with your attorney. Ask whether he or she has enough experience to manage a complex estate. If not, ask for the name of an attorney who specializes in estate planning.

You could also ask the trust department of your local bank or trust company to recommend one. If your estate is large, you do want your estate plan to be developed by an attorney with considerable expertise. Otherwise your assets may not go to the proper parties, and your estate may incur more taxes than necessary.

A lawyer should also be used for any real estate transaction you engage in, whether you are buying or selling.

## Insurance Agents

You should periodically review your insurance coverage. Not only will your need for insurance change throughout your life, but new insurance products are introduced periodically as a result of changes in the tax law and because of changing economic conditions and new competing products.

An insurance agent should be able to help you review your insurance needs and make appropriate recommendations. Make sure you select an agent who represents a company or companies that do business in your state. Insurance companies are not controlled by federal regulations; they are controlled at the state level.

You should select an agent who represents an insurance company whose costs are low relative to those of other companies for the type of insurance that interests you. Some agents are "independent," which means that they sell products of various insurance companies. Ask the agent to show on paper that the cost of his or her products is low relative to that of the competition. If the agent cannot provide that information or cannot explain how his or her product is superior to competing products, find a new agent. Costs among companies and among specific types of policies vary considerably. Accordingly, you should insist that your agent demonstrate to you that the products he or she is offering are priced competitively.

Although some insurance products are complex, a good agent should be able to explain clearly the advantages and disadvantages of each type of policy. Make sure your agent spends sufficient time explaining the policy to you in terms you understand. Ask the agent to discuss the disadvantages of the policy. Most agents are uncomfortable with this type of question, but a good agent should be able to answer you.

When an agent presents different options to you, keep in mind that cash-value policies generally pay much higher commissions than term policies pay. If an agent is biased in favor of cash-value insurance rather than term, find an agent who is not.

## Stockbrokers

When you purchase securities such as common stocks and bonds, you have two basic options: (1) use a full-service brokerage firm or (2) use a discount stockbroker.

If you want a broker to make recommendations to you regarding industries or individual securities to invest in, use the services of a full-service broker. The broker will tell you which type he or she is. You will pay a higher commission if you want the individualized service that a full-service broker provides than if you use a discount broker. The larger full-service brokerage firms have research departments that recommend investments in specific industries and individual securities.

If you intend to make your own decisions regarding what securities you want to buy or sell and when to do it, then you can use the services of a discount broker. Most major discount brokers advertise regularly in the financial section of newspapers that have comprehensive coverage of financial news. You can save up to 65 percent of the sales commission charged at a full-service brokerage firm. However, do not expect to have your hand held. The discount brokers will only execute your order. They will not offer you any investment advice.

If you do decide you want to use a discount broker, select a member of the New York Stock Exchange who has been in the business for several years. Some of the major discount brokerage firms that have been in the business for several years are subsidiaries of major banks.

Many brokers now sell insurance as well as stocks and bonds. Buying insurance from a broker can be a problem if the broker's main business is selling securities and the broker is not willing to spend a sufficient amount of time explaining insurance products. Many of these products are quite complex, and you need a representative who is willing to spend time with you, especially *after* you have purchased a policy. If a broker seems to race through the explanation of a product, you can be pretty sure you will have difficulty getting full attention later.

## Banks and Financial Institutions

Many banks and other financial institutions have been expanding their product bases. In addition to traditional banking services, they now offer products such as discount brokerage services, mutual funds, and financial planning services.

Some banks and financial institutions offer broader financial services to high-net-worth customers at only specific locations. You will find a wide range of product offerings that varies significantly among banks and even within the branch network of a bank, according to the anticipated demand for a specific product in a certain location. For example, a multibranch bank offering Keogh accounts may have specialists available only at locations that serve many self-employed people.

In general banks provide quality service for traditional products such as CDs, mortgages, and money-market accounts. For more specialized and sophisticated products, such as Keogh plans, you should restrict your banking to branches and locations that have personnel trained to manage these products. Do not hesitate to call branch managers to find out which locations have such specialists.

Some of the larger banks offer financial planning services. The quality of this type of service varies widely. Some banks simply offer a computerized printout for under $100 with no individual follow-up. This is unlikely to be of very much value to you. Other banks, such as Chase Lincoln First in New York state, offer much more comprehensive programs that include individual follow-up conducted by well-trained financial planners.

In some states, such as New York and Connecticut, savings and loan associations (S&Ls) are allowed to sell insurance on both individual and group basis. Within a specific state, the prices of the same insurance products at an S&L will be identical regardless of which one they are purchased at. These products are priced attractively and are generally less expensive than their equivalent bought directly from insurance companies. The insurance agents that sell at savings and loan associations are specialists—they do not provide any other services. Generally the agent at an S&L is not a high-pressure salesperson.

# Glossary

**Acceleration clause**   A provision in a mortgage that may require the unpaid balance of the mortgage to fall due immediately if the regular mortgage payments are not made or if other terms are not met.

**Accrued interest**   Interest earned but not yet paid; generally used to refer to bond interest earned between actual payments.

**Administrator**   Individual or institution appointed by the court to administer the estate of a person who died without a will (intestate).

**Amortization**   A payment plan by which the borrower reduces his or her debt gradually through monthly payments of principal.

**Amortize**   To reduce debt by making fixed payments on a regular basis over a given period.

**Annual percentage rate (APR)**   The cost of credit on a yearly basis expressed as a percentage of the amount borrowed.

**Annuity**   A series of equal payments at fixed intervals, generally to a retired person.

**Appraisal**   An evaluation of a piece of property to determine its value.

**Appraisal fee**   The charge for estimating the market value of property.

**Ask**   An offer to sell a security at a stipulated price.

**Asset**   Something that is owned by an individual or business and that has commercial value.

**Attestation**   Act of witnessing the signing of an instrument and subscribing to it as a witness.

**Automatic reinvestment**   A service offered by most mutual funds whereby income dividends and capital gain distributions are automatically put back into the fund, buying new shares and building up holdings through compounding.

**Bankers acceptance**   Negotiable time draft, or bill of exchange, accepted by a bank. The bank assumes the obligation to pay the holder the face amount of the instrument on the maturity date. Used primarily to finance the export, import, shipment, or storage of goods.

**Basis point**  0.01%

**Bear**  An investor who expects market prices to fall.

**Bearer bond**  Bond not registered in the name of an owner freely negotiable like currency with the issuer; a cash equivalent.

**Beneficiary**  Person named to receive funds or property from a trust, insurance policy, or will.

**Bequest**  A gift of personal property by will.

**Bid**  The highest price a customer is willing to pay for a security.

**Big Board**  The New York Stock Exchange.

**Binder**  A simple contract between a buyer and a seller stating the basic terms of an offer to purchase property. It is usually good only for a limited time, until a more formal purchase agreement is prepared and signed by both parties. A small deposit of earnest money is made to bind the offer.

**Blue chips**  Stocks with a long history of above-average growth and increase in earnings.

**Bond**  Promissory note issued by corporation or government; usually principal is paid off not earlier than 10 years and interest is paid periodically. Interest rate is fixed at time of issuance.

**Bond fund**  A mutual fund whose portfolio consists primarily of corporate, municipal, or United States government bonds. These funds generally emphasize income rather than growth.

**Book value**  A company's total assets minus liabilities.

**Broker**  Agent who executes orders to buy and sell securities for a commission.

**Bull**  An investor who expects market prices to rise.

**Buydown**  A lump-sum payment made to the creditor by the borrower or by a third party to reduce some or all of the consumer's periodic payments to repay the debt.

**Callable bond**  Bonds containing a recall provision allowing the borrower to buy back the bond at a price higher than the issue price within a set time. Corporations normally call bonds when interest rates have fallen and they are able to issue new bonds with a lower coupon rate.

**Capital appreciation fund**  A mutual fund that seeks maximum capital appreciation through investment techniques involving greater than ordinary risk.

**Capital gain**  Profit on the sale of a capital (long-term) asset.

**Capital gains distributions**  Annual payments of gains made on the sale of portfolio securities to shareholders in mutual funds.

**Certificate of deposit (CD)**  A deposit at a bank or savings institution with a specified interest rate for a specific period. Cannot be withdrawn before maturity without an interest penalty for early withdrawal. Small-denomination CDs are often purchased by individuals. CDs of $100,000 or more are often negotiable; they can be sold or transferred before maturity.

**Certificate of title** A document prepared by a title company or an attorney stating that the seller has a clear, marketable, and insurable title to the property offered for sale.

**Charitable trust** A trust in which part of a donor's estate is used for charitable purposes.

**Closed-end investment company** An investment company that offers a limited number of shares traded in the securities markets, usually through brokers. Price is determined by supply and demand. Unlike open-end investment companies (mutual funds), closed-end funds do not redeem their shares.

**Closing** The final step in the sale of a property, when the title is transferred from the seller to the buyer. The buyer signs the mortgage and pays settlement costs; and any money due the seller or buyer is paid.

**Closing costs** Sometimes called settlement costs—costs in addition to the price of a house (usually including mortgage origination fee, title insurance, attorney's fee, and prepayable items such as taxes and insurance payments) collected in advance of closing and held in an escrow account.

**Codicil** A supplement that adds, changes, or deletes provisions of a will.

**Collateral** Property offered to secure a loan or other credit and subject to seizure on default. (Also called security.)

**Commercial paper** Short-term unsecured promissory notes of $10,000 or more with maturity no longer than 270 days issued by corporations to fund short-term credit needs.

**Commission** Money paid to a real estate agent or broker by the seller in payment for finding a buyer and completing a sale. Usually it is a percentage of the sale price and is spelled out in the purchase agreement.

**Common stock fund** An open-end investment company whose holdings consist mainly of common stocks. These funds usually emphasize growth.

**Community property** A form of ownership in some states under which property acquired during a marriage is presumed to be owned jointly unless acquired as separate property by either spouse.

**Condominium** A residential or commercial real estate development in which individual apartments, townhouses, or offices are separately owned but common and public areas such as halls, elevators, grounds, and recreational facilities are communally owned.

**Conventional loan** A mortgage loan not insured by FHA or guaranteed by VA.

**Convertible security** Bond or preferred stock that can for a stipulated time be exchanged for a fixed number of common stock shares.

**Cooperative** An apartment building or group of housing units owned by all the residents (generally a corporation) and run by an elected board of directors for the benefit of the residents. The resident lives in a unit but does not own it; he or she owns shares of stock in the corporation.

**Cosigner** A person who signs for a loan with another person and assumes equal liability for it.

**Coupon rate** The interest rate specified on coupons attached to a bond.

**Credit** The right to defer payment of debt.

**Credit rating** A rating or evaluation made by a person or company such as a credit bureau based on the rated person's present financial condition and credit history.

**Current yield** The dividends or interest paid on a security divided by the market price of the security. The current yield of a stock selling for $10 and paying an annual $1 dividend is 10 percent.

**Custodian** One who has custody; a guardian or a trustee.

**Debenture** Corporate bond backed by the general credit of the issuing corporation.

**Decedent** A person who has died.

**Deed** A document stating ownership of a piece of property.

**Deed of trust** A document used instead of a mortgage in some states. It transfers the title of the property to a third party, the trustee, who holds the title until the debt or mortgage loan is paid off, at which time the title (ownership) passes to the borrower. If the borrower fails to make payments, the trustee may sell the property at a public sale to pay off the loan.

**Default** Failure to make loan payments on time as agreed in the contract. If a mortgage payment is 30 days late, the borrower is in default, and the lender may have the right to start foreclosure proceedings.

**Discount bonds** Bonds selling below their face value. If a bond was issued at $1,000, it is selling at a discount any time it is selling below $1,000.

**Distribution** Payment of income to the owners of securities.

**Dividend** Payment to stockholders of cash or stock in direct proportion to share ownership. The company's board of directors approves each dividend.

**Dollar-cost averaging** Process of investing a fixed sum of money regularly in the same security. The advantage of the system is that more shares are bought at low prices than at high prices, lowering the average cost per share.

**Donee** Person who receives a gift.

**Donor** One who makes a gift.

**Equal Credit Opportunity Act** A federal law that requires lenders not to discriminate because of race, color, religion, national origin, gender, marital status, or income from public assistance programs.

**Escrow** Money or documents held by a third party until all the conditions of a contract are met.

**Escrow payment** That part of a borrower's monthly payment held by the lender to pay for taxes, hazard insurance, mortgage insurance, and other items until they become due. Also known as impounds or reserves in some states.

**Estate** The assets owned by an individual at his or her death.

**Executor/Executrix** Person or institution appointed by person making a will to carry out the terms of the will.

**Face value** The principal amount stated on a debt instrument; the borrower promises to repay it at maturity.

**Fannie Mae (Federal National Mortgage Association)** An agency established by the federal government but owned by private stockholders; it issues mortgage-backed certificates in $25,000 denominations. Timely payment of both interest and principal are insured.

**Federal agency issue** Security issued by a federal agency. These bonds are second in safety only to United States government issues. Some are federally insured. They are generally exempt from state and local taxes.

**Federal Housing Administration (FHA)** A division of the United States Department of Housing and Urban Development whose main activity is to insure home mortgages made by private lenders.

**Fiduciary** An individual, corporation, or other entity that manages property according to a trust agreement.

**Finance charge** The amount one must pay to get a loan.

**Firm commitment** An agreement from a lender to make a loan to a particular borrower on a particular property. Also an FHA agreement or a private mortgage insurance company agreement to insure a loan on a particular property for a particular borrower.

**First-mortgage bond** Corporate bond secured by a mortgage on some or all of the property of the issuing corporation.

**Fixed rate** A traditional approach to determining the finance charge payable on an extension of credit. A certain predetermined interest rate is applied to the principal.

**401(k) plan** A tax-deferred retirement plan that can be offered to employees by businesses of any kind. A company's 401(k) plan can be a profit-sharing or stock bonus plan in which employees save a specific dollar amount or a plan in which employees save a percentage of salary.

**Freddie Mac (Federal Home Loan Mortgage Corporation)** A federally chartered agency that purchases residential mortgages from lending institutions and packages them for sale as securities backed by the pooled mortgages.

**General obligation bonds** Municipal bonds backed by the general credit of the municipality issuing the bond.

**Ginnie Mae (Government National Mortgage Association)** An agency of the United States Department of Housing and Urban Development that buys mortgages from lending institutions, forms securities, and sells them to investors. Ginnie Mae guarantees timely payment of both interest and principal.

**Growth-and-income fund** A mutual fund that seeks to combine long-term growth of capital with level or rising income.

**Growth fund** A mutual fund whose primary investment objective is long-term growth of capital. It invests principally in common stocks with significant growth potential.

**Guaranty**  A promise by one party to pay the debt of another if that other fails to do so.

**Income fund**  A mutual fund that primarily seeks current income rather than growth of capital. They tend to invest in stocks and bonds that normally pay high dividends and interest.

**Index fund**  A mutual fund that seeks to mirror general stock market perform- ance by matching its portfolio to a broad-based index, most often the Standard & Poor's 500-stock index.

**Individual retirement account (IRA) rollover**  Placement of lump-sum payments from pension or profit-sharing plans in an IRA. By the same provision, IRA funds can be transferred from one investment vehicle to another.

**Interest**  A charge paid for borrowing money. Also a right, share, or title in property.

**International fund**  A fund that invests in securities primarily traded in markets outside the United States.

**Intestacy**  Dying without a valid will. The decedent is said to be intestate.

**Joint tenancy**  An equal, undivided ownership of property by two or more persons. Should one of the parties die, his or her share of the ownership would pass to the surviving owners; that is, the joint tenants have right of survivorship.

**Junk bond**  A speculative bond rated BB or below by Standard & Poor's and Ba or below by Moody's Investor Service. Junk bonds are generally issued by corporations of questionable financial strength or without proven track records. They tend to be more volatile and higher-yielding than bonds with superior quality ratings. Junk bond funds emphasize diversified investments in these low-rated, high-yielding debt issues.

**Liability**  A debt or obligation stated in terms of money.

**Lien**  A hold or claim on property as security for a debt or charge; if a lien is not removed by payment of the debt, the property may be sold to pay off the lien.

**Listed stock**  Stock traded on a national securities exchange.

**Listing**  Register of properties for sale with one or more real estate brokers or agents; allows the broker who actually sells the property to get the commission.

**Load**  A sales charge or commission assessed by certain mutual funds known as load funds to cover selling costs. The commission is generally stated as a portion of the fund's offering price, usually on a sliding scale from 1 percent to 8.5 percent.

**Low-load fund**  A mutual fund that charges a small sales commission, usually 3.5 percent or less, to purchasers of its shares.

**Margin**  The down payment required for an investment in securities purchased on credit.

**Margin call**  A call from a broker requesting an investor who has purchased securities on margin to supply more capital to the broker. Margin calls are made when the price has gone down since the initial purchase. If the investor cannot put up additional capital, the security will be sold.

**Margin stock**  Any stock listed on a national securities exchange; any over-the-counter security approved by the SEC for trading in the national market system or appearing on the Big Board's list of over-the-counter margin stocks and most mutual funds.

**Money-market fund**  A mutual fund that aims to pay money-market interest rates. This is accomplished by investing in safe, highly liquid securities, including bank certificates of deposit, commercial paper, United States government securities, and repurchase agreements.

**Mortgage-backed securities**  Certificates backed by pooled mortgages. Issuing agencies buy mortgages from lending institutions and repackage them as securities, which they sell to investors. They are generally issued in denominations of $25,000 or more. Yields, which stem from interest and principal on underlying mortgages, are generally higher than those of Treasury bonds that provide comparable liquidity and safety.

**Municipal bond**  Bond issued by city, town, or state. Interest is exempt from federal income taxation. If you reside in the area in which the bond is issued, interest on your investment usually is exempt from state and local taxes as well.

**Municipal bond fund**  A mutual fund that invests in a broad range of short-term, intermediate, or long-term tax-exempt bonds issued by states, cities, counties, and local governments. The interest obtained from these bonds is passed through to shareholders free of federal tax. The objective of these funds is current tax-free income.

**Mutual fund**  An open-end investment company that buys back—that is, redeems —its shares at current net asset value. Most mutual funds continuously offer new shares to investors.


**National Association of Securities Dealers (NASD)**  A self-regulating organization with jurisdiction over certain broker-dealers. The NASD conducts examinations for compliance with net capital requirements and other regulations.

**Negative amortization**  Repayment schedule calling for periodic payments that are insufficient to pay off, or amortize, the loan. Earned but unpaid interest is added to the principal, increasing the debt. Eventually payments must be rescheduled to pay off the debt.

**Negotiable-order-of-withdrawal (NOW) account**  An interest-earning account on which checks may be drawn. Withdrawals from NOW accounts may be subject to a 14-day or more notice requirement although this is rarely imposed. NOW accounts may be offered by commercial banks, mutual savings banks, and savings-and-loan associations.

**Net asset value per share**  The current market worth of a mutual fund share.

Calculated daily by taking the fund's total assets, deducting liabilities, and dividing the remainder by the number of shares outstanding.

**No-load fund**   A commission-free mutual fund that sells its shares at net asset value, either directly to the public or through an affiliated distributor, with no additional charge.

**Open-end credit**   A line of credit that may be used repeatedly up to a certain limit, also called a charge account or revolving credit.

**Option**   The right to buy or sell securities at a specified price within a set time.

**Option income fund**   A fund that invests primarily in dividend-paying common stocks on which call options are traded on national securities exchanges. These funds seek high current return consisting of dividends, premiums from expired call options, net short-term gains, and any profits from closing purchase transactions.

**Overdraft checking account**   A checking account associated with a line of credit that allows a person to write checks for more than the actual balance in the account, with a finance charge on the overdraft.

**Over-the-counter (OTC) stocks**   Stocks not traded on a national securities exchange.

**Points**   Finance charges paid by the borrower at the beginning of a loan in addition to monthly interest; each point equals 1 percent of the loan amount.

**Portfolio**   Holdings of securities by an individual or institution.

**Preferred stock**   Category of stock with more characteristics of bonds than of common stock. Preferred stockholders receive fixed dividends. Preferred stock remains outstanding indefinitely unless called for redemption by company at a predetermined price. In case of liquidation, preferred stockholders' claims on assets are subordinate to bondholders' but come before common stockholders'.

**Premium bond**   The price above par—that is, face value—of a bond. If a bond sold initially at $1,000 par value is selling for $1,100, it is selling for a $100 premium.

**Prepayment penalty**   A charge made by the lender if a mortgage loan is paid off before the due date.

**Price-to-earnings (P/E) ratio**   The ratio of current stock price to company earnings per share.

**Principal**   The amount of money borrowed that must be paid back along with interest and other finance charges.

**Promissory note**   Negotiable instrument that is a written promise to pay.

**Prospectus**   Document filed with the Securities and Exchange Commission by a company when a new issue of securities is offered to the general public. The document contains highlights from the registration statement. The information is used by brokers and investors to evaluate the securities before purchase.

**Purchase agreement** A written document in which a seller and a buyer agree on a transaction. Certain conditions and terms of the sale are spelled out: sale price, date of closing, and condition of property. The agreement is secured by a deposit or down payment of earnest money.

**Qualified retirement plan** A private retirement plan that meets the rules and regulations of the Internal Revenue Service. Contributions to a qualified retirement plan are generally tax-deductible; earnings on such contributions are always tax-sheltered until withdrawal.

**Quitclaim deed** A deed that transfers some interest in or title to a property. A quitclaim deed does not warrant or guarantee a clear title.

**Rating** The evaluation assigned by a rating service regarding the quality of a debt instrument. The most respected rating services are Standard & Poor's and Moody's. Their letter evaluations are similar but not identical. For each service, respectively, AAA and Aaa are the best ratings; B ratings are lower in quality and C and D ratings are the worst.

**Real estate** Land and the structures thereon. Also, anything of a permanent nature such as trees, minerals, and the interest and rights in these items.

**Registered bond** Bond registered with the issuer in the owner's name. The issuer's paying agent mails a check directly to the issuer when interest payments are due.

**Rollover** See individual retirement account rollover.

**Sector fund** A mutual fund that maintains several specialized portfolios in a given sector of the economy, such as the oil industry.

**Securities and Exchange Commission (SEC)** A federal agency established by Congress to protect investors.

**Security** Any document that identifies legal ownership of a physical commodity.

**Seller's points** A lump sum paid by the seller to the buyer's creditor to reduce the cost of the loan to the buyer. This payment is either required by the creditor or volunteered by the seller, usually in a loan to buy real estate. One point equals 1 percent of the loan amount.

**Selling short** The sale of a security not owned by the seller. The short seller expects that the price will go down, borrows stock for delivery to the buyer and must eventually purchase the security for return to the lender.

**Serial bonds** Bonds redeemed on an installment basis in sequential order. Municipalities generally issue serial bonds.

**Series fund** A mutual fund whose prospectus allows for more than one portfolio. These portfolios may be specialized (as in a sector fund) or broad (as in a growth-stock portfolio along with a money-market portfolio). Management can create additional portfolios as it sees fit.

**Simplified employee pension (SEP)** A program that allows employers without qualified retirement plans to contribute up to 15 percent of compention or $30,000, whichever is less, to their employees' individual retirement accounts.

**Sinking fund**  A fund of money produced through regular payments by the bond issuer that will be used to retire outstanding bonds on a predetermined schedule.

**Specialty fund**  A mutual fund specializing in the securities of a particular industry or group of industries, special types of securities, or regional investments.

**Spread**  Difference between the bid and ask prices for a security.

**Stock dividend**  A dividend paid to stockholders in the form of additional common stock. The company normally uses this form of dividend to preserve cash for expansion.

**Street name**  A name in which a security is held but that is not the name of the actual owner. A street name may be fictitious or belong to an agent of the owner.


**Tenancy by the entirety**  Title in which the names of husband and wife appear on the deed to their real estate. Creditors cannot attach such property because of debt of either partner without the other; property cannot be split.

**Tenancy in common**  Title of a piece of property held jointly by two or more people. Each individual has control over his or her share and can dispose of the property independent of the other owner.

**Testamentary**  Pertaining to a will.

**Testamentary trust**  Trust established by means of a will.

**Testator**  Person making a will.

**Time deposit**  A deposit that is held by a financial institution and that matures within a certain time.

**Title insurance**  Special insurance that usually protects lenders against loss of their interest in property because of legal defects in the title. An owner can protect his or her interest by purchasing separate coverage.

**Title search**  An examination of public records to uncover the ownership of a piece of property. A title search is intended to make sure the title is marketable and free from defects such as an outstanding claim or encumbrance.

**Totten trust**  A trust in which the donor deposits funds in a bank in his or her own name as the trustee for another. The donor retains control over the account and can withdraw any part of the account at any time. Upon the death of the donor, any balance goes to the beneficiary.

**Treasury bills**  Short-term United States Treasury securities issued in minimum denominations of $10,000 and usually having original maturities of 3, 6, or 12 months. Investors purchase bills at prices lower than the face value of the bills and receive the face value at maturity.

**Treasury bonds**  Long-term United States Treasury securities usually having initial maturities of more than 10 years and issued in denominations of

$1,000 or more, depending on the specific issue. Bonds pay interest semiannually, with principal payable at maturity.

**Treasury notes** Intermediate-term United States Treasury securities having initial maturities of 1 to 10 years and issued in denominations of $1,000 or more, depending on the maturity of the issue. Notes pay interest semiannually, and the principal is payable at maturity.

**Treasury securities** Interest-bearing obligations of the United States government issued by the Treasury as a means of borrowing money to meet government expenditures not covered by tax revenues.

**Triple tax-exempt fund** A mutual fund, usually a municipal bond fund, whose dividends and interest are exempt from federal, state, and local income taxes within a particular state.

**Trust** The holding of property set aside for the benefit of those for whom the trust was created. The property is managed by the trustee for the advantage of the beneficiaries.

**Trustee** Person or institution designated by the trustor or assigned by a court to administer a trust.

**Truth in Lending Law** A federal law providing that the terms of a loan, including all the finance charges, must be disclosed to the borrower before the loan is signed.

**12b-1 Fee** Fee charged by some mutual funds to pay for specific expenses such as advertising, sales literature, and dealer incentives. This fee is permitted because of a 1980 Securities and Exchange Commission rule.

**Uniform Gifts to Minors Act** Legislation adopted by most states establishing rules for the administration and distribution of investment assets in a minor's name. Securities can usually be transferred from the account of a parent or other custodian into a Uniform Gift to Minors Act account in the name of the child. Earnings are then taxed at the rate applicable to the child, which is usually lower than that of the parent's. Unless otherwise stipulated, the child gains control of the assets upon reaching the legal age of majority or adulthood.

**United States government short-term fund** A mutual fund that invests only in United States Treasury and government agency issues.

**Variable annuity** A type of insurance contract that guarantees future payments to the holder, or annuitant, usually at retirement. The annuity's value varies with that of the underlying portfolio securities, which may include shares in a mutual fund. All monies held in the annuity accumulate on a tax-deferred basis.

**Variable rate** An interest rate that may fluctuate over the life of a loan. The rate is often tied to an index that reflects changes in market rates of interest. Fluctuation in the rate changes either the payments or the length of the loan term. Limits are often placed on the degree to which the interest rate or the payments can vary.

**Vested** Indicates the attainment of an employee benefit that is not contingent on continued employment.

**Veterans Administration (VA)** A federal agency that guarantees a certain proportion of a mortgage loan made to a veteran by a private lender. Sometimes called GI loans, these usually require very low down payments and permit long repayment terms.

**Warrant** Document conferring the right to buy a security at a specified price, normally within a specified time. Warrants usually are offered as incentives to investors to buy additional securities.

**Warranty deed** A deed guaranteeing that the title to a piece of property is free from any defects or encumbrances.

**Wraparound** A financing device that permits an existing loan to be refinanced and new money to be advanced at an interest rate between the rate charged on the old loan and the current market interest rate. The creditor combines the remainder of the old loan with the new loan at the intermediate rate.

**Yield to maturity** True rate of return, taking into consideration current market price, interest to be received, and the value of the bond at maturity. This yield is important, since it enables investors to compare the returns offered by bonds having various coupon rates and maturity dates.

**Zero-coupon bond** Bond sold at a fraction of its face value. It appreciates gradually, but no periodic interest payments are made. Earnings accumulate until maturity, when the bond is redeemable at its full face value.

# Index

Real estate, *continued*
  mortgage, 73
  postponing gains, 70
  rental property, 75
  residence, 69, 74–75
  retirement strategies, 71–72
  taxes, 70, 72–73
  vacation, 75–78
Real estate syndications, 85
Real estate limited partnerships, 85
Real estate investment trusts, 84–85
REIT, *see* Real estate investment
      trusts
Retirement Equity Act of 1984, 106–107
Retirement planning, 7–13, 14–19,
      20–28, 71, 92, 96, 99, 104
Return on equity, 53
Reverse Annuity Mortgage, 74
Riders, 174
Rollovers, *see* IRA rollover

Savings bonds, *see* U.S. Savings bonds
Scudder, Stevens and Clark, 57, 83
Self-employed plans, *see* Keogh
SEP, *see* Simplified Employee Pension
      Plan
Short-term assets, 2
Simplified Employee Pension Plan, 123
SLMA, *see* Student Loan Marketing
      Association
Social Security
  age, 93–94
  credit, 88–89, 90–91, 93
  disability, 47
  domestic employees, 89
  eligibility, 92–93
  earnings record, 91
  family members, 90
  farm employees, 89
  federal employees, 90
  income, 92, 94
  indexing, 15
  medicare, 97–98
  military, 90
  nonprofit organizations, 89–91

Social Security Tax, 8, 9, 92, 94, 99–100,
      146
Sources of information, 26, 28, 46, 50,
      56, 63, 150, 158
SSI, *see* Social Security
Standard & Poor's, 43, 46, 50
State and local taxes, 188
Stockbrokers, 209
Student Loan Marketing Association, 37
Surrender charges, 21, 145
Survivor benefits, 96

Tax Reform Act of 1986
  business interest, 187
  capital gains, 23, 189
  children's income, 189
  home equity, 182
  income tax rates, 179–181
  interest deductions, 180–187
  investment interest, 185
  medical expenses, 187–188
  miscellaneous deductions, 188–189
  mortgage, 180–181
  passive activity interest, 186–187
  personal exemptions, 180
  personal interest, 184
  standard deduction, 180, 182
  state and local taxes, 188
Ten-year Averaging, 139–140
Treasury bills, 27–28
Trustee, 198
Trusts, 198–203
Truth in Lending Act, 15

U.S. Savings bonds, 28–30
Unit trusts, 42–43

Vacation homes, 75–78
Value Line, 43, 46, 50
Vesting, 107

Wiesenberger Services, Inc., 56, 63
Wills, 199

Zero-coupon bonds, 79–81, 135

# About the Authors

**Elliot Raphaelson** has had more than fifteen years experience consulting, teaching, and writing on personal finance, specializing in retirement and financial planning for older persons. He is a Second Vice President at Chase Manhattan Bank in New York City and has conducted many seminars on retirement and financial planning sponsored by Chase Manhattan Bank, West Point, the American Institute of Banking, Dow Jones, and Executive Enterprises, Inc. He taught personal finance at the New School for Social Research in New York for ten years. His writings on the subject have appeared in *Vogue, Town and Country, Working Woman, New York Times, Savvy, Self, Working Mothers,* and the *Physician's Financial News.* His first book is entitled *Planning Your Financial Future* (1982). He lives in New Jersey with his wife, Arline, and his son, Mark.

**Debra Raphaelson West** has collaborated before with her father, Elliot, on writings about personal finance, however her chief occupation is language analysis for the U.S. Department of Defense. She has written articles for scholarly journals on the subject of humor and is working on a cookbook "for the realistic amateur." Her M.S. degree in linguistics is from Georgetown University in Washington. She and her husband, Stephen, live in Maryland.